Helping Families in Family Centres

of related interest

The Child's World
Assessing Children in Need
Edited by Jan Horwath
ISBN 1 85302 957 2

Effective Ways of Working with Children and their Families
Edited by Malcolm Hill
ISBN 1 85302 619 0

Family Support
Direction from Diversity
Edited by John Canavan, Pat Dolan and John Pinkerton
ISBN 1 85302 850 9

Childhood Experiences of Domestic Violence
Caroline McGee
ISBN 1 85302 827 4

Creative Responses to Child Sexual Abuse
Challenges and Dilemmas
Edited by Sue Richardson and Heather Bacon
ISBN 1 85302 884 3

Permanent Family Placement for Children of Minority Ethnic Origin
June Thoburn, Liz Norford and Stephen Parvez Rashid
ISBN 1 85302 875 4

Meeting the Needs of Ethnic Minority Children
Edited by Kedar N. Dwivedi and Ved P. Varma
ISBN 1 85302 294 2

Helping Families in Family Centres

Working at Therapeutic Practice

Edited by Linnet McMahon and Adrian Ward

Jessica Kingsley Publishers
London and Philadelphia

First published in the United Kingdom in 2001 by
Jessica Kingsley Publishers Ltd
116 Pentonville Road
London N1 9JB, England
and
325 Chestnut Street
Philadelphia, PA 19106, USA

www.jkp.com

Copyright © 2001 Jessica Kingsley Publishers

Library of Congress Cataloging in Publication Data
A CIP catalog record for this book is available from the Library of Congress

British Library Cataloguing in Publication Data
A CIP catalogue record for this book is available from the British Library

ISBN 1 85302 835 5

Printed and Bound in Great Britain by
Athenaeum Press, Gateshead, Tyne and Wear

Contents

Part Three: Managing the Work of a Family Centre

Part Four: Conclusion

Acknowledgements

We would like to thank all those students and colleagues within the University of Reading and outside who have played a part in developing our understanding of the work of family centres. Some of them have directly contributed chapters to the book. Others have contributed case study material. There are others too, unnamed, whose ideas have influenced our thinking and thus the contents of this book.

Note

In order to protect identities names of clients and children in the case studies and practice examples in the book have been changed, as have some other identifying characteristics such as children's ages and genders.

Introduction
Linnet McMahon and Adrian Ward

Finding a basis for the work of family centres

Our aim in producing this book is to produce a text which will be of use to practitioners and managers and thereby of benefit to the families who use family centres. We want this work to be well grounded, both in theory and in practice, which is why this book has been written in collaboration with experienced practitioners. Our own reason for working on this project is that we believe family centre work to be still new enough to be relatively under-developed theoretically. Family centre work does have a firm pragmatic base, in that the welfare system both nationally and locally is increasingly committed to early intervention and to an emphasis on 'the family'. The growth in family centres during the last 15 years has been enormous, but the range is also enormous, and we know that there is very little consensus as to what a family centre 'is'. The growth has been so rapid and so diverse that the thinking and planning have not yet caught up with the practice.

One result of this very rapid growth, then, is that, despite the best efforts of a small number of people (some of whom have contributed to this book), family centre work does not yet have a firm enough theoretical base. There is a small number of important publications, including a few books specifically on family centres, but it is mainly scattered in journals and other collections, and consequently fairly inaccessible to the average practitioner. It is also fairly 'incoherent', by which we mean not that any given paper is incomprehensible, but that the whole body of work has never really been brought together into a coherent whole. In this sense it probably mirrors one of the things which can happen in practice – in the sense that an organisation as complicated as a family centre can become fragmented and unco-ordinated, so that the whole risks actually becoming *less* than the sum of its parts. Where this does happen, people are missing out: service-users are not getting the best service, staff are not getting the job satisfaction, and agencies are not getting the best value for money.

The risk of fragmentation may become apparent if we briefly consider an example from practice. If you visit a typical family centre on a Monday afternoon, you are likely to find somebody offering individual counselling in one room, someone else doing groupwork in another, a group of children and mothers involved in craft activities in a third, a staff supervision session going on in a fourth, and so on. Every now and then, everybody moves round from one room to another, or they all come together for lunch, or some of them leave and another lot arrive – and on Tuesday there may be a completely different group of people using the place doing some of the same activities and some different ones, while on the Wednesday the whole place becomes a 'drop-in' centre with yet another change of focus. The question is, who and what is holding the whole thing together, how do all these activities contribute to the overall task of the centre, and how do the users make sense of the whole thing? It is our aim in this book to focus as much on the holding together as on the disparate parts, and we want to produce something which will help others doing this work to think about how the whole thing can be made to work. The paradox is that we want to retain focus on the detail as well as on the large picture.

The sense in which the literature mirrors the practice is that, for the most part, what you will find is disparate papers on all sorts of aspects of family centre work, but very little on how it all holds together. In fact, you will be lucky to find it at all, because you will also have to search all over the place to find this material. This is perhaps especially true of *therapeutic* practice in family centres, which appears to be particularly widely dispersed, and generally fairly absent from the literature.

A note on 'theory'

When we talk about theory we will always be meaning 'theory for practice', rather than some abstract and distant set of intellectual ideals. We are looking for clarity and effectiveness in practice, and we believe that this will be helped by clarity in thinking and effectiveness in putting that thinking into action. The goal of this project must be improved services for the families who use family centres – as well as for those who (for a variety of reasons) do not currently make much use of family centres, but who might benefit from their services.

Social policy: concern for children and prevention for families

Probably the prevailing view of children for the first half of the past century was that, in public at least, they should be 'seen but not heard'. That started to change with the 'discovery' in the second half of the century, first of 'the battered child' and physical abuse and severe neglect within the family, and in subsequent years a horrified realisation – after an initial shocked denial – of the sexual abuse of children by members of their families. In a parallel process, the developing understanding of children's emotional needs and in particular the damaging consequences of long separations from their families meant more attention to children's unhappy experiences in institutions and other forms of care away from home, in the course of which further evidence of abuse was found. The consequences have been more attention both to child protection and to listening to children and taking account of their wishes and needs. Poor outcomes for children in care and a recognition that most children in care eventually return to their families has meant more emphasis on the desirability of children remaining in the family if possible. This in turn has led to more attention to working with families and partnership with parents. These varied concerns were given voice in the 1989 Children Act and its broad emphasis on 'children in need'.

Public anxiety about children has been aroused for other reasons too. There is fear of and anger with children who are out of control at home or school, children who bully, or truant, or who get involved in substance abuse and crime and, in the rare case, even murder of another child. On the other hand, those closest to children are concerned about the effects of unsatisfactory relationships within families, emotional abuse of children, parental mental illness, domestic violence and the high level of family breakdown, on the mental health of children and young people. Mental health problems are exhibited not only in forms of socially unacceptable 'acting out' behaviour but also in high levels of anxiety and depression in young people, even increased suicide. There is a broader social context to this. Families often have few adults available for child care and general support, functioning in some isolation from the outside world. Poverty has not gone away and may well be aggravated by the wide gap between poor and rich. Racism is an ever present fact of life for black children and affects not only external relationships but acts as a threat to their identity.

The need for prevention through early intervention

We know enough about attachment and the development of a child's inner world to know that relationships established in the first year of life are significant for future development. Longitudinal studies of attachment show continuing and intergenerational effects (see Chapter 2). Problems identified in pre-school children predict later childhood difficulties (Richman *et al.* 1982), and problems in childhood foretell difficulties in adulthood (Rutter 1989). Farrington (1995) points to the childhood origins of later offending. It seems like common sense to intervene as early as possible, in the hope of helping families provide 'good enough' care to produce mentally healthy children. A number of studies support the efficacy of early intervention (McGuire and Earls 1991). The Department of Health (1998, p.1) 'piloted and promoted new ways of supporting families with young children, especially children in need,' under the Refocusing Children's Services Initiative. The work within its 43 projects focused on: putting children in need at the centre of practice; intervening early to support families and pre-empt crisis; and encouraging parents to support themselves and each other. Evaluation of these projects concluded that 'the early intervention strategy works' in the task of helping and supporting families and, although not necessarily quick or cheap, is likely to be cost-effective in terms of the prevention of further dysfunction. A particularly influential study has been the long-term follow-up of the US Head Start pre-school programme which revealed positive 'sleeper' outcomes as the children involved reached early adulthood (Berrueta-Clement *et al.* 1984; Offord 1987). The UK's turn-of-the-century Sure Start programme hopes for similar gains and is predicated on even earlier intervention with families in areas with a high level of need, with support and help to parents from the beginning of their children's lives.

The need for long-term work with the most needy families

The 1990s saw a national growth of parenting skills programmes to support families in early parenting (Joseph Rowntree Foundation Findings 1996 and 1998). Evaluation of outcomes of these short-term behaviourally based programmes, for example the Leicester Fun and Families programme (Neville *et al.* 1996) suggested that typically about *half* the parents who attended showed clear benefits in their relationships with their children. A Barnardo's report on effective interventions for children and their families noted failures in maintaining good outcomes which appeared to be 'attributable to too narrow an approach in response to complex problems', particularly where there were severe or long standing difficulties within the family which affected relationships (Macdonald and Roberts 1995, p.35). For outcomes to be effective and sustainable within these families, parent training alone is not likely to be a sufficient response, even when we take into account the benefits of emotional support from sharing difficulties in a group of people who have similar problems. This would seem pertinent to many of the cases referred to family centres, where dysfunctional family systems and relationships have become established and issues are indeed complex.

A similar conclusion was reached by Murray and Dymond (2000) in relation to early brief intervention to prevent or relieve post-natal depression. While some mothers feel better and communicate better with their baby, brief treatment is not good at preventing depression in mothers with severe attachment histories. Van IJzendoorn *et al.*'s (1995) review of attachment based interventions showed a wide range of outcomes. Although brief focused interventions appeared more successful in improving the immediate mother–infant relationship there was a strong possibility that these were only short-term improvements; longitudinal studies are awaited to find out what kinds of intervention lead to fundamental change, especially for those mothers with the most damaged attachments.

A literature review of treatment of child physical abuse concluded:

> We know that the treatment of an abusive family is complex. We know that it is not like a lotion that can be rubbed on, or a medicine that can be taken for a short time. When one realises that the abusive behaviour has often been learned by the parents over several years in their own childhood, it becomes clear that treatment, even if the intensity of the treatment becomes less, most likely it will have to take place over several years as well. This means that with a problem as large as child abuse, with only a relatively small number of people available to provide treatment, only a small proportion of families will be able to be properly treated. However, there is great value in some clinical insights that can be derived through careful treatment, insights that might generate ideas for better prevention as well as treatment programs. Even for the relatively small number able to be helped, the investment of time is worth it if the cycle of abuse can be prevented from appearing in the next generation. (Oates and Bross 1995, p.473)

In a further review of studies of the long-term consequences for children of physical and sexual abuse, and of neglect, and on the outcomes of various kinds of therapeutic treatment, Stevenson (1999, p.106) confirmed the need for long-term work, concluding 'that the evidence only strengthens the case for endorsing such a recommendation [Oates and Bross] and the results of studies published subsequently have not led to the need to revise these conclusions'.

The most vulnerable families are those with long-standing difficulties, often with extensive histories of deprivation, abuse and mental illness. Their children are the most 'at risk' of being neglected or damaged physically or emotionally. These families need the kind of in-depth and reliable longer-term support that can help them change the way they care for their children rather than just get by until the next crisis. Despite such evidence many family centres are having to justify their existence to cash-starved local authorities and are under pressure to move to short-term work only, which centre workers know from experience is not enough for the most needy families.

The development of family centres[1]

The growth of family centres in the 1970s was a response to a shift in values in society as a whole and social work in particular towards working in partnership with and empowering parents. Some families centres grew out of community playgroups and the self-help ethos, others from closures of day and residential nurseries and children's homes, as local authorities and the big non-statutory organisations such as The Children's Society, Barnado's and National Children's Homes (now NCH Action for Children) redirected their work towards supporting families. By the 1980s a wide range of services and activities was being offered, with much attention to users' views (Phelan 1983; Willmott and Mayne 1983; De'Ath 1985; DiPhillips and Elliott 1987; Downie and Forshaw 1987; and Cigno 1988).

The Children Act 1989 required every local authority 'to provide such family centres as they consider appropriate in relation to children within their area'. The subsequent Guidance and Regulations 2:19, 3:20 referred to Therapeutic, Community and Self-help centres, a broad categorisation of the many different family centre or family support projects that have developed since (Warren 1991; Cannan 1992; Hardiker 1996). Issues of user empowerment, gender roles and parental involvement were well explored in writing and in practice. There was growing recognition of the need to think about race and culture. Institutional racism, however, was not widely understood, as reflected, for example, in the limited use of family centres by black families and the small number of black staff, mainly in less senior positions (Butt and Box 1998).

The findings from 'Child Protection: Messages from Research' (DOH 1995) led to a national move to refocus services to provide child protection within the context of family support. The Audit Commission report 'Seen But Not Heard' (1994, p.28) gave family support a high priority, recommending that family centres should be developed as a suitable focus for this work. A Department of Health report (1999, pp.3, 5), following the inspection of the delivery of social services-based family support services, noted general high levels of satisfaction from users who were surprised that social services could be so helpful. Many parents had been helped both to respond more effectively to the needs of their children and to take more control over their lives. The report commended family support within family centres, which 'were offering an increasingly wide range of innovative services' and making 'extremely good use of scarce resources…'. Work with disadvantaged groups was also noted with approval: 'Family centres generally gave the best attention to promoting the individual identity of black and minority ethnic and disabled children.' Pithouse and Lindsell (1995 and 1996) noted the improved outcomes for families who had used family support services at a family centre in comparison with those who received a field social work service only. Smith's (1996, p.6) study of users' views in six family projects illustrated 'the difficulty of making rigid distinctions between "outcome" and "process"'. Parents viewed the process in terms of what had been helpful to them overall rather than identifying a particular service, and what mattered most was the quality of the relationship between worker and user.

What is 'therapeutic' work in family centres?

In thinking about therapeutic work we need first to ask what 'therapeutic' means. It is clearly about offering help, but what kind of help, to whom, by whom, under what circumstances, and for how long? Many family centre workers explicitly reject any suggestion that their work might be therapeutic. This seems to be based on a notion that therapy is carried out by experts behind closed doors, and, moreover, that it is something that is 'done to' people rather than empowering or supporting them. In this book we take a broader view of what it means to work therapeutically, and examine what kinds of work are helpful – therapeutic in the wider sense – in enabling parents to feel better about themselves and to be a 'good enough' parent to their children.

Family centres are often described as a 'preventive' service. Many accounts of family centres give a great deal of attention to ways of offering help to families *before* problems have developed or become entrenched (Smith 1996). Where such work helps families to function better and their members to become happier this could be said to be therapeutic. A further level of prevention consists of helping families with existing and long-standing problems, that is, the most needy families (Caplan 1964 in Offord 1987; Phelan 1983; Stones 1994; Sinclair *et al.* 1997). It is here that a family centre's work can most clearly be identified as therapeutic (Speller 1994). These are the families in great distress, where parents are violent, abused or mentally ill, and who in turn may abuse and neglect their children, or in other ways fail to meet their emotional needs.

How can family centres help the most needy families?

Many family centres provide a wide range of services within an existing social and geographical community, identifying individual and group needs for information, support, advocacy, play, and so on. Since family centres are generally sited where they are particularly accessible to vulnerable families they are often working to help families with high levels of need (and this is may well be their *raison d'etre*). Then a social work model of targeted intervention of family support services may become incorporated into the community work model of these 'integrated' family centres (Gill 1988), helpful in offering the flexible and non-stigmatising service recommended by the Audit Commission report (1994). Other family centres have different specialisms and some may concentrate on assessments or more avowedly therapeutic work while others take on a more educational role in teaching parenting skills. On the whole family centres are the friendly acceptable face of social services. They are able to engage families who would avoid a formal child guidance clinic or fear a child-protection field social worker.

What parents find most supportive and helpful from their family centres are: working in partnership, having time to build trusting relationships with staff in a safe and secure environment, feeling empowered, having strengths identified as well as weaknesses, working openly and honestly – with effective communication, and having their needs met as well as their children's. There are tensions between the parallel tasks of child protection and family support. Parents, however, seem to accept the family centre's role in child protection, preferring it to be taken by people they have come to trust (Chrystal 1998; Chrystal and Ward 1999).

The most needy families have always been part of many family centres' work but the demands they make on workers are extreme. Neither community work nor general social work models provide an adequate guide, although elements of each may still be needed. Family centres provide their services from under one roof and largely from the resources of their own staff team. How can they decide what to provide? What difficulties arise in the work, for example conflicts between meeting the needs of the parent and the immediate apparent needs of a child for emotional support, perhaps embodied in the form of splits between staff members? What anxieties does the work engender, and how are these worked with rather than defended against? How can the staff be supported and managed to work as a team? Where can issues of culture, race, gender, and difference be thought about? What is oppressive and discriminatory practice and how can it be addressed? How can the families be part of a whole family centre community? Can a family centre be a therapeutic community?

Much of this book will necessarily be focused on the detail of the work undertaken with children and/or their parents in family centres, looking, for example, at the use of a range of methods for assessing the attachment patterns between children and parents, or at the use of play and other methods in helping children to realise and integrate the nature of the experiences which may be troubling them. It may appear that much of this work is similar to what may happen in clinical settings, such as Child and Family Clinics or Child Guidance Clinics as they used to be known, and this is indeed true, although the work of a family centre is usually quite different from the work of a clinic in some key respects. But family centres have other origins and parallels too. Many of them have developed out of day nurseries, and although they have needed to leave behind some of the assumptions about practice in those nurseries, there remains a strong element of planned daily care for young children and their families which is quite separate from the clinical connections of some of the therapeutic work, and this tradition also has connections with early childhood education. Many 'referred' family centres, meanwhile, have clear connections with the Child Protection teams in Social Services Departments, and some of these draw quite strongly on the office-based mode of practice typical in such departments, while others have their roots more in the Community Work camp, and conceive their task far more in terms of offering a neighbourhood resource for local families. Staff in this last group often reject the notion of 'therapeutic work' as inappropriate to their model of mutual support and community action, although some of the observable activities going on within such centres may appear surprisingly familiar to those working in those centres with a more avowedly 'therapeutic' task.

Family centres are therefore a hybrid creation, and perhaps they might be thought of as the offspring of a number of different traditions and cultures, some of these traditions overlapping, and some of them apparently competing. They have grown rapidly, and the different centres and the agencies responsible for them have evolved different ways of integrating (or not) these different traditions. Some centres are more clearly linked to one tradition or another, but all have had to find a way to create an appropriate identity out of the range of possibilities.

Why family centres and why 'therapeutic family centres'?

It may appear from the above that all family centres are different from each other and that it will therefore be hard to generalise about them, and there is a grain of truth in this view. However, many centres do also have a lot in common, especially those centres which are attempting to carry out therapeutic work. If we return to our question, 'Why family *centres*?', we might say that what they have in common is that there is a group of staff in a particular building engaged on a shared task of trying to help a group of troubled children and their parents. By focusing like this on what these centres have in common – the group of staff and the group of families, the shared task and the particular building – it should be possible to identify more precisely what is distinctive and special about the services which such centres can offer. This will be the focus of the rest of this book: the special and distinctive characteristics of therapeutic family centres, and the ways in which such qualities can be understood so that they can be consciously planned for and developed.

Addressing such issues will mean thinking about what family centres are asked to do by the people and agencies who refer families to them, in other words by focusing on the *task* of the centre. It will also mean thinking about how this task can be carried out by the centre as a whole as well as by its constituent parts. Perhaps we normally think about these parts as the specific sessions and programmes and the people running them, but we also need to think about the bits in-between these sessions, such as the pattern of informal interactions between people, and the ways in which everyday life is managed in the place, as well as thinking about more general and perhaps less tangible factors such as the quality of relationships within the staff team and between the staff and the parents and children, and the overall atmosphere in the place. Thinking about factors such as these can also be aided by placing them all within some conceptual framework for making sense of the patterns. In other words we need a theory base which will help to explain how the *whole* centre works as well as how its individual bits operate.

For this discussion we will be drawing on a number of different ideas in different but overlapping ways, and using 'theory' in different ways – ranging from theory as a general set of ideas to its use for specific concepts as well as for an underlying framework of ideas. Starting with the distinctive qualities of family centres, then, we will be drawing on ideas about group care, and hoping to show what practice in a family centre may have in common with practice in other day and residential settings. Here the 'theory' of group care will be used as a general framework for thinking about the context of the work. Getting more specific about the *therapeutic* task in family centres, we will be outlining the concept of the therapeutic community, using theory now in the sense of drawing on a specific set of ideas and practices as a model for practice. These discussions will necessarily lead us into thinking about the psychodynamic and attachment theory frameworks underlying them, and we hope to show how some of the insights from these approaches can help to explain the complexities of practice. The argument here will be that these ideas can contribute a helpful underpinning theory for practice.

We have been working with some of these questions at the University of Reading where senior family centre workers have joined other day and residential child care workers and managers, teachers, psychiatric nurses, and field social workers on our MA in Therapeutic Child Care. We have been writing in a general way about therapeutic child care (Ward and McMahon 1998) and about family centres in particular (McMahon, Dacre and Vale 1997), and have at various times provided consultancy to some local family centres. In 1998 a number of practititioners in family centres who know about both theory and practice, *and* about the continuing struggle to hold them both together, and some social work academics from the University of Reading met for two days at Charney Manor in Oxfordshire to explore the possibility of together writing a book that would provide a theoretical basis for practice and address *how* therapeutic work can be provided and managed. While we were writing, the climate around family centres was changing, with pressure to abandon long-term work with families. The distress of those who felt that their work was devalued and that vulnerable families were being left unsupported included some of our contributors, and made the process of writing difficult, and for some impossible. It is time for the pendulum to swing back in favour of intensive and, where necessary, long-term work with the most needy families. We hope this book will help.

Note

1   Thanks to Denise Ledger (Ledger 2000) for help with this section.

PART 1

A Framework for Therapeutic Practice

Chapter 1

Theory for Practice in Therapeutic Family Centres

Adrian Ward

The theory: some starting-points

'Theory for practice' is an ambitious topic to cover in a single chapter, and perhaps not one which will excite all practitioners, admittedly. In the midst of the complex demands of everyday practice, the idea of drawing on 'theory' can feel like just another demand, and a rather remote or alien one at that. For this reason, however, my starting point will be just this very complexity. Why is it that practice can seem so complicated and at times difficult? How can the whole thing begin to make sense? But also, why is the work potentially so rewarding and worthwhile? What I want to offer here are a number of ways of thinking about these complexities, in order to find a way through them.

In this chapter, then, I will be outlining various types of idea which, when taken together, should create an overarching framework for thinking about therapeutic practice in family centres. Later chapters will focus more closely on the detail of such practice and its theoretical underpinnings, focusing, for example, on ideas about attachment and about family systems, whereas my focus in this chapter is much more on the overall framework.

I will begin with that complicated overall picture and the need for a *general* context for understanding what happens in family centres, by drawing on ideas about group care. The group care framework offers a generic approach to analysing practice in all residential and day care settings, and sets the context within which the work is carried out. It does not in itself presuppose any particular theoretical orientation, however, and since this book focuses on therapeutic work in particular, we need a more focused theory base which can underpin that task. For the theory base in this book we shall be drawing strongly on psychodynamic thinking, so in the next part of this chapter I will focus on the application of such thinking to therapeutic practice in group care. Whereas later chapters will show how psychodynamic thinking helps in explaining the details of therapeutic work with children and families, here I will be concentrating on its application to groups and organisations, and on the idea of the holding environment as an organising principle. I will also refer to the concept of the therapeutic community as an especially relevant version of the holding environment. The picture is starting to get complicated again, so finally I will draw on 'systems-thinking' as a way of holding the whole thing together.

There are therefore several different approaches encompassed in this chapter, and my argument is that they all need to be taken together, as they interweave with each other in practice.

Group care as the context for practice

The first question which arises is: what *sort* of work is family centre work, especially in therapeutic family centres, and in what ways does this context affect the ways in which the workers need to think about and plan their work? Another way to pose this question is to ask 'What is the mode of practice?'.

The answer is that it is certainly not the same as field social work or care management, but neither is it clinical work (although it has some elements in common with both of these); nor is it community work, although many neighbourhood family centres do draw extensively on community work traditions and practice. In other words, the mode of practice does not typically consist of individual staff based in offices seeing individual service-users and families in their own homes or in 'interview rooms' – it has a more open ethos than that. Neither is it primarily clinical work in the sense of trained therapists offering individual appointments to 'patients' – although some 'direct work' will certainly be part of the overall programme in therapeutic family centres. Equally, it is not principally community work, especially in the therapeutically oriented family centres, because these tend to work with a group of identified and 'referred' families, whom they often have a statutory duty to assess or 'treat', whereas community workers do not typically hold such statutory duties. Family centre practice may of course entail some element of each of the fieldwork, clinical and community work approaches, but these are not likely to be the *primary* mode of practice.

What this practice does consist of is a team of staff from a number of professional backgrounds working together with groups of families within a building which has a range of facilities and opportunities. Sometimes these staff work as independent individuals, but at other times they need to rely closely on each other for practical and emotional support and exchange. Some of the work is done on the basis of planned sessions either for individuals, families or groups, while some of it may be done on a 'drop-in' basis, and some of it happens in the informal in-between times, over cups of coffee, or as people move from one room or session to another. The planned work may happen in 'sessions' behind closed doors, although some of it may also take place in a more open or public forum. In many family centres other events such as lunch-time provide further opportunities for interactions between staff and service-users. This pattern, or what has sometimes been called a 'mosaic' (Brown and Clough 1989), of planned and unplanned interactions sometimes seems closer to residential care than to fieldwork or clinical work. It also has much in common with other types of day care. In other words, family centre work can be viewed as a form of what has been called 'group care' – a generic term covering both residential and day care settings (Ward 1993).

It may therefore be helpful to explore further what is distinctive overall about working in group care settings, in order to set the context for the other approaches covered in this chapter. It is worth pointing out straight away that the concept of 'group care' is not in itself a theory, it is just a label to indicate a broad area or context of social care practice. It is a means towards identifying what there is in common between a number of different settings, and thus to discover what may be distinctive about the methods of working in these settings.

Although there is much diversity within the broad field of group care, there are certain common and distinctive themes, variations upon which will be found in all such settings. I have suggested elsewhere (Ward, *ibid.*) that there are a number of these characteristics which distinguish group care as a context for practice, as follows:

1. The network of relationships between the team and the group of service-users

2. The close interdependence required of the team

3. The public or semi-public nature of much of the work

4. 'Opportunity-led work' – using the opportunities for useful work in the informal everyday life of the centre

5. The co-ordinated use of time

6. The planned use of space and the physical environment.

1. The network of relationships between the team and the group of service-users

The first distinctive feature of group care is that most of the service-users have regular contact and interactions with most of the staff group, and vice versa. This is in marked contrast to the fieldwork or clinical settings, in which the service-users are typically seen only on an individual-case basis (i.e. either as individuals or as families), with the same (usually solo) worker always working on the same case. In group care, however, each service-user is likely to relate to more than one individual worker, and even in those settings where there is a 'keyworker' or similar system, each worker may work simultaneously with many different service-users within the group throughout the day, as well as carrying responsibility for other types of work, including management and administrative tasks, etc. There is often an emphasis on working with groups and groupings of service-users (see Brown and Clough, *op. cit.*), and sometimes with the whole group, rather than solely on working with them as individuals.

This is why this field has become known as group care – not because people are subjected to what has been called 'batch-living', but because there are constant interactions between *groups* of staff and of service-users. There are enormous implications here for the workers in terms of the awareness they need to develop of the way these groups may interact and influence each other for better and for worse. The group is the greatest resource in any group care setting, yet it is often under used because people do not fully recognise its strengths or know how to harness them. There are also implications for the ways in which the work needs to be organised, and for how the team members need to be able to work together to support each other.

2. The close interdependence required of the team

This 'group-focus' therefore leads us naturally into the second distinctive feature of group care practice. By contrast with many clinical and office-based settings, where each worker works autonomously for much of their day's work, and only gets together with others for occasional team meetings, in group care team work typically means that workers need to be able to rely *directly* upon each other in their everyday work with service-users. Thus in a family centre one person can only focus on her interactions with a group of mothers if she knows that someone else is with the children, or supervising the student or whatever else is happening in the place. This applies not just in terms of the planned sessions but also in terms of all the other events and informal activities of the day, where people may need to call upon each other's support or intervention. This means that workers need to cultivate the ability to know what each of their colleagues is doing at any given time, to know who they can call upon for support if there is a crisis or some unexpected arrival at the centre, and to have a sense as to who may need support following a difficult session, and so on. They need to know how to work with each other collaboratively and flexibly, moving rapidly between, for example, a planned group meeting and a conflict between two parents arising from the everyday interactions between groups of parents and children.

This sort of ability may seem to come naturally to some people (particularly those who have grown up in large families!), but it certainly does not do so for everyone, and it often needs to be learned by people new to the work. Without it the 'knitting together' of the fabric of the place soon becomes unravelled. Again this factor has widespread implications for the management of the centre, for instance in terms of the appropriate arrangements for staff meetings and supervision.

3. The public or semi-public nature of much of the work

Not only is the work of group care units such as family centres based on group interactions between the team and the service-users, but much of the work happens in a public or semi-public forum. Colleagues witness each other's practice as they work alongside each other, and the service-users (and their relatives and friends) will also be aware of how other service-users' needs, rights and wishes are responded to. Again, this is a very different context from the mostly 'private' practice of fieldwork and clinic-based work, and one which brings its pressures as well as its rewards.

This is not to say that all the work of a family centre is or should be conducted in a public forum. Indeed there are many aspects of the work which demand meticulous attention to confidentiality, especially where child protection issues are involved. But confidentiality is not the same thing as privacy, and certainly not the same as secrecy – for many families, secrets are potentially very painful things. What this all means is that the issue of what is public and what is private is a constant dilemma in family centres, and is rarely straightforward to handle (Chapter 5 contains an example of the sensitive introduction of personal material from one family's history into the group arena). Workers need to be able to help service-users decide what can be talked about in a 'closed' group discussion, what belongs in a private session, and what can be known more informally among the whole group; they will also need to give regular attention to the question as to how the confidentiality of a large and changing group can be maintained.

4. 'Opportunity-led work' – using the opportunities for useful work in the informal everyday life of the centre

In many forms of professional practice there is a strong emphasis on the formal interview or the planned group session as the main mode of direct practice. In group care, on the other hand, whatever planned work is carried out, there is usually also a strong emphasis on the purposeful use of everyday interactions and events as opportunities for intervention, as in the concepts of the 'life-space interview' (Redl 1966) and the 'Work of the Day' (Kennedy 1987). I have described this as 'opportunity-led' work (Ward 1995b and 1996), to emphasize the skill which is needed on the part of the workers to spot and use these opportunities when they arise. In fact there are many skills involved in this mode of work, ranging from the careful observation required for noticing such opportunities, the assessment skills involved in weighing up the possible interventions, the decision-making skills needed to select an appropriate thing to say or do, and so on.

Opportunity-led work arises out of the handling of incidents and exchanges in everyday 'living alongside' in group care settings, including small-scale as well as larger or more dramatic incidents. The skill of the worker lies in the scrupulous attention to detail in the management of everyday life, and the spotting thereby of occasions which may indicate a need to communicate on the part of a child or parent, or which might create the opportunity to initiate such communication. Typical examples might include:

- a tense exchange between a mother and child over a meal-time, which might have echoes of similar difficulties they have experienced at home

- an angry conflict between two of the children over use of a toy, which might provide the occasion for the worker to help both children develop some skills in negotiating with peers rather than attacking them. (See Stones, Chapter 11 in this book.)

The above examples are just provided to indicate something of the range and focus of opportunity-led work, whereas fuller examples which have arisen in actual practice are described by various authors in the later chapters of this book.

5. The co-ordinated use of time

There are two further ways in which group care workers need to think differently from those in office- or clinic-based settings. The first is in the way in which time is handled. In field social work the individual worker's time is usually her own responsibility to organise and plan. By contrast, in most group care settings time is organised into an overall co-operative routine, within which service-users' and workers' activities are co-ordinated. Individual workers are still responsible for managing their own work-time, within the demands set by the agreed routine, but their work is also likely to be organized (and especially in residential care) within a staff rota of shifts, etc. There may be less shiftwork in family centres (although the recent emergence of some residential family centres has changed this situation again), but there is certainly a lot of detailed scheduling to be done.

A family centre's routine, or pattern of the day, may be formal or informal, overt or implicit, and it will usually include a mixture of formal and informal times. As we have just seen, in many group care settings including family centres, the workers will be with the clients during these informal times as well as during the formal sessions, and will aim to capitalize on the opportunities which these offer. These distinctive elements of 'prolonged exposure' to service-users throughout a day's work, together with the need to be continually accountable to other colleagues for where you are and what you are doing, can be experienced as quite stressful, especially for new or inexperienced workers.

6. The planned use of space and the physical environment

The other way in which group care workers need to think differently from those in office- or clinic-based settings is in terms of the physical environment itself. This environment is much more than just the 'four walls' within which the work is done – it has potential and meaning in its own right. Most group care units are 'centre-based' – i.e. workers and clients all use one building or 'centre' for most of the working day, rather than most of the work being done either in an office or clinic. According to how this space is arranged, used, valued and maintained, it can significantly help, hinder or frustrate the work.

For example, most group care settings have both public and private spaces, and some spaces which are used for formal work as well as others which are mainly used informally by service-users and workers together during 'in-between times'. A contrast can be drawn with the fact that many other professional settings specifically exclude such informal use of space – e.g. staff do not use service-users' waiting-rooms, service-users and staff do not share refreshment facilities. In a place like a family centre, however, there is much more fluidity but also subtlety in the use of space, and decisions about the use of space, and issues arising from its use, often assume major proportions both on a daily basis and in the longer term. Some buildings (but not always the purpose-built ones) seem to lend themselves especially well to therapeutic work with families – perhaps the buildings which have more the feel of a large family house than those which feel more like a school or office, although for some service-users a more 'neutral' atmosphere may actually feel less threatening if associations with 'family' are especially painful.

The distinctive features which I have outlined start to indicate what a rich mixture of elements group care offers, and thereby highlight some of the complexity of the work. I have focused largely on the fact that practice in this context is about groups, both formal and informal, and about the network of relationships between the various groups and sub-groups and the individuals who comprise them. The argument is that in any group care setting, such as a family centre, all of those involved in using or working in the centre will affect each other, for better or worse, and that we should therefore pay close attention to the ways in which these effects work and to how we can understand, influence and maximise the benefits of these effects.

Psychodynamics as an underpinning theory

While the group care framework offers an approach to thinking about practice, it does not in itself presuppose any particular theoretical underpinning. I emphasize this point because there are group care settings which use all sorts of different theoretical perspectives, as well as some which do not appear to use any explicit theory base. Since our focus in this book is on therapeutic practice, we will need a more precise frame of theoretical reference for this, and it will probably be evident by now that our preferred theory base is the psychodynamic one. Our argument is that there is within the extensive literature on psychodynamic thinking about individuals, families and organisations a large amount of work which can be applied very productively to the work of therapeutic family centres.

Relationships and attachments

The most obvious of these connections is perhaps in the work of Winnicott and others on the relationships between mothers and children and on the consequences for children of early disturbances in these relationships (Winnicott 1965). Winnicott was a paediatrician and psychoanalyst who studied early developmental processes in infancy. He focused especially on those processes and developing relationships through which children are helped by their parent(s) to move from their earliest state of absolute dependency towards becoming relatively independent physically and emotionally, and able to function as an autonomous being. He talked about the 'holding function' which (usually) the mother provides, by which he meant both literal physical holding and metaphorical holding of the child's powerful feelings, and he argued that it is through this holding that the child is enabled to gradually establish itself as a person in relationship with others. In parallel with this approach, John Bowlby (1969 and 1982) focused on the instinctive processes of attachment, through which the relationship between child and mother become established. More recently, the burgeoning literature on attachment provides both the research evidence to flesh out the theoretical work of Winnicott and others (see Chapter 2) and some fairly clear lessons for practice in terms of both the assessment and the treatment aspects of family centre work (see Chapters 3 and 4). Psychodynamic thinking of this sort can provide workers with the means of unravelling the sometimes enormously complicated patterns of relationship and conflict within families, and thus with a 'way in' to begin helping families to resolve their difficulties.

Staff dynamics and anxiety

Beyond the detail of the work with individual children and their families, though, psychodynamic thinking can also help us to unravel and explain some of the staff dynamics involved, by highlighting the ways in which, for example, unconscious anxiety may impinge upon the work of individuals or whole teams. Here the work of authors such as Isabel Menzies Lyth (1988) is helpful in tracing the connections between the task of an organisation and the anxieties which that task may generate in the staff. Menzies Lyth argues that these anxieties may influence the whole operation of an organisation (such as a family centre), because individual staff tend to unconsciously pool their anxieties into what is known as a 'collective defence', which then disrupts or inhibits the work.

In the case of a therapeutic family centre, for example, the task of the organisation may in some cases be defined as 'to help families in which children are at serious risk of abuse to become families in which there is a much lesser risk of further abuse'. When we reflect on the reality of a task such as this, we start to realise how fraught with anxiety it may be, with all its connotations of violence, disturbance and distorted relationships. The underlying anxieties associated with such a task, for example, might include the fear that a child may be killed or that a parent may commit suicide, or perhaps the fear on the part of individual staff that they may be attacked or that their mental health may be undermined by prolonged contact with such troubled people. Anxieties such as these which belong with the task may find especially fertile ground, of course, in particular staff members, bearing in mind the sorts of motivations which people may have for doing this sort of work (such as the unconscious need to re-work their own traumas or other disturbances from their own childhood).

The risk to the organisation is that such anxieties may come to predominate in people's attitude to their work in general and/or to the clients in particular. If individual staff members are excessively anxious about the sorts of issue outlined above, or if these understandable worries are not sufficiently contained, they may start to instinctively protect themselves against the anxiety – by, for example, avoiding too much direct contact or emotional involvement with the mothers, or by keeping themselves somewhat distant from the distress and fears of the children, and thus possibly missing signs and symptoms of potential abuse when these arise, because unconsciously they 'don't want to know'.

For individuals to handle their anxieties in this way would be problematic enough, but the more serious scenario is when a whole team or organisation adopts a collective defence of this sort. Such a situation is not so uncommon, in fact, since the anxieties are real and people do need some defences, and are likely to instinctively seek some form of group cohesion. What is needed, therefore, is a mechanism by which the team or organisation can become collectively aware of such tendencies and then find more productive ways of dealing with the anxieties – such as acknowledging them, and reflecting on them together, with the help of supervision or consultancy. In fact, it can be argued that this sort of support and developmental learning is needed on a regular basis by all teams engaged in work of this sort, if they are to prevent the slide into defensive practice, and to remain truly focused on their task.

I have given here only a rather general example of the sorts of anxiety which may be operating in family centres. Other anxieties may be associated with some of the other main themes in this book, and especially around the strong feelings associated with the recurring themes of attachment, separation and loss. Further discussion of this theme can be found in Rosemary Lilley's account in Chapter 12.

The holding environment

We have moved in the above discussion from looking at how parents provide 'holding' for their children to enable them to develop a healthy personality, to focusing on staff anxiety and how it needs to be contained through supervision and consultancy. These two themes might appear to be totally disconnected, but they are in fact directly linked through the concept of the 'holding environment'. This is the term that Winnicott originally used to refer to the totality of the mother's provision for her young child, and here it was intended to convey that 'holding' goes well beyond literal physical holding and beyond the immediate reassurance that a warm cuddle can provide to a distressed child. It refers rather to the whole quality and importance of the human context in which the young child begins its developmental journey.

The link with professional practice is one which Winnicott himself made, in two ways: first by drawing a direct parallel between what the mother provides for her infant and what a therapist may need to provide at an unconscious level for their patient; and second by drawing a further parallel with the sort of 'holding' of a staff team and its anxieties which we saw above. In the context of individual therapy, this 'emotional holding' (Greenhalgh 1994) is provided by the therapist through the medium of deeply attentive listening plus the offering of insightful and well-timed responses which convey to the patient the sense of being understood without being intruded upon. At the broader level of an organisation with therapeutic aims, Winnicott extended the metaphor on to incorporate the total treatment 'environment', or the whole human and physical context in which care and treatment is provided in a range of settings – including, in our case, family centres.

What needs 'holding' in these settings, then, is not only the individual child or parent and their own distress, but also the groups of children and parents, and their interactions with each other and with their communities and broader networks, as well as the group of staff, whose own strong feelings both as individuals and as team members will be aroused through working with the children and their families. Since the staff need to provide emotional holding for the families, they will also need some element of holding in their own right if they are to feel sufficiently secure and resilient to provide for the families, and if (as we saw above) the anxieties inherent in the task are not to overwhelm or divert them.

To be more specific, the aspect of 'holding' in each of these contexts will consist of a number of elements, including the following:

- providing suitable boundaries on behaviour and on the expression of emotion so that strong feelings can be expressed but do not get 'out of hand'

- meanwhile also providing an element of 'giving' and tolerance in relationships, so that people will feel genuinely cared for and, where appropriate, looked after

- the appropriate containment of anxiety (see above, and Bion 1962), which might mean communicating to the other person 'Let's think about that anxiety together until you can find a way or an opportunity to manage it for yourself'

- working towards complete clarity in communication, by aiming to clarify and resolve any misunderstandings or confusions as soon as possible – people under extreme stress are highly likely to interpret things in quite distorted ways, and for those prone to feeling 'unheld' these distortions will often consist of variations on the theme of being persecuted or in other ways undervalued.

Providing a holding environment for a group of troubled children and their families will therefore be a complicated task, involving a mixture of conscious and unconscious elements; and when we also take into account the provision of appropriate 'holding' for the staff team who are themselves engaged in the holding process, it will become evident why the role of leadership in such settings is such a complex and demanding one. Eric Miller offers two related thoughts in this context:

1. The quality of the holding environment of staff is the main determinant of the quality of the holding environment that they can provide for clients.

2. The quality of the holding environment of staff is mainly created by the form of organisation and by the process of management. (Miller 1993b, p.3)

Providing an appropriate holding environment for staff can therefore be seen as the overall framework within which therapeutic care is provided for children and their families. In practice, the holding environment in a therapeutic family centre will be provided through the whole pattern of arrangements for one-to-one, group and inter-group relationships, as well as through the containment of these relationships through a network of arrangements for supervision, staff meetings, consultancy and management (see Ward 1995b). In addition, 'holding' will be conveyed through less tangible means such as the 'atmosphere' of the place and the spirit in which the work is conducted, as well as through those more tangible means such as the quality of the physical environment. In everyday life in group care settings, there is sometimes a real and difficult challenge to be met in trying to maintain the quality of 'atmosphere' in the face of the diversionary and even subversive interventions which may come both from troubled children and their families and from anxious or exhausted staff. Here again we see the crucial role of good leadership. In Chapter 8 Sarah Musgrave offers a more detailed account of the 'holding' function in working with the families attending family centres, while in Chapter 11 Christine Stones explores the role of management in creating a therapeutic environment.

The therapeutic community as a model for practice

The concept of the holding environment provides a theoretical foundation upon which practice can be built, but it might be objected that it is still couched in rather vague terms, and that it is not yet clear exactly what such an approach would look like in practice. To some extent this is inevitable, and our aim is that the remaining chapters of this book will help to fill out the detail in various different ways. One model of practice in a related field, however, which has a great deal to offer family centres is the model of the therapeutic community. This is a model with a long tradition in the fields of both adult psychiatric care and the residential care and treatment of children, although it has not often been explicitly applied to the family centre context. For this reason, some readers may be surprised to find this approach emphasized here, and may have assumptions about therapeutic communities which make them appear rather different from or even irrelevant to practice in family centres. Some people, for example, retain an impression of the therapeutic community as somewhere between the imagined 'let it all hang out' ethos of an encounter group and the unboundaried permissiveness of some religious cults. By contrast with such stereotypes, however, the therapeutic community model of practice is actually very clear and disciplined. It is also a model which fits well within the 'group care' approach, since it focuses very much on the nature and quality of interactions between the various groups and groupings in the place (Hinshelwood 1987).

What is meant by the therapeutic community approach is a model in which the 'whole is greater than the sum of its parts', and which places great emphasis on establishing a 'culture of enquiry' (Main 1946). This means that all members of the community (or in this case, of the family centre), whether staff or 'clients', work together on understanding and resolving whatever difficulties and conflicts may arise, whether for individuals, for groups or for the community as a whole. The aim is that at every level within the organisation, practice will be conducted in an open and equal spirit, based upon a system of regular and frequent 'community meetings' of everybody involved. If this starts to sound rather idealistic, there may be some truth in that, and what is probably closer to reality is that many places do adopt a 'therapeutic community *approach* (see below) though they may not all meet every characteristic of the ideal model (see the 'Audit Checklist' developed by Kennard and Lees 2000, for an overview of these characteristics).

In truth, there is no such thing as '*the* therapeutic community'. What there is, is a set of ideals, beliefs and working practices which (like the group care characteristics, but in this case in closer detail) can be identified as typical of the therapeutic community approach. The central principle of this approach is the belief that *all* members of the community (service-users as well as staff) can give as well as take in therapeutic exchanges and indeed that it is *the community itself* which is therapeutic, rather than (as is more traditional in clinical work) that it is primarily only *the staff* who engage in therapeutic endeavour. The focus of the work thus becomes the task of enabling people to realise and apply their own ability to help as well as to be helped.

In the case of family centres, this approach seems especially appropriate in the context of an aim of helping parents both to improve their ability to care for and support their own children, and to develop in their own right. Experience in family centres certainly bears out the reality that many parents can and do contribute to each other's growth and development in very important ways, and many examples of this will be found in the rest of this book. Perhaps the best documented evidence of this ethos being applied in action is in the work of NEWPIN (Cox 1987; Pound 1994), and in Chapter 13 Anne Jenkins Hansen outlines one aspect of this approach when she describes the 'soft structuring' style of management in that organisation.

In general, however, the ways in which the principles of the therapeutic community are applied in practice include the following (Ward and McMahon 1998):

- an emphasis on the value of *groupwork* as a medium both for therapeutic work and in some places for decision-making with the service-users

- a specific commitment to the use of the daily *community meeting* as a medium for both practical and therapeutic business between service-users and staff

- an emphasis on the potential for therapeutic communication between staff and service-users to arise from *everyday interactions* in daily 'living alongside' each other (i.e. opportunity-led work – as above)

- in daily practice, a commitment to a *personal* and involved style of working, in which the quality of the relationships between service-users and staff is seen as playing a central role in the treatment process

- a commitment to the value of the physical and personal '*environment*' for its contribution to the therapeutic task

- in internal management structures, an emphasis on each person's role and *potential contribution* to the agreed task and philosophy rather than mainly on status, rank and formal titles

- a commitment to the value of a full system of staff support and supervision, including the use of *consultancy* for senior managers

- the use of *psychodynamic* rather than solely behavioural or cognitive theoretical frameworks to underpin the treatment philosophy.

None of these working practices is offered as a perfect ideal, however, and in reality even the longest established therapeutic communities are continually adapting them to manage the constant tensions between ideals and reality. For many family centres it may be more appropriate to explore the use of the 'therapeutic community *approach*' rather than to become what has been called a 'therapeutic community proper'. In terms of the unfolding argument of this chapter, the therapeutic community approach can be seen as an example of how the concept of the 'holding environment' can be applied in practice, and as one version of how psychodynamic thinking can inform therapeutic practice in a group care setting.

Systems thinking as a model for holding the whole thing together

Since the aim of the chapter is to provide theoretical frameworks which will help practitioners to hold together the complexities of therapeutic practice in family centres, it seems appropriate to conclude this part of the discussion by thinking about systems theory. Indeed the principle value of taking a systems approach to practice is that it encourages us always to think about 'the interconnectedness of things', which is extremely valuable in the context of the potential complexity of the work as outlined at the start of the chapter.

The basic premise of the systems approach is that every human organisation, such as a family, team, or indeed a family centre as a whole, may be envisaged as a 'system' consisting of many parts. All of these parts or 'sub-systems' are interconnected and affect each other (although sometimes in unexpected ways), and the whole system is in some senses greater than the sum of its parts, and can be said to have characteristics of its own. One of the images which has sometimes been offered as a concrete example of a system is that of a central heating system. Thus it has been pointed out that, while the separate components of a central heating system are not much use by themselves, once they are properly connected-up and functioning together they become an effective system for heating a house.

Systems-thinking focuses on such properties as the boundaries and connections between sub-systems, and on the extent to which a system is 'open' or
'closed' to interaction across these boundaries. A further characteristic of
systems relates to the issue of change. The systems approach is based on the
view that since all the parts of a system are connected, change in any one part is
likely to affect all other parts. The implications of this simple idea are
enormous, especially in therapeutic family centres, for example, where change
is usually a central preoccupation. At the same time, systems are seen as
naturally tending towards 'homeostasis', or maintaining a steady and un-
changing state. Thus all systems are said to be inherently geared towards
preserving themselves intact by keeping their various parts in a state of balance.
Taking these last two characteristics together may help us to explain, for
example, why an attempt to change a whole system (such as a troubled family,
or an unhappy staff team) by 'pushing' all the parts at the same time may fail,
while by contrast a well-aimed 'nudge' of one small part of the system may set
in motion much greater changes in the system as a whole.

Straightforward examples of the systems and sub-systems in a family centre
would include: the centre as a whole (all the people within it); the staff team;
the groups of children and of mothers, the family system of any given child, etc.
The systems approach can help to explain the ways in which 'systems' such as
these operate both within themselves and in interaction with each other.

The connections between the parts of a system, and the ways in which these
parts influence each other, can all be studied within the systems approach,
although the approach itself does not presuppose any single theoretical basis
for the connections. In fact, it is an approach which allows for the use of many
different theories, and is not really a theory in its own right at all, more a way of
looking at the world: it will not in itself provide answers, but it can provide a
more productive way of framing the questions.

There are therefore many different ways in which systems-thinking can be
applied to family centre work. Perhaps the most obvious of these is in terms of
the dynamics of the families attending the centre, and the strategies which staff
can use in order to engage with the families and promote appropriate change.
There is an extensive literature on family systems and family therapy to draw
upon, and some centres do explicitly make this the basis for their practice,
although perhaps not many have fully trained family therapists on their staff
team. In Chapter 6 Yvonne Bailey-Smith provides an example of this approach
in working with black families.

Even where family centres are not offering formal family therapy they can
still draw usefully upon family systems thinking, since looking at the family as
a system (rather than as a mere collection of individuals) enables us to

understand more about the ways in which family members influence and affect each other. Thus, as in all systems, change in one person in a family may have a profound effect on other family members, and the system as a whole may try to protect itself from the impact of this change by trying to retain its balance or established order at all costs. Sometimes, for example, a family system tries to maintain this balance by pushing out the individual who is challenging it: perhaps a troubled child or a troublesome partner. The appropriate professional response to such dynamics may involve examining and challenging the assumptions in the whole system rather than being caught up in the pressure to exclude (see Preston-Shoot and Agass 1990).

Beyond using systems theory to look at individual families, however, we can also apply it to the ways in which other 'sub-systems' of a family centre interact, for example for looking at how the group of mothers and the group of staff affect each other in various ways, or at the relationships between different groups of staff such as 'domestic' and 'professional' staff. Likewise, we can look at the relationship between the family centre as a whole and other systems with which it interacts, such as key organisations in the local community, or the 'parent' organisation which funds the project.

In fact it is perhaps in terms of these relationships between the family centre and its organisational and societal context that systems theory can make its most useful contribution. Writers such as Eric Miller (1993) and Isabel Menzies Lyth (1988) use an 'open systems' approach to address the primary task of organisations. This model can be summarised into a few key concepts as follows: any organisation is viewed as an 'open system' with one central or primary task, this task being achieved through a number of co-ordinated 'systems of activity', or sets of arrangements for carrying out the various functions of the unit (Miller and Gwynne 1972). Clarity about the primary task is seen as essential to the proper operation – and indeed the survival – of the system.

The concept of the 'open system', on which this model is based, simply represents the fact that most organisations function by being 'open' to their surroundings: they take in or 'import' materials at one end, 'process' or 'transform' them, then send them out or 'export' them again at the other end. (The term 'materials' is used metaphorically, since in a group care organisation it is people [families in this case] rather than inanimate materials who come in at one end and go out again at the other: this is obviously an important difference between group care organisations and other kinds of human organisation – factories, insurance companies, etc.) A closed system, by contrast, would be one in which nothing comes in or goes out – the stereotype of a monastery is very nearly a closed system, although it has been pointed out that 'there is no perfect closed system, because there is nothing that is not affected by influences from outside' (Bruggen and O'Brian 1987, p.56).

Applying this framework to the problem of defining the task of a unit such as a family centre, the open systems approach proposes that the central or primary task of the unit should be expressed in terms of the 'throughput of materials' – i.e. the 'process' of each family's stay at the family centre, from admission through to departure. It is in relation to this process that the primary task is seen as 'the task which the enterprise must perform in order to survive' (Rice 1958) – in other words, the primary task is that which it must be seen to be achieving if it is not to lose its supply of referrals or even to be closed down.

What this approach highlights is both the need to be absolutely clear about the task of the centre, and the difficulty of doing so, since so many competing expectations often have to be met. For example, what the families may want from the centre staff may differ in subtle but significant ways from what the external managers or the employing agency may expect, and both of these may differ again from what any given referring professional may hope for. One hypothetical example of the primary task of a therapeutic family centre was offered above (p.31), but for any given unit the primary task cannot usually be lifted 'off the shelf', it has to be thought through and negotiated. It will usually be the responsibility of the centre manager, in consultation with all parties, to negotiate and re-negotiate the task in order to keep the work of the centre properly focused, and to be aware of the ways in which the anxieties inherent in the task can affect its achievement (see the discussion on pp.31–32). Like most welfare organisations, many family centres struggle to be clear about their primary task, and it often happens that the organisation drifts off task or becomes preoccupied with secondary or even apparently trivial aspects of the task (Menzies Lyth, *op. cit.*). For further discussion of this theme, see Rosemary Lilley's chapter (Chapter 12) on task and anxiety.

Conclusion

I began with an acknowledgement that some practitioners may approach the topic of 'theory' with caution and reluctance, and perhaps another indication of this caution is that many people prefer to describe their approach as 'eclectic' rather than being tied to any one particular framework. Eclecticism, meaning the judicious choice from within a range of ideas, is certainly an appropriate approach, so long as we are clear about why and how we are choosing the approaches which we do. The aim of this chapter has been to outline a range of ideas which can be used for different purposes: group care for its account of the overall context and mode of practice; psychodynamic thinking as an underpinning theory, with the concepts of the holding environment and of the therapeutic community as increasingly specific models of practice; and systems-thinking as a way of holding the whole thing together. I would not wish to be prescriptive about which particular blend of ideas a family centre staff team should draw upon, but I would argue that such choices should be made explicitly and on the basis of clear judgements about what will work best in the given context. It will be the responsibility of the staff team as a whole to aim to be clear and explicit as well as eclectic in drawing on different frameworks for different purposes.

Chapter 2

Understanding Parent–Child Relationships

Attachment and the Inner World

Linnet McMahon

How can we understand the needs of troubled children and parents? Our aim in this chapter is to offer a way of doing so which draws on two related sets of ideas, attachment theory and psychodynamic thinking. In family centres we often see children and parents firmly entrenched in mutually unhelpful, even destructive, patterns of behaviour. Sometimes this behaviour has simply become a habit which both child and parent are relieved to put behind them when offered teaching in positive parenting. For other families this help is not enough, and interventions which draw on understanding of children's and parents' troubled 'inner worlds' and on the way in which these affect their relationships offer more possibility of hopeful outcomes. At the same time we need to remember that families exist within a wider social context; their lives affected by issues of race and culture, social class, poverty and isolation, gender and sexual orientation, disability and mental illness. We need to be constantly aware of the whole gamut of prejudice and power, both in their direct effects on families and in their more subtle influences on the inner worlds of parents and children.

John Bowlby's (1969, 1988) pioneering work on attachments in infancy has inspired a vast pool of research which is producing important findings about the formation of attachments and the long-term effects of early relationships. Much of this research relates too to psychodynamic studies of infancy largely based on case material, and it has been valuable in clarifying, supporting and sometimes challenging these ideas. The findings have significant implications for family centre practice, in particular in pointing to the importance of giving help to families experiencing difficulties in parent–child relationships as early as possible in a child's life if lasting problems are to be avoided.

The foundations of attachment

Attachment theory starts from observation of how child and parent behave in their relationships with one another, from which inferences are drawn about what is happening in the inner worlds of child and parent. By inner world we mean that 'mixture of the conscious and less-than-conscious: thoughts and feelings, fears and imaginings, understandings and misunderstandings, dreams and nightmares, images of people and places and assumptions about their meaning or importance' (Ward 1998, pp.11–12). Attachment refers to that profound emotional relationship which develops between a baby and one or more parents or caretakers. The main parent or caretaker is not necessarily the biological mother, or even a woman since 'mothering' can come from fathers. However we shall use the word 'mother' in referring to the most usual first relationship. Whereas *bonding* refers to the mother's tie to her baby, *attachment* is concerned with the child's need for the person in his or her life who provides a secure base. An important feature of this relationship is that it persists over time (even over a life-time) and involves someone who is seen as stronger or wiser. Clearly we are concerned here with some aspects of love but the concepts take us to basic instinctual needs so that the feelings part of love have to be inferred.

We now know that most mothers do not fall in love with their babies at first sight, but that over the first weeks most mothers develop a strong bond. Bowlby suggested that infants' behaviour such as crying, smiling, raising their arms, clinging, and later on following, is an evolutionary built-in survival mechanism which hooks in most mothers to provide responsive care. The classic Bowlby view was that the proximity seeking of attachment behaviour served to protect the infant from danger rather than meet needs for nourishment and shelter. So attachment behaviour is a response to fear and anxiety. This is not, of course, the whole story. Relationships between parents and young children also grow out of shared good experiences, as we shall see.

A key recognition in attachment theory is that almost *all* children develop attachments to their mothers/caretakers. *Non-attachment* is rare and only occurs when mothering has never been provided. This is the case for some children raised from infancy in institutions, more frequent in war-torn societies or those in extreme poverty. Thus what is in question is the *quality* of the attachment. Some attachments are more secure than others. Over the first year of life the baby is learning from experience about how others respond to him or her. Out of this experience the baby develops an expectation, an '*inner working model*', of the parent, generalised to the world, as responsive and helpful (or not), and so builds up a picture of themself as worthy (or unworthy) of love and care. Bowlby called these two contrasting types *secure attachment* and *insecure* or *anxious attachment*. He identified different kinds of insecure attachments, and others built on this work, but we will come back to this later. What is important to note here is that attachments are probably best regarded as a *continuum* from very secure, to more or less secure, to moderately anxious, to very anxiety-provoking and frightening, including all the stages in between (Crittenden 1995). While discrete categories can be useful in helping us think, we need also to pay attention to the complexity and individuality of people's experiences.

Holding and containment – the basis for secure attachment

If we are to offer effective help when the relationship between parent and child is in trouble we need first to understand the processes involved when the relationship between parent and child is 'good enough' and the child forms a secure attachment.

Although babies differ according to the exact age at which attachment behaviour appears we know that even very young infants, with their inherent capacity for relating (Stern 1985) recognise and prefer their mothers. In its waking hours a baby experiences the distress and pain of hunger and physical discomfort inside or outside its body, the excitement and pleasure of feeding, and after urgent needs have been satisfied an attentiveness to the world, and an urge to explore and play with its own and its mother's body and find its physical edges. Emotional edges take longer to find, since the baby's intense feelings of pleasure and pain, of love and anger, are bound up with the mother.

The 'good-enough' mother initially meets her baby's needs totally. She is able to do this through her *primary maternal preoccupation* in which she 'gives the infant the illusion that there is an external reality that corresponds to the infant's own capacity to create' (Winnicott 1971, p.12). The baby feels comfortably omnipotent rather than helpless. The mother attends to her baby's feelings, good and bad, to such an extent that she experiences them as if they were her own. Bion (1962) calls this process *maternal reverie*. The mother is 'open to being stirred up emotionally by the baby'. For example, most parents can recall the compelling anxiety produced by the sound of their baby's crying.

When the baby is upset the mother acts as a *container*, holding on to without being overwhelmed by her baby's feelings. She thinks about how the baby is feeling, sometimes consciously but probably more often without consciously doing so. By the way in which she responds she gives these feelings back to her baby in a more bearable form. For example, if her baby cries angrily when undressed, she may pick her up or touch her gently, or hold the baby with her voice saying soothingly something like 'You don't like being all exposed do you, but you are quite safe and I'll soon have you dressed'. Whether or not she puts it into words like these she conveys her own good feelings. She gives back more good feelings than bad ones, more experiences of love than anger or hate. The predominance of loving feelings from the mother enables the baby to begin to bear and manage angry and anxious feelings. She no longer has to get rid of them and project them onto someone else. In addition, the baby 'takes in the feeling of "being contained", of maternal space having been available for his anxieties to be born and thought about' (Copley and Forryan 1987, p.241). This *emotional holding* or *containment* enables the young child to take in and integrate both good and bad feelings into the self.

We know now that infants thrive on sensitive and responsive care involving reciprocal interaction. Stern (1985) describes this as *attunement* or inter-subjectivity. The mother who is tuned in to her baby paces her overtures and responses, avoiding either being overcontrolling or undercontrolling, but keeping in synchrony with her baby, in a sort of mutual dance (Brazelton and Cramer 1991). For example, a mother playing peepbo with her baby pauses to anticipate his response. His delight encourages her to continue, and one day he will initiate the game himself. As the infant finds the space for *his* turn so his sense of self grows.

Holding the child in mind as a separate person

Research suggests that more than responsive care is involved in secure attachment. The mother must also be able to hold her child in mind, to think about her child as a separate person from herself (Fonagy *et al.* 1994). Such emotional containment allows the child to become emotionally as well as physically separate and to establish his or her identity. Sometimes this is described as developing a psychological self as well as a physical self, or as Winnicott (1965) puts it, a sense of 'me' and 'not me'. This need may help to explain why some mothers do well with their baby in the early weeks but have difficulties later. They identify with their new-born baby's need for nurture which matches their own need, but cannot bear the rejection implied by the child's development of a separate self.

The 'good-enough' mother's gradual and inevitable failure to match her infant's every need 'enables the infant eventually to relinquish the illusion of unity and omnipotence', to find their own emotional edges and to explore the reality of the outside world. A 'perfect mother' who remained totally adapted to her infant's needs would not allow her baby to start to experience themself as a separate person. From the initial state of merger with the mother, the edges of the infant's self become more defined. Eventually the child in turn becomes a container for his feelings, able to hold on to them and think about them, a process helped by putting them into words. From the original state of merger with the mother the child becomes an emotionally separate person and achieves an integrated self, reaching Winnicott's age of concern.

Multiple attachments

Bowlby and Winnicott referred mainly to the 'mother' but we need to understand how attachments develop in families and cultures where the mothering function is shared among several people, including fathers, grandparents, aunts, siblings, childminders or nursery workers. What seems to happen is that a child builds up a hierarchy of attachments. Only the primary attachment figures are able to comfort the child in severe distress but others can provide reassurance for lesser upsets. However, multiple mothering where the child has several primary attachment figures may contribute greatly to the child's overall sense of security and belonging (Rashid, in Howe 1996; Gaber and Aldridge 1994; Gambe, Gomez *et al.* 1992; Harwood and Miller 1997).

Some children demonstrate secure attachments to both parents, others to only one parent. Occasionally an older sibling becomes an important attachment figure, as may others such as grandparents, aunts, childminder and so on. A child may have a different kind of attachment to each parent (Fonagy *et al.* 1994). (This suggests too that the child's temperament is not an over-riding factor.) Where a child has an insecure attachment to one parent, he or she may be protected to some degree by a secure attachment to the other. People may also have different roles beyond attachment; for example a father who might be a less significant attachment figure than the mother may be crucially important as someone to play and talk with.

Separation anxiety and attachment seeking

The formation of attachment begins in the first weeks and months of a baby's life. From about four months a baby's attachments are becoming clearer, shown in their preferences for particular people, especially when in need of comfort. By about six months, most babies are starting to show fear of strangers. They also start to show separation anxiety. If the parent moves out of sight or leaves the room a child may cry, or (once mobile) attempt to follow. The child's anxiety is greater if the surroundings or the people remaining are unfamiliar. It can be upsetting to parents who see their up until then sociable baby who 'would go to anyone' become much more discriminating, and they fear they have done something wrong to cause this. Yet such attachment-seeking behaviour is an essential part of normal development, and has survival value – the child is less likely to run into danger or get lost, and most parents would ultimately be very anxious about the safety of a child who would 'go with anyone'.

Separation anxiety and protest occurs at about the time the young child gets the idea of object permanence. It probably starts as the baby realises that mother is a separate person and can leave him. The child's feeling of security depends on keeping mother in view, at an age when the child is unable to hold on to the idea of 'mother' if she cannot be seen. Strong secondary attachment figures can support a child at the stage of separation anxiety, unless the child's anxiety is extreme. Where these attachment figures are high in the child's hierarchy of attachments, as in some forms of multiple mothering, the occurrence and severity of separation anxiety may be much reduced.

Where the child's distress and anxiety on separation are high it helps if the caregiver can tolerate the painful feelings of the child's protest without defending against them. A crying or angry child is very painful to be in touch with and to avoid this carers can busy themselves with mundane tasks or be falsely cheerful, when what the child needs is comfort, the reassurance of the familiar, reminders of the parent (including a physical reminder like a purse or photograph) and the child's 'transitional object', the soft blanket or teddy, which helps the child to recreate part of the mother in her absence. Then the child may be 'held' well enough emotionally to manage their anxiety. Protest is a healthy stage. Only if the separation is prolonged or not well managed does the child risk withdrawal into quiet despair and eventual detachment, unable to retain the memory of 'good' mother as opposed to the 'bad' mother who has left them (Robertson and Robertson 1989). A well managed and not too lengthy separation need not impair a child's security of attachment.

Separation anxiety and attachment seeking remains high from around six months through the next two years, diminishing only towards the age of three as the child's memory and sense of time develop, and a mental image of mother and being mothered can be sustained for longer, while developing language ability means the child is more able to ask questions and grasp explanations of what is happening. While ages vary a little, this pattern occurs in widely varying cultures (Bretherton and Waters 1985; Waters 1995).

Secure attachment and the inner working model

The value of a secure attachment is that, paradoxically, it frees the child to play and explore the world. The secure child does not have to spend time and energy monitoring the parent and trying to get his own emotional needs met. Attachment provides a safe base from which to find out about the world. Thus *dependence* is the essential foundation for the development of autonomy and independence.

Bowlby suggested that by the end of the first year a child has developed an inner working model, a generalised expectation based on experience, of the mother as available and responsive (or not) and, in turn, a complementary model of the self as worthy (or unworthy) of care and love. Attachment is linked to self-esteem. 'Thus an unwanted child is likely not only to feel unwanted by his parents but to believe that he is essentially unwantable' (Bowlby 1973, p.204). This mental image becomes a blueprint both for other attachments later in life and the feelings a person holds about themself. Studies of the pre-school years show that securely attached children are more confident with adults and with their peers, and that they tackle difficulties with more confidence and in the expectation that help will be available if they need it. (It may be of course that such optimism is unrealistic. However the securely attached child tends also to be likeable, which goes a long way to ensuring the support of others.)

Research studies suggest that a secure attachment confers not only social but also intellectual skills – the ability to think. An aspect of the inner working model of the securely attached child is that she seems better able not only to develop her own reflective ability but also to think about other people thinking. This 'theory of mind' has been found significantly more developed in five-year-olds who are securely attached, in contrast to those with insecure attachments (Fonagy 1996). The securely attached child is able to connect thinking and feeling.

Early difficulties in parent–child relationships

So far we have been concerned to understand how a 'good-enough' relationship between child and parent leads to a secure attachment, with the emotional and intellectual strength which this confers. We go on to look at some of the difficulties in parent–child relationships which lead to children having insecure and anxious attachments. We need to do this without in any way attributing blame to the parent. Sometimes the 'mother' is overwhelmed by the baby's distressed or angry crying. This may happen if she too is anxious or angry and does not have enough good experiences and feelings from her own past experience to hold on to and to draw on. It may happen too if her own 'holding environment' is inadequate, for example if she is struggling with poverty or isolation, especially if she herself is not 'contained' by a close confiding relationship with someone else, whether a partner, relative or friend. It may also occur if she is physically or mentally ill or depressed, or has drug or alcohol problems. Sometimes real difficulties in the recent life of the parent or of the child have impaired the development of a secure parent–child relationship. For example, post-natal depression, housing or financial stress, or a separation or loss of someone close, may affect a parent's ability to provide responsive care. Equally a child's illness, or developmental delay or disability may create anxiety or grief which may affect both the parent's bonding with their child as well as the child's capacity to respond. While a child's temperament will always be a factor, children's responses to different kinds of containment or its lack are reflected in their attachment behaviour.

Recognising secure and anxious attachment – the strange situation

How can we know how secure or anxious a child's attachment to a parent is? We need to spend time observing, listening and thinking if we are to make sense of the relationship between a particular parent and child. Some additional diagnostic tools may help. Young children at 12, 18 and 24 months have been observed in Mary Ainsworth's (Ainsworth et al. 1978) 'strange situation', a test which has provided the basis for numerous research studies. A child is left alone for up to three minutes with an unfamiliar person, the question being what happens when the child loses their secure base and becomes anxious. The child is then reunited with mother, and it is the child's behaviour on reunion which is the indicator of the child's attachment status. This behaviour is classified as follows:

SECURE ATTACHMENT

The young 'secure' child responds to the separation with more or less distress, some crying and seeking the mother and others showing some capacity for response to care from the 'stranger'. The key indicator of secure attachment is the child greeting their mother positively on her return and being readily reassured or comforted, and then going back to playing and exploring. The child prefers mother to the stranger, but responds to the stranger unless distressed. Secure attachment is the most common attachment pattern.

ANXIOUS (INSECURE) ATTACHMENT

Sometimes children have learned defensive responses which do not communicate directly to the mother how they are feeling. These can take different forms.

1. Some young children show little distress or protest when their mother leaves, although a raised heartbeat has been noted. Their play may be very superficial and they are likely to respond positively to the stranger. *They initially avoid their parent on return and do not seek contact.* This is described as anxious *avoidant attachment.*

2. Other young children show much distress on separation, and wariness of the stranger. More important, they *continue to show distress on mother's return, with prolonged crying and clinging, together with moments of anger.* They are not easily comforted and their subsequent exploration and play is limited and passive. This is described as anxious *ambivalent* or *resistant attachment.*

3. Mary Main (Main *et al.* 1985) later identified a small third group of young children with what she called *disorganised* or *disoriented attachment.* On reunion the child shows contradictory behaviour either at the same time or in quick succession, incomplete or undirected movement or stereotypes, confusion and apprehension, or 'stilling'. For example, a child moves towards her mother while looking away with momentary strong expression (of fear, anger, or a dazed look), rapidly followed by putting her expression into neutral to look at her mother. Another child may crouch motionless. Some of this behaviour may appear dissociative.

A word of warning here. Some children with *autism* or other impairments may show similar behaviour to anxiously attached children, for example approach/avoidance conflict. This does not necessarily mean that they have insecure attachments. Listening to parents' views and prolonged observation are needed to distinguish these children.

Situations similar to the 'strange situation' occur naturally all the time in family centres. A parent leaves the room to get a cup of coffee or to take part in a conversation or group. The young child is meanwhile cared for by other people. If these are familiar people the child may not be anxious unless something happens like falling over or getting hurt by another child; and a child beyond toddlerhood is usually capable of holding the parent in mind for longer and so can better tolerate absence. But after a brief separation involving some stress, *observing the child's behaviour on reunion with the parent* can give useful clues to the child's security of attachment to them. Where assessment is part of the worker's brief, for example in observing contact visits, informal versions of the 'strange situation' can give useful information.

While the 'strange situation' test becomes less useful as children get older, other indicators such as the picture tests and story completions provide a glimpse of a child's attachments and inner working models of self (see Chapter 3).

Anxious attachment as a child's defensive response to a parent's difficulties in providing emotional holding

We can understand differences in children's attachment behaviour as a response to their different experiences of parental holding and containment. We have seen how the 'good-enough' parent is able to be attuned to her child and to help the child manage difficult or painful feelings, so that the child builds up an inner working model of the parent, and so the world, as responsive and helpful, and of themselves as worthy of love and care. The child is helped to use both thinking and feeling and to make connections between them. In contrast the anxiously attached child has learned that their parent is unavailable and unresponsive for all or some of the time. Without the resources to be other than egocentric the young child sees themself as the cause of the parent's behaviour. The child develops an inner working model of the world as unresponsive and unhelpful and themself therefore unworthy of love and care. Depending on the parent's response the child may be able to use *either* thinking *or* emotional strategies to get some of the care they need, but thinking and feeling remain unconnected. In the extreme case there is no possible action the child can take to get adequate care, and the child's thinking and feeling are both desperately confused and impaired.

Let us look at some of Ainsworth's patterns in more detail, while remembering that parents and children are individuals and therefore are unlikely to fit exactly into a particular pattern. Our aim is not to slot children and parents into boxes, which would avoid the important task of reflection, but rather to draw on general models which may help us in our task of understanding a particular relationship.

Children with anxious *avoidant* attachment tend to have mothers who give basic physical care but are predictably unresponsive, emotionally unavailable, often depressed, or rejecting of physical contact with the baby, teaching their children not to cling because they cannot bear it. The child's communication may pass straight through the mother like a 'sieve', or their distress be simply wiped away ('teatowel') or met by a 'brickwall', a lack of or mis-timing of maternal response (Copley and Forryan's (1987) metaphors for non-containment). The children have learned that their parent is *predictably* unavailable to meet their emotional needs and that expression of feelings is ignored or disliked. Crittenden (1995) suggests that the parent's predictability enables these children to develop their intellectual skills – thinking can be trusted, although feelings have to be so denied as to become repressed into the unconscious.

The child's *core anxiety* is *abandonment*, with feelings of grief and loss, and underlying deep sadness, and also anger and emptiness. The best defence against this is to bottle up your feelings, smile brightly, behave well and keep your distance. If the parental rejection is not too severe (concern may be there but emotional warmth lacking) the child may use positive coping strategies such as getting buried in the worlds of books and stories, playing with friends, telling themself they're all right, getting absorbed in the world of things rather than people, achieving at school. More thoroughgoing defences involve developing a 'false self' (Hopkins 1987), with a false cheerfulness and denial of pain. If the parent's withdrawal from the child is the result of depression or other turning inwards, then looking after the parent becomes one way in which the child can get closer, often generalised to the child becoming a 'compulsive caretaker'. A more dangerous parent means the child is safest if compliant or good, idealising the parent through projective identification, and blaming themself, or derogating the other parent (Crittenden's 'compulsively compliant' child). The question remains as to whether the child's real emotional self exists and has to be hidden or, in the direst case, whether it never had the chance to develop at all. In the long run the child or young person has difficulties with making intimate relationships. In adolescence, promiscuous sexuality can ward off isolation, although depression and suicidal thoughts are a real risk. Compulsions and addictions, such as eating disorders or drug addiction, keep feelings at bay.

Children with anxious *resistant* or *ambivalent* attachment tend to have mothers who give inconsistent care, at one time sensitively responsive and at another angry and rejecting (for instance if the infant cries a lot). The mother may sometimes fail to notice an obviously upset child ('sieve'), or be frightened by the child's distress and so act as a 'sponge', soaking up the distress but taking away some of its meaning. At other times she may be intrusive, interrupting a child happily playing or dumping her own feelings of anger or distress on him ('dustbin'). Some mothers have learned to view the world as an unsafe place and discourage exploration, so the child becomes less competent and more frustratedly angry and anxious. All these children have learned that their parent's availability and response is *unpredictable*, which leaves them with no consistent intellectual strategy for getting the care they need. Their only effective way of getting care and attention is to raise the emotional temperature, with crying and clinging or angry tantrums. These, as Crittenden points out, are intuitively chosen and alternated between to match the parental emotional response. Children are so preoccupied with monitoring the parent's emotional state that their independent play is often impoverished. The child learns to trust the language of emotion but not of thinking.

The severely rejected or abused child for whom their first attachment figure was both the source and the solution to alarm is likely to have a *disorganised* attachment, or an attachment which *combines elements of extreme avoidance and resistance*. This group is perhaps to be equated with Winnicott's *'unintegrated'* child. These children can reliably use neither thinking nor feeling, which remain disconnected. Such very uncontained children find bad feelings unbearable, experiencing 'nameless dread' or 'falling to pieces'. They continue to get rid of these feelings and project them into other people in order to find relief. Dockar-Drysdale (1968) describes such unintegrated children as *frozen*, broken off rather than grown away from the mother and unable to form a reciprocal relationship. Their greatest fear is of *annihilation*. They may try to preserve what is left of the self by annihilating others, mentally as much as physically. Or the child may hold or cling to an object such as a bright light (or to a person treated as an object), or use sensuous feelings or body movements to hold her together against the terror of falling apart (Copley and Forryan's (1987) *adhesive identification or merger*). Some retreat into phantasy and dissociation. Dockar-Drysdale also identifies *archipelago* children who have isolated islets of ego functioning which are not linked up into a coherent self. *False-self children*, described by Winnicott, operate with a front which conceals and protects the turmoil within.

Continuities in attachment

Attachment behaviour persists through childhood and adult life, extending to partners, work colleagues and friends, and even god. It is a normal not a pathological response, reflecting the human need to seek other people to ensure survival. As they get older children develop skills that enable them to protect themselves. Over time most children make additional attachments and previous attachments may become more or less secure. More 'holding' from a better 'held' parent (with a new supportive partner, for example) or other carer (such as a foster carer) may help a child develop a more secure attachment (Hopkins 1999, Howe 1995, 1996). In contrast some children who experience severe trauma later in childhood or a series of adverse life events may have the foundations of a secure attachment severely damaged (Waters, Weinfield and Hamilton 2000). Yet there are strong continuities in attachment patterns. Research studies suggest that a child's early attachment status tends to persist through childhood into adolescence and adulthood, and has lasting effects (Main, Kaplan and Cassidy 1985; Waters *et al.* 2000).

The avoidantly attached child becomes the adult who *dismisses* the significance of past and present relationships – their problem with intimacy continues. The ambivalently attached child becomes the adult who is *enmeshed* and *preoccupied* with earlier and current relationships – the difficulty with separation and individuation remains. There is some indication that men are more likely to be avoidant of feelings (the culture of the 'stiff upper lip', 'boys don't cry') while women are more likely to be enmeshed, as a consequence of the 'push-pull' of the maternal relationship (Eichenbaum and Orbach 1983). More bleakly the unintegrated child ('disorganised' attachment) may become an adult who is dissociating and mentally ill, or violent and abusive. Such attachment histories are in turn likely to be reflected in these parents' relationships with their children.

However, most infants classified as anxiously attached will not develop psychiatric disorders or become delinquent or deviant citizens. Many varieties of insecure attachment are not pathological, although they may have consequences. For example, some avoidantly attached children appear to focus on things rather than people and so may fail to resolve attachment issues or avoid intimacy, yet compensate with high physical or mental achievement and have successful careers. Some children seem *resilient* despite apparently severe early emotional deprivation and insecure attachments to both parents. It looks as if they have developed a *reflective self-function*, probably because *someone* has held them sufficiently in mind (Fonagy *et al.* 1994). This 'holding in mind' may be provided in the family centre.

Parents' attachment: the 'ghosts in the nursery'

Parents of course have their own attachment histories from their childhood which can influence their relationships with their children in the present. They risk replicating unresolved attachment problems with their children. Selma Fraiberg described parents' repressed memories of their own childhood which may be revived by the birth of their baby as 'ghosts in the nursery'. She wrote:

> In every nursery there are ghosts. They are the visitors from the unremembered past of the parents, the uninvited guests at the christening. Under favourable circumstances, these unfriendly and unbidden spirits are banished from the nursery and return to their subterranean dwelling place. The baby makes his own

imperative claim upon parental love and, in strict analogy with the fairy tales, the bonds of love protect the child and his parents against the intruders, the malevolent ghosts. (Fraiberg 1980, p.164)

Fraiberg wanted to understand how the parental past may interfere with the present mother–infant relationship. She realized that a parent's feelings from a past relationship can sometimes be transferred to the child. The child has come to represent a figure from the parent's past or a part of the parent's hidden self. Children always carry subjective meaning for their parents, but sometimes the parental projections may be damaging, so that 'parents endow a baby with characteristics that are totally at odds with the baby's nature: the baby is seen as having well-defined intentions or harbouring adult characteristics, or even endowed with supernatural forces. The strength and nature of the parents' projections determine to what extent parents are able to recognise the infant's own individuality', or whether 'their unconscious takes over, casting the infant in the role of hero or villain' (Brazelton and Cramer 1991, p.135). The 'ghosts' prevent the parent from being able to respond appropriately to their own child's needs but instead repeat and recreate their own past experiences in the present.

Some ghosts are mere mischief makers who break through from the past in unguarded moments. Those of us who are parents can recall those moments when we caught ourselves sounding exactly like one of our parents, using the same words and even the same tone of voice, probably despite our clear intention to do the opposite to what they had done. We can be surprised at the powerful feelings which parenthood evokes, and the forgotten memories of childhood which are uncovered. More troublesome ghosts seem to cause difficulties at 'flash points' – eating, sleeping, toilet training, discipline, or other areas ripe for conflict.

Fraiberg (1980, p.165) describes another group of families who appear to be possessed by their ghosts. 'While no one has issued an invitation (to the christening) these ghosts take up residence and conduct the rehearsal of the family tragedy from a tattered script.' These parents neglect or damage their children because they are unable to see them for whom they are; instead they are perceived as the uncaring, greedy, demanding, all-consuming parent, or the attacking and persecuting one, the critical and rejecting parent, sometimes as a rival sibling, or sometimes as the split-off bad child that the parent perceives herself to be. Other parents may see their child as the reincarnation of someone who has died (perhaps a previous child), or, if the child is physically or mentally impaired, as a changeling for the perfect child they were expecting. The problem is that 'such an intrusive ghost creates a major source of mismatch between parent and infant. The parents are unable to respond to the infant's signals, because they are busy communicating with a ghost' (Brazelton and Cramer 1991, p.139).

The Adult Attachment Interview

Yet 'history is not destiny'. The fact of having had a traumatic or abusive childhood does not necessarily mean that a parent will repeat the pattern with her own children. What seems to be important is the sense a parent has made of her own past experience. Research uses the Adult Attachment Interview and a version of this interview may be useful to family centres in their assessments, as Chapter 3 shows. This structured interview asks about memories of childhood relationships and the feelings involved, and goes on to ask about experiences of rejection, separation and fear. In thinking about the response, attention is paid not so much to the content of someone's childhood but to the way they talk about it. The question is how well is someone able to tell their story. If they can do so in a way that makes sense, using general descriptions (drawing on semantic memory) together with memories of particular situations and their feelings at the time (episodic memory), the story becomes a coherent narrative, rich with thinking and feeling. Such a story is an indicator of someone who is emotionally integrated, whether or not their childhood was actually happy. These parents are more likely to have securely attached children.

In their research, George, Kaplan and Main (1985) used 'strange situation' assessments of children's attachment and compared them with the Adult Attachment Interviews with their mothers. They found that mothers who *dismissed* their childhood and reported it in a split-off way tended to have anxious avoidant children. Mothers *enmeshed* or pre-occupied with early relationships were more likely to have anxious-resistant children. A mother who had *not resolved* mourning a death or other loss was more likely to have a child with disorganized attachment. Later work has shown a link between disorganized attachment and abuse, for example the mother who was an abused child and then becomes either an abusive parent or a parent who has relationships with partners who abuse her and their children.

Further indication of the connection between child and parent attachment status comes from Fonagy's (Fonagy *et al.* 1994) Adult Attachment Interviews with mothers during pregnancy. He found that they were a good predictor of the subsequently born child's attachment in the 'strange situation'.

The Adult Attachment Interview may turn out to be a valuable diagnostic tool, and give some indication of the kind of help needed. Someone who *dismisses* feelings and memories is likely to need more help with managing intimacy in relationships, while someone *preoccupied* with the past may need more help with becoming a separate autonomous person (Holmes 1993). Where someone is *dissociated* from reality or has very confused and *disorganised* feelings they may need a period of time in which they can receive good experience without any pressure to form attachments. This is what Dockar-Drysdale (1990) calls the *provision of primary experience* – which is what therapeutic communities and some family centres try to offer. Only when someone can hold on to the good experience are they able to form relationships.

Conclusion

Children who are insecurely attached lack an inner sense of being worthy of care and so have little expectation of care. What they need as children, and as the parents they become, is emotional holding and containment, although they will not behave as if they expect it. We may then find ourselves drawn into re-enacting unhelpful parental relationships. By making sense of behaviour through understanding the dynamics of the parent–infant relationship and the attachment histories of both children and their parents, we are better able to find a way of relating to both in a helpful way. How to offer such help is the subject of Chapter 4. First, Chapter 3 looks in more detail at attachment-based assessments and the implications for intervention.

Chapter 3

Assessment and Implications for Intervention Using an Attachment Perspective

Steve Farnfield

This chapter looks at ways of applying attachment theory to assessment and the implications for therapeutic work with children and their families. The emphasis is on structured approaches but the thinking and methodology are readily transferable to opportunity-led work grounded in the daily living experiences at the centre.

A related aim of this chapter is to promote techniques which have been largely designed by developmental psychologists for research purposes and have not found their way into the common currency of general practice. This aim does bring with it problems, not least the difficulty of interpreting results that require, in research terms, a manual and, with an instrument such as the Adult Attachment Interview (AAI), considerable training. However, all the approaches outlined here have been used successfully in family centre and social work teams as they are currently organised. Nonetheless they do come with a number of caveats.

What follows is an outline of some of the more effective approaches. However, nothing develops practice so well as sharing current case problems with a facilitator or trainer familiar with the techniques to be explored. Further, there is a tendency for practitioners, who spend most of their working day with at-risk children, to normalise behaviour that is actually pathological. Trying these approaches with children from 'normative' populations does bring home the, at times, depressing difference between children able to enjoy and explore the world and those desperately trying merely to survive in it. Finally, recording interventions, by means of audio or video tape, allows for further reflection and learning with colleagues as well as ensuring that the very difficult decisions that have to be made about children's welfare are based on hard evidence and the judgement of more than one person.

An overview of assessment

Bowlby's (1973, 1985) 'internal working model' can usefully be restricted to the description of children between one and two years of age who enact what they have learned to expect from carers. In developmental terms, children then move from enacting learned behaviour to representing models of their key relationships by symbolic means such as play and then, later, language. For older children and adults the term 'internal representational model' (IRM) is thus preferred. These are models of attachment relationships which become capable of re-presentation to the self and thus become more accessible to conscious reflection as the child develops. A developmental perspective is thus an important starting point for both assessment and therapeutic interventions.

Between the age of one and about two years children in the Ainsworth Strange Situation test (Ainsworth *et al.* 1978) are demonstrating learned behaviour that is pre- or unconscious. Rather like driving to work and then not remembering how we got there, the child's behaviour, when anxious or upset, unconsciously reveals what has already been learned in previous interactions with carers. For these children, assessment is based on observation. By about 37 months the child's capacity for symbolic thought is such that representational models can be revealed in a doll-play exercise or narrative stem. The school years (five to puberty) see increasing sophistication in the use of language so that by ten, a securely attached child should be able to give you a coherent story of their life (Main 1991, p. 148). At this stage a combination of doll play and a facilitated interview (e.g. Farnfield 1996, 1997) can provide good results; a child attachment interview has proved successful from about seven years onwards. From puberty onwards increasing reliance can be put on attachment interviews that may also incorporate projective tests, such as the Separation Anxiety Test (SAT) (e.g. Wright, Binney and Smith 1995), until, for adults, formal assessment can be built around linguistic forms of representation by using the AAI. This progression from observation through play and then projective tests to interviewing is given in Table 3.1.

	History	Observation	Play	Tests	Interview
0–12 mths	•	•	•		
12–18 mths	•	SS	•		
18mths–3 yrs	•	SR	•		
4–6 yrs	•	SR	•	SAT Animal Stems	Facilitated
6–puberty	•	R	•	SAT Doll Stems	Facilitated CAI
Adolescence	•	•		SAT	CAI Modified AAI

Table 3.1: Assessing attachment in children

Abbreviations/terms:

SS	Strange Situation	SAT	Separation Anxiety Test
CAI	Child Attachment Interview	SR	Separation and Reunion
Stems:	Narrative stems	AAI	Adult Attachment Interview
R	Reunion	Facilitated:	Combination of interview and prompts

A theoretical model

Attachment theory is heavily biased towards the effects of actual experience in that dangerous environments are believed to heighten the risk of developmental problems. It is just not possible, in attachment terms, to be a psychopath who had a happy childhood! This does overlook the degree of fantasy we all use to come to terms with reality and which does appear in the narrative stems discussed below.

The model of attachment theory that is preferred here is based on Crittenden's extension of the Ainsworth categories (Crittenden 1995) but incorporates object relations theory for a better understanding of those few extremely disturbed children who appear to have no organised pattern of relating to carers when under duress.[1] The thinking behind this is as follows: while useful to describe the behaviour of very young children, the term 'disorganised' attachment is not always very helpful in trying to understand children, in their third year and upwards, from dangerous backgrounds. A medical diagnosis such as Reactive Attachment Disorder (RAD) provides a helpful list of symptoms but tends to highlight pathology at the expense of the meaning of the behaviour to the child. Crittenden's model, on the other hand, explains many of the features of 'disorganisation' in terms of organised defences under extreme circumstances. While reference will be made here to disorganised attachment in research studies the term is, ideally, reserved for children exhibiting the 'manic defences' described by Klein and Bion (see Briggs 1997 Ch. 1 and Shuttleworth 1989 Ch. 2 for discussion). Essentially these are high fear states during which a child experiences a free floating sense of persecution by just about everybody in his environment and, therefore, has no organised defence.

Following on from this it is important to avoid judging families from the perspective of balanced security (B) when the other two Ainsworth categories, avoidant (A) and ambivalent (C), discussed in Chapter 2, are also normal within the population at large. For assessment purposes the goal would seem to be to identify those parents and children who have pathologically insecure attachments that put them at a greatly increased risk of major psycho-social problems.

Get the history – dangerous environments

Crittenden's developmental model of attachment (1995) is based on the belief that human beings have survived by adapting to dangerous environments. This means either changing behaviour to placate others (A) or else forcing other people to meet our attachment needs (C). What looks like disorganised behaviour is, Crittenden argues, actually an organised response to dangerous circumstances. Therefore, when scrutinising the history of both child and parent, a key question is 'how dangerous is (or was) the environment, and how predictable is the danger from the child's point of view?'

Danger which is predictable affords the child the possibility of organising a defence; usually one of the compulsive dismissing patterns (A+).[2] Here the child inhibits behaviour likely to displease adults and emphasises a bright, cheery exterior. In Ferenczi's terms (Ferenczi 1933/1999, p.301) such children become little psychiatrists, able to read and adapt to the behaviour of mad adults at the cost of remaining out of touch with their own feelings.

Danger which is unpredictable demands constant vigilance until, in extreme circumstances, everything becomes a potential threat. The vagueness that characterises more normative ambivalent attachments (C) is, however, not protective, and children living in an unpredictably dangerous world focus on one aspect of their feelings, or a particular characteristic of a carer, in the attempt to simplify information processing. This is the basis of the obsessive preoccupied patterns (C+) which demonstrate a split between fear of abandonment and desire for nurture, on one side, and anger on the other. Whereas the compulsive dismissing child (A+) appears ashamed of herself, her preoccupied brother appears to blame everyone else; he is either so angry he seems unaware that he wants to be loved, or else a professional victim who gains attention by using exaggerated displays of helplessness.

These patterns will be elaborated as the chapter unfolds and are represented in figure 3.1.

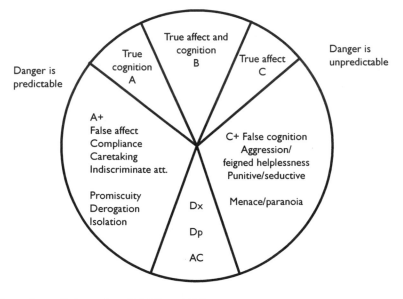

Based on Crittenden (1995, p.397)

Dp: DEPRESSION   Dx: DISORGANISATION

The A, B and C segments at the top represent the Ainsworth infant categories. In the pre-school years the compulsive (A+) patterns develop to include compulsive compliance or frozen watchfulness, compulsive caretaking and indiscriminate attachment. The obsessive (C+) pattern includes aggression/feigned helplessness. In the school years this pattern may be extended so that it becomes punitive or seductive (tricking people with helpless strategies). In adolescence and adulthood the A+ pattern may be further extended to derogation (claiming not to need a hated attachment figure), compulsive self reliance and sexual promiscuity. The C+ may further develop into menace and/or paranoia whereby everything and everyone is experienced as a threat. The argument here is that from infancy onwards disorganisation (Dx) can be viewed in the terms of menace/paranoia. Depression (Dp) is part of the human condition and not tied to any one pattern. In Crittenden's model the balanced (B) pattern integrates true affect with true cognition while, in adulthood, some extremely disturbed (psychopathic) people integrate false cognition with false affect (AC).

Figure 3.1. Model of attachment patterns

Some of the more common dangerous occurrences are as follows:

- Physical or sexual assault, real or threatened.

- Neglect.

- A carer who is physically or psychologically unavailable (psychological absence involves some learning disabled parents and depressed carers).

- A carer who is frightening or frightened; this may include a parent addicted to alcohol or drugs (frightening) and psychotic illness or domestic violence (frightened). Note that in domestic violence the aggression in the room arouses the child's attachment-seeking behaviour while simultaneously the mother, whom the child seeks for protection, is herself frightened and unable to help. The effects are therefore similar to direct abuse of the child.

- Rejection of the self as a person (the difference between 'go away I'm busy' and 'bugger off you little shit – I wish you'd never been born'.)

- Abandonment, real or threatened, including being put into care. This includes 'ambivalent' parents who will only accept the child of their fantasies rather than the child of reality.

- Overprotection from unknown or non-existent danger. The following fragment is taken from a child observation:

Anna (age 5) then sat down next to me and asked if I had ever seen a ghost. I said no and she then proceeded to tell me that there had been a ghost in their last flat and that Mum had 'felt it'. Anna then suggested that we all draw a ghost and gave me a piece of paper and a pen. Charley (age three) began to draw immediately, saying that she was drawing a 'Mummy ghost'.

- Role reversal in which the child becomes the psychological parent to the adult. Children who carry out practical domestic tasks for a physically disabled parent would not be included unless they were also the psychological parent; that is the parent looks to the child for protection. Likewise older children bringing up younger siblings are not axiomatically parenting their parents.

- Spousification in which neither party has the parental role and psychological boundaries are blurred.

- Inappropriate socialisation ranging from involving the child in adult criminal or sexual activities to, say, valuing violence in a boy. Some (C+) adults and children become both proud of their anger and obsessed with revenge against perceived wrong-doers.

- Failure to protect the child from predators; this includes the social services. Sudden removal from home, dawn raids, frequent or unplanned moves of placement, all indicate to the child that their parents (later substitute carers) cannot protect them.

Assessing children's attachment

Observation

Mary Ainsworth developed what became the 'strange situation test' (Ainsworth *et al.* 1978) following an extensive period of observing young children in their own homes. Family centres offer optimum conditions for observing children in natural, rather than laboratory-induced, encounters and so, while the thinking behind the strange situation needs to be retained, the formal procedures are usually unnecessary. Contact arrangements, between looked after children and their parents, frequently replicate the more formal conditions.

The key component is that the child's attachment-seeking behaviour must be aroused through anxiety or distress. When they are hurt, ill, worried or otherwise vulnerable, small children need an adult to help, comfort and protect them. If anxiety is pushed to the point of fear then, of course, flight/fight or 'manic defences' operate and the assessment will be meaningless. Ainsworth was particularly concerned with reunions or what happens in the first few minutes when the child's parent becomes physically available.

For children up to about 18 months a useful blueprint for classifying 'disorganised' attachment patterns has been provided by Main and Solomon (1990). They employ seven thematic headings, the key feature of which is an experience of stress which is not accompanied by any behavioural strategy that *either* increases proximity to the attachment figure (C) *or* organises attention away (A) from her. In utilising this approach it is important to observe children's approaches to carers carefully: for example walking towards the parent with arms raised but at the last moment dropping the arms and attending to a toy can happen in a second; likewise freezing, in mid movement, or stilling (the cessation of movement in a restful posture) can be a momentary occurrence.

About the end of the second year more sophisticated patterns start to make an appearance and the patterns described by Crittenden (1995; Crittenden and Ainsworth 1989) become observable. Children of predictably dangerous carers demonstrate frozen watchfulness and those with a withdrawn or helpless parent role reversal, both of which demand a false self (A+). Observers will also notice indiscriminately attached children, who go to anyone to have their basic needs met. In the pre-school years some ambivalent (C) children amplify the Ainsworth pattern becoming either aggressive with adults and other children, or using exaggerated helplessness; sometimes switching between the two patterns to maximise caregivers' attention (Crittenden 1995). More guidelines for assessing attachment in infants aged between twelve and twenty four months can be found in Schneider-Rosen (1990, p.200), and a recent overview of the field has been provided by Solomon and George (1999).

By six years children assessed as 'disorganised' at age one show up as either controlling or caretakers (Solomon, George and De Jong 1995). Such children feature prominently among family centre clients and it seems likely that this is actually a split whereby the child alternately controls an ineffectual parent in a, sometimes, outright punitive way (C+), or protects her from his own rage by acting as a caretaker (A+). What therefore appears as disorganised behaviour is actually the employment of two alternating strategies: caretaking and punitive control (A+/C+).

However, punitive children do sometimes work themselves into extreme states whereby they get out of everyone's control, including their own. In effect their 'magic omnipotence', the belief that they can force other people to do what they want, has broken down and they are in a high fear state or truly 'disorganised'. A few such children seem not to have developed any capacity for meaningful relationships and instead plunder the centre for food and immediate gratification as if they were pirates looting a ship. In addition, the child's behaviour or conversation may sometimes muddle up basic functions, such as eating, defecation and sex.

To further complicate matters pathological patterns are not restricted to poor families. The difference is that children from affluent homes often have elements in their environment, such as private schools, numerous extra curricula activities, the opportunity to succeed at something, which offer compensatory features unavailable to children in need. Indeed, the function of the family centre is frequently to provide that extra protective layer to enable children to function more successfully.

Observation of separation and reunion behaviour is a key tool in the pre-school years and provides good information about the extent to which children can make appropriate use of adults, both attachment figures and centre staff, to meet their emotional and physical needs. In the school years, behaviour alone becomes increasingly difficult to interpret because the children themselves become more adept at masking their feelings.

Play

The main function of secure attachment is that it allows the child to explore. Exploration begins with play and, as the child develops, continues into exploration of relationships and ideas. Children who are constantly vigilant, wary that they will be abandoned or suddenly threatened, have little in the way of attentional resources left to explore their environment.

Simply sitting in a play room with a child new to the centre will tell the worker a great deal about how the child expects the world to treat him. Procedurally the child has to fall back on previous encounters, as a guide, as the adult quietly says: 'Explore the room, play with what you like. I'm just going to sit here.' Very soon the worker can pick up something of the child's expectations built on past relationships (the transference). All the worker is required to do is tune in to the child's feelings about her. She may have a sense that the child wants to please her or take care of her in small ways (indicating compliance or care taking, A+), or quickly find herself in a struggle for dominance more typical of coercive children (C+). Frightened, possibly disorganised children, may find the confines of the play room too threatening and the whole session is spent negotiating with the child about boundaries or, in everyday language, trying to keep the child in one room.

Narrative stems

In these exercises the child is asked to choose a doll figure or animal about whom the interviewer tells the beginning of a story and then asks the child to 'tell me or show me what happens next'. Various batteries of attachment story procedures are in existence, and for pre-school children, stems using animals, or a combination of animal and doll people vignettes, are recommended (see Appendix 1), whereas children over six seem to respond better to story stems using doll families (see Appendix 2). Bretherton and colleagues give a full account of procedures with three-year-olds (Bretherton, Ridgeway and Cassidy 1990), Buchsbaum with four- and five-year-olds (Buchsbaum et al. 1992) and Green and colleagues with children aged five to eight (Green et al. 2000).

As can be seen in the appendices, narrative stems are biased towards experiences where attachment-seeking behaviour is activated. If we take, for example, the lost little pig story, the interviewer sets up the farmyard with the big and little pigs, who are taken to represent children and adults, and then deliberately heightens the child's anxiety by introducing the story in a dramatic fashion. 'Little piggy goes for a walk. She looks at all the flowers and the other animals and Oh dear! Little piggy's lost. She doesn't know how to get home. Show me or tell me what happens next.'

In analysing the story completions the interviewer is looking for relatively benign resolutions and, increasingly as the child gets older, coherence of content or presentation. While aggression in children's narratives is not unusual, relatively secure children manage to resolve stories in a way that depicts adults as both comforting and protective. The stories of preoccupied (C) children frequently exhibit busyness without getting to the point of resolution (Solomon, George and De Jong 1995), while dismissing children terminate attachment-seeking behaviour prematurely and their stories are characterised by the unavailability of attachment figures and the minimal need for help in resolving the story issues. Dismissing children may also change the story or cut it short, as in 'she doesn't get lost' or 'she does get home. That's all'.

At the end of each story the interviewer asks 'how does the (doll) child or animal feel?' This question, and the surrounding material, assesses the degree to which the child is open to discussing painful or frightening emotions (Main, Kaplan and Cassidy 1985; Wright, Binney and Smith 1995; Oppenheim, 1997).

Idealisation of carers rarely appears in children's stem material, which makes this approach very useful in assessing children from dangerous backgrounds who, if asked outright, invariably say positive things about carers who are clearly not protecting them. Of particular importance for subsequent treatment are the sudden catastrophes which impinge on stories of maltreated children for no reason. While all children may introduce violence and danger, the stories of maltreated children are frequently characterised by frightening adults, or big animals, who appear without warning and from whom the child in the story has no satisfactory means of self-protection (see Solomon, George and De Jong 1995; Wright, Binney and Smith 1995). Catastrophic fantasies do seem to appear only in the stories of children with unresolved trauma or parallel representational models; these should be taken very seriously and further investigation for post-traumatic stress disorder is necessary (see Sauter and Franklin 1998).

As well as narrative coherence and emotional openness, a third area for consideration is the degree to which the child co-operates with the interviewer. Compulsively dismissing (A+) children will generally co-operate with the task even if their stories are pithy and defensive because their basic strategy is to avoid antagonising powerful grown-ups. Coercive (C+) children are much more likely to confront the interviewer by refusing to co-operate or challenging the task.

Simon is four and the interviewer arrives at the high point of the hot gravy story.

> Interviewer: What happens next?
>
> Simon: He calls his Mum. (*agitated*) 'Mama! Mama!'
>
> Interviewer: Does he right. Then what happens?
>
> Simon: And he gave himself a plaster on…it

The lost keys story:

> Simon: Well Mummy does…well when he got out of…um…outside and um he couldn't get in because he wouldn't…he couldn't have some keys.
>
> Interviewer: Right, so what happens next in the story then?
>
> Simon: Um…um…they call…um…the…um the baby (*calling*) 'Baby! Baby!' and they um…and the baby um comes along and takes them um with them, takes them in.
>
> Interviewer: Right. Do you want to do another one?
>
> Simon: (*enthusiastic*) Yes.

The hot gravy story is highly arousing. Simon appears caught up in the drama but the doll child has to tend his own wounds and there is no sign of comfort or acknowledgement of the child's pain. In the lost keys story he is clearly struggling to give a coherent narrative and finally the baby, the weakest member of the family, saves the day. Taken together these two stories suggest self-reliance and start to build a picture of a dismissing (A) child. Note too that he cheerfully co-operates with the request to do another story.

Kathy is five and chooses to tell stories about some of the Beanie babies Spunkey, Lips and Opal Fruit.

> Interviewer: Lips has done a nice picture at school and she takes it home and knocks on the door. Tell me or show me what happens next.
>
> Kathy: (*silence*)
>
> Interviewer: What happens next? What do you think her Mummy says?
>
> Kathy: Her PC's broken. She's down loading her PC.

The interviewer tries again with Opal Fruit.

Interviewer: What happens next?

Kathy: They can't get in.

Interviewer: They can't get in. What does he do then?

Kathy: If the back door is open they can go down the alley way, come round, unlock it with the key...but they haven't got a key lock.

Interviewer: What happens then?

Kathy: Um...Has to climb over into the next door neighbour...and he waited at the front door and...they got a stick. He pushed as hard as he could and open the door came.

The interviewer gives the stem for the lost keys story and asks what happens next.

Kathy: (*silence*) You tell.

Interviewer: I'd like to hear your story

Kathy: No. (*appealing baby voice*) You tell.

Although, on the surface, Kathy appears to be stuck or maybe avoiding the task, her manner demonstrates a struggle for dominance with the interviewer (see procedural memory, below). Her risqué choice of dolls has a slight mocking quality and the struggle continues with coercive attempts to get the interviewer to do the work, switching from silence, and then bossiness, to seductive appeal. Note too that the restarts to the first story meander off topic until, instead of taking a picture home, Kathy is more concerned with getting into the house. All this is indicative of an angry coercive (C+) child. Kathy's account of the children getting in through the neighbour's garden feels real.

Clara is six and has made one of the bears in her stories herself.

Interviewer: Clara has all these nice bears in her family and one day she goes out for a walk all by herself and she walks and walks (*make actions*) a long way and...

Clara: (*interrupting*)...then there was a tiger...

Interviewer: ...and what happens next?

Clara: Then she saw a tiger and rrah Clara's dead.

Interviewer: Mummy, Daddy and all the little bears have been out for the day. They come back to the house but O dear, Mummy and Daddy can't find the key, who's got the key for the front door, they can't find it...

Clara: (*interrupting*) Clara finds it, Clara had the key, you didn't know Clara had the key…you didn't see them under the cushion, that's what happened silly Mummy, that's what happened you silly old Mum (*Clara laughs*).

The lost keys story gives us an omnipotent Clara with a very low opinion of her mother and, as with Kathy, her frequent interruption, indeed control of, the interviewer suggests a coercive strategy. Clara's tiger illustrates a catastrophic fantasy that arrives suddenly in the story and is not resolved.

A similar procedure is the Separation Anxiety Test (SAT) which uses photographs of attachment issues (Hansburg 1986; Wright, Binney and Smith 1995). Main and colleagues took a family photograph and then showed it to the children to explore the security of their relationship (Main, Kaplan and Cassidy, 1985, p.80). Another well established measure of family relationships is that of Anthony and Bene (1957).

Implications for interventions with the child

- Aggressive, controlling and punitive (C+) children, like Clara, pose an immediate management problem. Talking about their feelings is not always productive and personalised commands, such as 'don't please scream it upsets Mum's nerves', may only offer Clara more ammunition to drive her Mum crazy. Instead more global directives such as 'that's good' may be more effective. The child needs to learn to modulate feelings rather than offer a dramatic response whatever the eliciting cause of distress (see particularly Crittenden 1992).

- What is on offer here is a crash course in thinking, where great attention is paid to cognitive processes and semantic statements (see semantic memory, below). In particular, workers can identify whether the child misses out bits of information, and jumps to conclusions, or actually distorts information usually in the direction of over-identifying other people as a threat. Help can then be offered on the lines of a stop – think – do programme (see Peterson 1995) which teaches the child to identify feelings associated with, say, rage, stop and then act on all not part of the information. For boys in pedal cars, the use of a working traffic light is both fun and effective.

- Children using feigned helpless strategies (passive C+) may also benefit from cognitive behavioural programmes that reinforce independence and acknowledgement of angry feelings.

- Compliant children (A+) need to get in touch with their own feelings, not mother's, and may benefit from the gradual introduction of emotional experience, starting with messy or sensory play and building up to naming feelings and exploring actual incidents as they crop up in the centre.

- For all children, great use can be made of everyday encounters, starting with minor incidents and working up to the more dramatic and threatening ones. Books, films and stories are also an effective way to introduce the child to what are often new ways of thinking or feeling about their world. This work is of crucial importance for the under-fives, whose internal representational models are still plastic and susceptible to change.

- The sudden appearance of the tiger and Clara's death suggest she might have a parallel model of violent behaviour by adults over which she has little conscious control. Unresolved trauma in children should be treated by a qualified therapist. Of particular importance in everyday living is the ability of the adults in the care-giving environment to validate the feelings the child actually has rather than those other people think she has or ought to have. Carers need to give an account of the abuse that accurately portrays the reality of the child's experience, otherwise the child is left with a kind of madness whereby she either cannot process what happened or cannot square her version with that of her carers.

Assessment interviews with children

When working with pre-schoolers the interviewer is working predominantly in what Vygotsky termed the zone of proximal development (Vygotsky 1978, p.86); that is filling the gap between what the child can achieve unaided and what she can do with the help of an adult. This demands a combination of props and questions about attachment issues. By the age of six the majority of children are able to give a coherent narrative about important aspects of their lives and assessments can therefore use a combination of narrative stems and an interview. Saywitz and Snyder (1996), working with seven- to eleven-year-olds, developed a series of prompt cards for when children got stuck, and this writer has developed a facilitated interview format, including attachment questions, for children aged six to puberty (Farnfield 1996, 1997). Main has outlined an autobiographical interview for 10- to 11-year-old children (Main 1991, p.150) and there are a number of child attachment interviews under development for school years children.

Attention deficit hyperactivity disorder (ADHD)

Family centre workers will not need their attention drawn to the increase in diagnoses of ADHD. Although the contribution of environmental, as opposed to organic, factors is imperfectly understood, some writers give insecure attachment a role (Crittenden 1995; Greenberg *et al.* 1997). In practice, whatever other deficits they may exhibit in terms of attention, these children are brilliant at keeping attention on themselves and so, to the extent that attachment thinking may be useful, they present as coercive (C+) children requiring a highly structured environment using cognitive behavioural, that is cause and effect, models of intervention (for example Van der Vlugt *et al.* 1995).

The assessment of parenting

Attachment behaviour is meaningless unless it refers to a relationship between, at least, two people. From the above it is clear that approaches useful in the assessment of attachment in children are at the same time assessing the type of parenting they are receiving. This section focuses on the parent.

The assessment of parenting can be reduced to a somewhat crude formula, written as follows:

The meaning that the child has for the parent + parent's own representational model of attachment + unresolved loss or trauma = the care-giving environment.

Each component will now be briefly discussed in turn.

The meaning of the child to the parent

To gain any pleasure from parenting it is necessary to fall in love with our children. Parenting can, for sure, be a demoralising and unhappy experience for anyone at times, but the bad times are usually endured because of the generally positive meaning the child has for the parent. Some parents and step-parents experience the child in predominantly negative terms. This is particularly serious when the child is perceived to be the cause of the parent's difficulties or a threat to a new love relationship. Sometimes only one child out of a sibling group is selected, as if this child carries all the negative parental projections. In the early months of a child's life it is useful to investigate the extent to which a parent has a 'theory of mind' about their baby: that is crediting the infant with an interior life or 'mind of his own' even though he cannot yet speak. Questions around whether the child was wanted, the birth and subsequent problems, particularly feeding and sleep, are frequently illuminating (see particularly Reder and Duncan 1995, also Fonagy et al. 1994).

The adult's representational model of attachment

George, Kaplan and Main (1985) designed the Adult Attachment Interview (AAI) to measure the adult's state of mind with respect to attachment by asking a series of questions about the speaker's childhood relationships with attachment figures. The interview is designed to 'surprise the unconscious' by asking the subject to give serious consideration to issues that frequently remain unexamined. For research, each interview is transcribed and then subjected to a detailed discourse analysis (Main and Goldwyn 1994) where judgement as to the degree of attachment insecurity is based not on what happened to the speaker in the past but how they think about their childhood now, as an adult. In this approach coherence of mind is assumed to be indicated by coherence of speech: dysfluencies, beyond the usual 'um...err...', transform meaning by hiding information about the past or exaggerating one aspect at the expense of another. The interview has been developed for use with at risk populations by Crittenden (1999) and some of the AAI questions are given in Appendix 3.

At its simplest, some familiarity with the AAI is a very useful exercise in that most basic of skills: *listening* – listening, that is, not just to the content of a parent's story, but how it is related. Of crucial importance is whether the parent can take a step back and view their childhood experiences from an adult perspective, or whether they are still so trapped in aspects of a painful childhood that they continue to think as they did when they were a child. Likewise the listener can ask herself, 'what would this story be like told from a more balanced perspective?' and measure the discrepancies.

Analysis of the AAI is built around Grice's (1975) four conversational maxims of:

1. quantity (be succinct, yet complete)
2. quality (truthfulness)
3. relevance (to the topic in hand)
4. manner (co-operation with the interviewer).

In essence a parent is asked to talk about their early life while the listener asks herself a series of questions:

'What do I feel listening to this person? Do they enjoy the chance to talk about themselves (possible B)? Are they trying to please me or look after me (possible

A+)? Do I feel I want to rescue them (passive C+) or is there a struggle for power going on here (aggressive C+)?'

'When the speaker stumbles or is lost for words what is the function of the dysfluency?'

'What is being left out here?'

'Is this story over long (C) or too brief (possibly A)?'

'Is the speaker wandering off topic? (C)'

'Does the story focus excessively on the self (C) or away from the self (A)?'

'Is this story psychologically sound? In other words, do I believe it?'

Memory systems

The AAI asks parents to access information about their childhood using five memory 'systems' (see particularly Crittenden 1999; Nelson 1996; Tulving 1972):

1. procedural
2. imaged
3. semantic
4. episodic
5. working.

Procedural memory is similar to the use of transference/counter-transference in that it refers to the echoes of previous relationships in the way the parent relates to the interviewer. *Imaged memory* concerns not just the cinema in the head but smells, feelings associated with objects, fragments of conversation from long ago. Preoccupied speakers tend to use animated, vivid images whereas for dismissing speakers, images are absent or else stand in for attachment figures. For example:

'What did you feel when you heard your mother was dead?'

'I remember this vase of blazing daffodils.'

The story stems of pre-school children are largely completed in terms of scripts or generalised accounts of past experience based on *semantic memory*. Adults are asked to tap into semantic memory when giving five adjectives to describe their childhood relationship with their parents. They are then asked to tap into *episodic memory* by providing examples of specific episodes which support the adjectives. Whereas preoccupied people tend to focus on episodes or parts of episodes, without providing a semantic conclusion, dismissing people tend to do the opposite. However, people who have experienced predictable danger cannot discount dangerous episodes and instead exonerate their attachment figure by taking responsibility or seeing events from their parent's point of view (A+).

The integrative questions ask people to bring together information from different parts of their experience using *working memory*. Parents who have had traumatic lives but have resolved most of their difficulties (what in AAI terms are called 'earned B's') are able to take a step back from the past and give due weight to their own and other people's part in past problems. Less secure subjects give the impression that defences, which were functional in childhood, are still employed now as an adult. In effect they think about their life as they did as a child.

Unresolved loss and trauma

Many parents attending family centres have unresolved thoughts and feelings with regard to loss, usually death or abandonment, and/or trauma, usually abuse. Lack of resolution is most commonly manifested in two forms, dismissing and preoccupied, and would usually be expected to conform to internal representational models of attachment; that is dismissing people dismiss loss or trauma and preoccupied people exhibit preoccupation.

Preoccupation involves the belief that the matter is not over and can still be put right: the dead mother will return or the abusing father will be controlled. Hence the matter is ever present, sometimes even talked about in the present. The dismissal of loss or trauma requires that memories are either repressed (rendered inaccessible to conscious recall) or disavowed ('Okay she's dead, but what of it?'). While this functions to decrease mental pain it leaves important information unavailable for use in self-protection should the danger reoccur. Hence some compulsive people (A+) take too much responsibility for abusive things that happened to them in order to feel in control.

Where the usual defensive processes breakdown then a person may switch to another strategy, for example a preoccupied parent who dismisses the loss of a stillborn child. Where clients exhibit unresolved trauma, consideration should also be given to post-traumatic stress disorder (see Sauter and Franklin 1998).

Family centre clients have frequently had childhoods overfilled with dangerous episodes. For assessment purposes, claims that past losses and traumas have been resolved should be supported by psychologically plausible evidence as to how resolution came about. This can include a secondary attachment figure, such as an aunt or teacher, therapy, a love relationship and, eventually, the family centre worker herself. Current models of counselling suggest that resolution demands at least partial forgiveness of past abusers, acceptance that the matter is in the past and retention of aspects of the experience that will be useful for self-protection in the future.

Implications for interventions with parents

An overarching principle is that children's attachment patterns are functional for their survival and that nothing should be attempted with the child unless current dangers in the care-giving environment can be significantly modified or removed. This means, in practice, that the bulk of focused interventions are concentrated on parents; particularly the three aspects of the care-giving environment discussed above.

In terms of counselling parents the chosen approach should challenge, and thus be the opposite to, the parent's predominant defensive pattern, otherwise interventions risk collusion or the endless perpetuation of the problem.

- Preoccupied people (C+) tend to have a low cognitive component to their self histories. Enmeshed in feelings and episodes, psycho-dynamic counselling that invites further preoccupation is perhaps less likely to succeed than a more cognitive–behavioural approach.

- Dismissing clients (A+) who take too much responsibility, and who exonerate their own parents, and abusive love partners, are, essentially, good at reading other people's feelings but not their own and should respond to identifying their own feelings and revisiting past episodes.

- Using this line of thinking, coercive (C+) clients should be encouraged to explore the split-off parts of themselves (anger or desire for comfort), while distortions in their own thinking can be challenged using a cognitive–behavioural approach. In terms of parenting, showing parents a video of their own child doing a narrative stem exercise may help them appreciate just how frightened or muddled their child really is.

- Unresolved loss or trauma requires attention and withdrawal from the centre because these issues are too distressing to work on may indicate a poor outcome.

- Severe distortions in thinking, including Munchausen by Proxy Syndrome, present a huge challenge which may be out of the range of the centre staff or indicate further treatment is unlikely to change anything.

There is an inevitable tendency for the workers to try and solve relationship problems with clients by using the same defensive strategies as the clients themselves. When we feel bored, angry or desperate to rescue family members we usually have good information about feelings that are being split-off or dismissed and so indicate areas for attention, for example angry people who have lost touch with their desire for nurture, or, perhaps more crucially, passive, victim-like parents who render the people trying to help them feeling useless and frustrated, thus experiencing the anger they do not show themselves.

Assessing attachment is difficult but ultimately rewarding for clients and workers alike. Mistakes are most likely to occur when confusing the compliance of dismissing people (A+) with the co-operation of balanced people, and the cold anger of punitive aggressive people (C+) as dismissing. While the concept of dangerousness (Dale et al. 1986) has gone out of fashion, the current Department of Health guidelines still demand assessment of risk (2000). Using the approach outlined here, parents whose representational model of attachment is fearful and aggressive, and who distort thinking to render the world more dangerous than it is, and who also see their child as malevolent, would present an unacceptably high risk. Finally, in the Crittenden model, psychopaths integrate false cognition with false affect (AC) to give a seamless performance based around what they intuit centre staff want to hear. The greater the performance the greater the chance of their material being misclassified as balanced.

The parent–child game

The parent–child game (Forehand and McMahon 1981; Jenner and McCarthy 1995) is effective with children up until the age of seven and, most probably, with the mid to more difficult range of parenting problems. Centres that use this approach no doubt vary aspects of it to suit client need, and the personal style of the workers, but it is useful to have a video suite so a tape can be made of the parent and child at play. This provides a discussion point for use with the parent and a baseline for professionals against which further progress can be measured. There follow a series of sessions in which the parent, who is equipped with an ear bug to keep her in touch with the worker behind the screen, plays with her child. In the first phase, the child's game, the child chooses the activity and the parent is encouraged to attend to the child in various non-directive ways. Phase two, the parent's game, involves the parent in learning how to give 'alpha' commands that accentuate the positive and the imposition of consequences for non-compliance. Emphasis is put on the importance of 'catching your child being good'.

This approach mixes the teaching of parent craft with a cognitive–behavioural approach to child-rearing. However, the parent's ear piece, in transmitting encouraging words and suggestions from the worker while the play session is actually in progress, does have features of an 'inner parent' who is, it is hoped, trusted and gradually internalised. Along with the parent–child game, individual counselling can be offered to the parent and, if necessary, individual work to the child.

Finally

Family centres offer a real opportunity to work with families in ways that are both meaningful and have a genuine chance of promoting lasting change. They also put the staff in the position of having to make judgements about parenting while simultaneously not discriminating against clients. In this light it is salutary to recall Bowlby's words:

> The position adopted here is that, while parents are held to play a major role in causing a child to develop a heightened susceptibility to fear, their behaviour is seen not in terms of moral condemnation but as having been determined by the experiences they themselves had as children. Once that perspective is attained and rigorously adhered to, parental behaviour that has the gravest consequences for children can be understood and treated without moral censure. That way lies hope of breaking the generational succession. (Bowlby 1973, 1985, p.321)

Acknowledgements

For case examples: Tina Lynam, Shona McGarry and Mairead Panetta

Notes

1   Attachment theory can be termed a branch of object relations theory that has shed its psychoanalytic roots, particularly in its emphasis on reality over fantasy. While bringing aspects of the two closer together will, hopefully, prove useful in the long term, the focus of this chapter is largely on attachment theory.

2   To denote the more extreme or pathological forms of attachment a plus sign will be added to the Ainsworth A and C categories.

Chapter 4

Working Therapeutically with Children and Parents in Family Centres

Linnet McMahon and Viv Dacre

Introduction

In this chapter we look at ways of applying ideas from psychodynamic and attachment theories to working therapeutically with children and with parents in the family centre. It is not easy to respond helpfully in the complex day-to-day situations which occur in practice with parents and children whose personal autonomy and self-esteem may be low and who have difficulties in relating to one another. We examine the opportunities and constraints of therapeutic work in such a public context, examining the nature of family centre practice, the anxieties associated with it and the connections this has with the way that the process is managed, drawing on the concept of 'containment', the 'holding environment', and the notion of reflection on the feelings not only of family members but also of workers. We consider ways of helping children and parents, drawing on understanding of different kinds of anxious attachment and of the projections involved in the process of working therapeutically. We illustrate these with case studies of work, first with children, second with parents. We explore some ways of working with the parent in the presence of the child. One approach uses 'relationship play' to repair attachment between child and parent. Another draws on parent–infant psychotherapy, an approach well suited to the family centre setting, which has been found helpful in enabling a parent to see their child as the real person he or she is, rather than as a representation of something from the parent's past.

The context: the family centre as a holding environment

In therapeutic family centre settings where there is intensive work focusing on the welfare of the child, associated with concerns about the care that the child is presently receiving, a number of families may attend for the whole day, and sometimes for several days a week. Work may be directed to assessing the nature of current parent–child relationships (see Chapter 3), to helping a child develop a more secure attachment to a parent (often termed preventive work), and to repairing emotional damage both to the child itself and to the child within the parent. Often these processes are taking place simultaneously. A whole range of types of intervention is possible – individual work separately with a parent or with a child, or with a parent and child together, or with a family as a whole. Group work may take place with parents only or children only, as well as with groups of families. The whole group of families and staff may come together in community meetings or at meal-times. As we saw in Chapter 1, the group care setting of a family centre lends itself to opportunity-led work as well as to pre-planned interventions. The 'holding environment' of the family centre may be able to offer sufficient emotional containment to both parent and child to resolve their relationship problems.

One of the central dilemmas for workers in a family centre setting concerns whose needs to address, those of the parent or of the child. While the child's needs are of course paramount, the question arises as to whether these needs should be met directly by the worker, or by the parent as a result of intervention by the worker with the parent. In a sense this illustrates the complexity of defining the primary task of the family centre; there is a multiple task for the worker or team when addressing the differing needs of the family members which affects both the way in which the team works and the service it provides.

Managing the apparent conflict between the needs of child and parent is a recurring issue. The neediness for emotional support of both can often lead to envy and rivalry in which meeting the needs of one appears to be at the expense of the other. At the very least there is often a dilemma over timing. While effective long-term help to the child may involve meeting some of the parent's needs and restoring or developing their ability to provide good-enough parenting, the child has immediate needs which if not met put development at even greater risk. For example, a parent may be struggling with intense feelings of anxiety and anger, and may find it difficult to respond to her child who may need comforting. A worker or the team are then faced with a decision as to how to respond – should they intervene and comfort the child at the risk of undermining the parent, or respond to the parent's needs so that she can be helped to respond to her child?

often related to *their* feelings about someone in their past or
emselves – which trigger an emotional response in us, so tha
hem as our feelings. This is sometimes called the *diagnos*
e, because it can be useful in guiding us as to the possibl
or present relationship difficulty. We need too to distinguis
om other feelings which arise out of our *own* history of bein
ir sense of self (*personal counter-transference*). Such reflection
sy task when painful feelings are involved. Recognition of th
ted feelings and understanding the extent to which our ow
te in others may enable us to make sense of what is happenin
ur engagement in the therapeutic process. The 'holdin
f the staff team including the sharing of reflection within th
in keeping the focus on the task.

environment' for reflective practice – team
supervision and consultancy

o be helped to be responsive to children's and parents' needs an
e defences against anxiety which inhibit thought (Menzies Lyt
l 1995) she needs the support of her own 'holding environment
The way workers are expected to respond to the feelings o
amilies needs to be mirrored in the way in which they are treated
to; management needs to be democratic and involve staf
994; Richman and McGuire 1988). Planned structures for staf
help people hold on to and bear the feelings which the work
ploring personal feelings through individual reflection in a journa
an also promote understanding and self-awareness when trying to
issues in an honest way (Dacre 1996).

ngs and the reflection process

re exposed to vulnerable families need the support of regular team
ime at the beginning and end of each day for the whole team to
aluate the day's work can enable workers to off-load concerns and
out things that have happened and to gain insight into some of the
t work within the centre as a whole. Understanding of the *reflection*
which 'the processes at work currently in the relationship between
worker are often reflected in the relationship between worker and
' (Mattinson 1975, p.11), can further help the individual worker or
ake the connections between what is happening within different

Workers are likely to be responsible for particular families and pieces of work. During the course of the day the worker will be presented with a variety of situations. Her day may have started with a family arriving in distress; she may then be involved within a counselling situation; then straight back into the work with the group of families, maybe participating in a creative activity such as some artwork; then lunch with the families; later she may be running a group with a colleague for parents or caring for the children while the group takes place. The worker may also see the families for whom she is the allocated worker at other more informal times in the week, for example at a 'drop in' session where the people using the service may have responsibility for running it. While these 'multiple roles and relationships' can present a dilemma for the worker and/or the parent in terms of roles and boundaries there are advantages: 'the opportunity they afford staff and users to get to know one another in a broader and deeper way', enabling staff 'to be aware of strengths as well as difficulties', and so allowing 'the possibility for a more equal relationship' (Stones 1994, p.172).

One instance of difficulty is that which may arise in those family centres where staff are allocated roles *either* with the child *or* with the parent, because it is too often the case that the work with parents is seen as 'more important'. This is compounded in those centres where the parent worker is a qualified social worker and the child worker is a nursery nurse; not only is the status of the children's worker lower but so is the pay. All staff in a family centre team need to share the same values and practice principles when it comes to the work with children.

In a group care situation, where families are together with workers for a large proportion of the day, it is important that discussion and debate happen in both the parent groups and the staff groups. There needs to be space to analyse situations, to think about how they arose and were responded to. For example, there needs to be a mechanism for people to test their value base regarding managing children's behaviour: all adults will have their own set of values about child care depending on their experiences and the cultures to which they belong. The structure of the week will include a range of meetings, for example supervision, staff meetings, planning and evaluation times, reviews and possibly consultancy. Workers and families may also be involved with outside meetings such as case conferences. Wider issues that at various times affect practice include the morale of the team and whether the workers feel their work is valued. So do inadequate resources and a lack of staff.

Staying on task – workers' anxieties

Much family centre work takes place within a very public arena. Things that happen in groups are on display to the group. Parenting skills are on show to other parents and staff. A worker's practice is on show to other work colleagues as well as to parents and children. This in itself can create its own anxiety and feel very uncomfortable, but on the other hand it can also provide a range of possibilities for working in a very direct, spontaneous and creative way. Workers are presented with a range of complex issues daily, and while some responses can be planned, other incidents can happen without any apparent indicators and a worker or the team then need to make some immediate decisions and quick responses (see Chapter 1 or Ward 1998). The responses will depend on a range of factors, such as the relationship between parent and worker, the other families that are present, as well as any other issues and dynamics around at the time. The noise level may be high (likely if all the families are in and if it is raining and the children cannot get outside to play). There may be a lack of workers available, one off sick, one on a training course, one dealing with a telephone enquiry, and so on.

The families bring with them their own issues and anxieties and during the course of the day many incidents occur. How these incidents are responded to may affect what else arises within the group and so has an impact on the work of the day. Thinking as a team about the impact of these incidents and their effect on the individual worker and the team can provide more informed strategies for helpful response. The task with families is often focused on the relationship between the parent and the child and promoting 'good-enough' child care. It can be very stressful containing the emotions that this interaction can generate. It can feel particularly difficult when a child arrives at the centre with an injury that is given a confused or inconsistent explanation; so can working with a child or children who exhibit signs of disturbance through their behaviour, whether overly excitable and aggressive or in contrast very passive and watchful. Working closely with families can provide exciting opportunities but it also brings with it the stress of being with families who are hurting.

In such situations we are exposed to the child's and parent's distress, which is communicated in a range of ways. Feelings can be projected on to the worker on an unconscious level. Work teams can sometimes mirror the families' behaviour, for instance not discussing some issues because they feel too painful or too big, and they need to be able to reflect on these. It is important that workers see themselves as effective and capable but at the same time aware of themselves and the impact they have on the people around them.

Uncertainty then is one anxie[...] sometimes feel anxious if a partic[...] equally feel anxious if this same fa[...] means exclusive to staff. The famil[...] uncertainties, for example a new pa[...] her, or she may feel anxious because[...] may seem friendly but busy. The ch[...] anxiety and feel anxious themselves a[...] the parent. The blurring of boundarie[...] fulfils throughout the working week [...] parent. For example a parent who [...] situation and then sees the same worke[...] something lighthearted may feel that [...] parent placed in her. Likewise the p[...] attention on a family support day where[...] may not be so attentive, which can be [...]

In order to stay on task and help [...] children (assuming that this is the spe[...] knowledge base from which their practi[...] that children need? When is parenting 'g[...] parenting capacity? Why is it that parents[...] children's needs? These require kno[...] parent–infant relationships and attachmen[...] (see Chapters 2 and 3). Yet such knowledg[...] prevent a worker from being drawn into a[...] parents and children who are hurting can e[...] bad. Parents or children who lack an inne[...] express their feelings in the way they b[...] themselves re-enacting unhelpful parenta[...] generated, for instance, by working with 'out[...] them into a power struggle with the childrer[...] with intense feelings of rage with a parent[...] ignores or shouts at an unhappy child. Or we n[...] family feels by becoming ambivalent about t[...] conflicts and splits may get re-enacted in the[...] between child protection and therapy when 'the[...] with a 'protection' hat on or too permissive and [...] very real' (Trowell 1995, p.130).

We need to be aware of these feelings and[...] meaning. Often these are projections of feeling[...]

the other person[...] hidden part of th[...] we experience t[...] *counter-transferen*[...] nature of a past [...] these feelings fr[...] parented and o[...] not always an ea[...] power of proje[...] feelings origina[...] and support [...] environment' [...] group can help[...]

A 'holding[...] meetings, s[...]

If a worker is t[...] so overcome t[...] 1988; Trowe[...] (Ward 1995)[...] children and [...] and listened[...] (McMahon [...] support can [...] involves. Exp[...] or portfolio [...] face difficul[...]

Team meeti[...]

Staff who a[...] meetings. [...] plan and e[...] anxieties a[...] dynamics [...] *process*, in [...] client and [...] superviso[...] team to [...]

groups, for example the family group and the staff group. There needs to be attention to ways of helping a team to identify and understand this mirroring process. There are certainly times in these meetings when it is possible to find 'reflective' connections between feelings within the staff group and equivalent feelings which seem to belong within the group of families. Where we find these connections, we can often use what we discover to help us decide how to respond to what is happening. At other times it is more difficult to make these connections – but even here, the reason for the difficulty is sometimes to do with the team feeling stuck or 'blocked', which may itself reflect issues that the families are bringing with them. What is needed is the time and space for the team to do this.

Practice example

One of the young children who attends the family centre had a heart operation. The team had discussed and responded to the anxiety in the family that this situation generated. One worker realised that she had found it very difficult to be involved with this and felt concerned that she had been unable to say goodbye to him before he went off for the operation. As the team thought about this the worker realised that there were two other things that could be significant. Her brother had died two years previously and she had not realised that the anniversary had arrived. She had also applied for another job and found it difficult to discuss this openly within the team. Through reflection with the team this worker was able to understand that it was her own anxieties she needed to deal with so that she could respond appropriately.

Supervision and consultancy

A further necesary support structure is supervision – both planned and impromptu – and consultation. The support of regular planned individual and group supervision needs to be built in. There may also need to be a mechanism for impromptu supervision in for example a situation where a child has arrived with an injury and some negotiation is needed with a senior worker about the immediate course of action that is needed. Using a consultant can be a way of helping the group explore more complex processes.

Practice examples – Anti-task action

A social work student on her final placement said hello to a four-year-old boy on the stairs and was met with 'fuck off bitch'. She reached the foot of the stairs, turned to look at him and registered her mouth was open, closed it and realised she was shocked. She felt angry with herself for feeling shocked, although she did ignore the swearing. Then she felt helpless and thought she could have thought of a better response than shock. Later, working in the group of families and staff she felt isolated from the team, believing that they would be able to handle such a simple situation. In supervision she explored these feelings and realised that she had unconsciously avoided the boy for the rest of the day. While this is a small incident the impact for the student was not small. There were anxieties associated with her task which were to do with fearing failure. The consequences were that by avoiding the boy her actions could be described as 'anti-task'. Supervision provided her with support and an opportunity for reflection which enabled her to get back on task.

In another example, it was agreed that a worker would provide a three-year-old girl with a 'special time' for half an hour in the playroom, because of the amount of time that this child was being ignored due to the stresses and strains in her family. During the worker's supervision when she was asked how the play time had gone she said that the child had 'just played'. When this was explored it transpired that directly before the session she has been approached by a very distressed parent. The worker's mind had been on this parent's anxiety during the session and she had unconsciously ignored the child, thereby re-creating the same experience for the child that the worker was trying to compensate for. Being able to recognise this helped the worker to avoid further re-enactments of this situation.

Using ideas about attachment and the inner world to help children and parents

To work with a parent or child we need to build up a trusting working relationship, which to some extent mirrors a good parent–infant relationship. Using attachment thinking can help us build on this task by identifying specific therapeutic aims and by indicating the likely difficulties in the process of work. While the securely attached child or parent can manage both the intimacy and autonomy which mature relationships involve, the anxiously attached person needs help with one or both (Holmes 1993 and 1996). The avoidantly attached child or dismissive adult longs for but also fears and cannot achieve intimacy. The ambivalently attached child or preoccupied adult longs for but also fears autonomy and individuation. At the extreme is the unintegrated child or adult with unresolved trauma and loss who fears annihilation, and for whom the possibility of either intimacy or individuation seems remote. Holmes' model used in conjunction with Crittenden's (1995) can be useful in thinking about how to respond helpfully. It is their thinking which we draw on in the following discussion.

Working therapeutically with children

Helping a child with anxious avoidant attachment

We can all recognise the child who is very quiet and good, usually shy and withdrawn although some specialise in taking care of other often younger children. Such children are not much trouble and so tend to get overlooked. However, if their difficulties are not addressed early on, while they may get through their school years without causing concern, difficulties are likely to arise in adolescence and adulthood.

The *core anxiety* of the child whose relationship with the parent is best described as an anxious *avoidant* attachment is *abandonment*, with feelings of grief and loss, and underlying deep sadness, and also anger and emptiness. A positive option for the very young child is to make an additional attachment to someone else as well as the parent. Here the family centre may help directly. The therapeutic aim is to help the child with intimacy. However the child has learned to *fear contact*, a transference projection which in turn makes the worker feel bored, angry and rejected. These then are likely to be the feelings the worker (or other carer) needs to struggle to hold on to and think about in offering emotional containment. Therapeutic strategies involve accepting the child's rage and grief. Cognitive behavioural work may be useful later because the child can use thinking. Sensory and symbolic play can help the child start to connect thinking and feeling.

Practice example – Learning to trust and coming to life

Nazia (age 3) had learned not to expect a positive response from her very distant mother, who was depressed and isolated, living in a cramped flat after a lifetime of moves, short of money and feeling that 'life is a nightmare'. Nazia's behaviour seemed to be based on 'not winding mum up'. If upset she would cry momentarily and then stop abruptly. When accidentally hit hard on the head with a toy by her baby brother she simply looked ahead at the television screen in a dreamlike trance. In the family centre her state could be described as compulsive self-reliance. She did not show any reaction when her mother left the room. She avoided anything messy like painting. Her keyworker joined her in her pleasure in books and in play with dough, and over time she became more animated, allowing herself to enjoy a wider range of activities, even finger painting. Occasionally she even dared to show she was upset when another child bumped into her, and allowed her keyworker to comfort her.

Helping a child with anxious ambivalent attachment

Family centre workers are unlikely to overlook the child whose attachment to their parent is ambivalent. There is always something happening, crying, whining, a tantrum, interspersed with periods when the child may be a real pleasure to be with. All these occur too in securely attached toddlers who are experimenting with autonomy or who become anxious when a parent's attention is elsewhere, but in anxiously attached children the behaviour is more intense and extreme.

The child's *core anxiety* is *impingement* by or *enmeshment* with the parent. Blurred boundaries make them unable to digest experience. The child's coercive defence against these feelings may involve, on the one hand, splitting people into good and bad, blaming others, denying their own responsibility, angry acting out and threatening. On the other hand they may use coy, helpless, charming, and seductive behaviour – another version of a false-self. Young children often alternate rapidly between the two states, unconsciously manipulating the carers as they have been emotionally manipulated (also for the most part unconsciously) by their parent.

The child's transference is *fear of separation*, which makes the worker feel smothered, manipulated, taken over, unable to think. The therapeutic aim for the child is autonomy or individuation – the development of a separate self. Because the child can use the language of feeling, the worker can use the relationship to provide emotional containment and clear boundaries, but will have to struggle to avoid collusion. For example, Blaug (1989) describes how easily a worker can get drawn into a power struggle with angry and 'out of control' children. The child can be helped towards thinking if the worker names feelings as they are expressed symbolically in play. Sometimes simple cognitive-behavioural strategies (see Chapter 3) can help a child better manage their behaviour.

The case study of Daniel below indicates an extreme form of ambivalent attachment.

Helping the unintegrated child – the child with anxious 'disorganised' attachment or severe avoidant or ambivalent attachment

A child who has lacked any real emotional containment from earliest infancy is the truly unintegrated child. The child's core anxiety is *annihilation* – fear of falling in pieces – arising from unresolved trauma, abuse or deprivation, or early loss. The child has no real defence against these feelings although may be both controlling and care-giving at times to obtain a precarious sense of self. For example he or she may try to engage a dissociating mother by controlling behaviour, either hypervigilant and nurturing, or by punitive control and deviance, both resulting in the child producing a 'false-self', covering up the chaotic self within.

The child's transference is *fear*, amounting to panic, of both contact and separation. There is no trust in anything or anybody, only a terrifying emptiness. The worker's counter-transference is to feel helpless and wiped out. The therapeutic aim for the child is the development of a real and integrated self with a 'reflective self-function'. For this to happen the environment has to change because the child alone cannot change. The child needs *primary experience*, sometimes in substitute care which must offer therapeutic child care which is *more* than good child care. Every part of the child's daily life from getting up to bedtime and sleeping needs careful management with predictable and reliable care.

Hence Dockar-Drysdale's (1990) sequence of the processes which must be gone through in order to reach integration: good experience, realisation, symbolisation, conceptualisation. The child must first have a good experience of being cared for; then they need to be able to hold on to that good experience and believe that it really happened, rather than deny or spoil it. They are helped to remember and store the good thing inside them by representing it symbolically, but eventually need to be able to put it into words so that it can be thought about and communicated. Play or individual psychotherapy can normally only be used as a supplementary part of the provision of primary experience. Since the child needs to learn how to think as well as taking the risk of learning to feel, cognitive work in the course of daily life is necessary to help the child acquire a view of the world based on reality. The therapeutic family centre centre can play a part in all this. The 'holding environment' which it offers will be essential to enabling workers and carers to bear the painful feelings of being in touch with a child who is empty and terrified.

Practice example – An inner world 'in fifteen pieces'

Daniel's mother had been ambivalent about him from before his birth. She regularly left him with his grandparents or demanded foster care and then insisted that he go back to her again. As Daniel got older his mother's calls for care were because he was 'out of control'. He would have angry tantrums, he wet his bed and soiled, and showed some sexualised behaviour. At the same time he was terrified of separation from his mother. There were questions about violence and abuse in the home. Family centre staff viewed Daniel with considerable apprehension. He scowled, spat, and could be controlling and destructive. He received individual play sessions at the family centre in parallel with work with his mother. In an early session he showed indications of his fragmented inner world; one drawing was of a person in 15 pieces. He repeatedly regressed in these sessions, asking to be fed and making use of the baby equipment in the room. In symbolic play he would put on a 'robber's' hat and use a bat to beat a beanbag, or a doll (perhaps a sign of anger at his own lost childhood), or build a Lego house which he always destroyed eventually (perhaps a reflection of his endless moves between home and care, none of which contained him for long). Over time he became more relaxed in his play sessions, able to think about some of his terrible fears of death and annihilation (he was fascinated by graveyards and brain surgery) and his worker became very fond of him. However, the lack of containment in Daniel's outside world led eventually, at the age of seven, to his going into therapeutic residential care where he could receive the more continuing primary experience which he so much needed.

Working therapeutically with parents – banishing the 'ghosts in the nursery'

The family centre as a whole and the relationship between an individual worker and parent within it need to reflect the way in which a 'good-enough' mother interacts with and understands her baby. We can draw on Winnicott's (1965) notion of maternal preoccupation and 'the holding environment' and Bion's (1962) concepts of maternal 'reverie' and 'containment' (see Chapter 2). These have parallels in Carl Rogers' (1958) model of individual counselling, where the paramount qualities needed are active listening skills and empathy, that is, being able to feel for someone as if we were in their shoes while remaining in our own. Work with a parent may take place in opportunity-led work, an individual session or groupwork.

Practice example – Containing fear of rejection

Mary came to the family centre each Monday morning. She would stand facing me, looking straight into my face, just a few inches from my nose. She would talk very quickly about her current worries, her anxiety level rising all the time. I would feel as if I wanted to break this flow of words, and sometimes to make an excuse to leave her in mid flow. However, my impression was that this behaviour was because Mary felt 'no one ever listens to her'. Just as I felt I could not get her to possibly stop talking and listen. After talking at me for five minutes she would stop, and say, 'I'll just go and get a cup of tea now, Bye.' This left me feeling tense and exhausted and rather bewildered.

I decided that Mary really did need someone to talk to about her anxieties but it seemed that she was unable to contain anxiety in any way and relied on coming to the centre to project her 'bad feelings' out, so that she could then forget about them for the rest of the day. She was not able to contemplate changing and would not discuss problems. To make the situation more controlled and contained, and so that we could build more of a working relationship, I suggested that we went off to a quiet room for one hour every Monday morning with a cup of coffee so that she would have a space to 'offload' and more space to explore issues further if she wished. She said she was pleased to have this space and attention. After a few weeks we began to be able to explore her problems more deeply within a safe and contained relationship and environment.

A worker without some understanding of projection and containment of feelings might have become tense and angry about being 'cornered', unable to think about the meaning of Mary's communication, and so might have missed the opportunity to help Mary contain and think about her anxieties.

Practice example – Bearing loss and grief

Carol, a parent who attended the family centre with her three younger children (who were on the child protection register), had revealed to her worker May that she had a baby who died at birth and because of the circumstances at the time had blamed herself for the death. She had not been allowed to see the baby at the time and had not discussed this or anything else to do with this episode in her life with anyone before. Carol felt that the child had been on her mind a lot recently because it was coming up to what would have been his eighteenth birthday.

After talking about this together, Carol and May went to visit the Snowdrop Garden, which was a place where babies who had died were remembered. As they sat in the peace of the garden, Carol recalled the events as they had taken place. As she listened, May was aware of her own total preoccupation with Carol and the intense feeling of sadness. She became aware that she was beginning to feel anxious and started to wonder whether she could bear Carol's sadness. May then wondered whether in fact it was Carol who was struggling with feelings of panic. Carol sometimes would self-harm by cutting herself with razor blades. As May registered this thought she said to Carol 'What would you like to do?' Carol said she wanted to cut herself to release the awful feelings and confirmed that she had some blades in her bag. Keeping her voice calm but registering her own internal panic as an indication of what Carol was feeling, May acknowledged the difficult step Carol had taken and the feelings that had gone unexpressed for so long. Carol began to weep, and May comforted her and praised her courage. As Carol cried the panic passed and they both sat for a while longer in the quiet of the garden.

Here the worker attempted to hold the parent's painful feelings by being thoughtful or preoccupied with the parent. She recognised her own panicky feelings – which she felt were the mother's projected unbearable feelings – but was not overwhelmed by them, conveying the message that although the feelings were painful they could be tolerated. Change is made possible because the parent is able to take in the feeling of being contained and so becomes more able to bear her loss

Practice example – Finding the real child

Susan asked for help with her relationship with her two-year-old son Adam, a fourth child and a longed-for son. She was confused by the hostility she felt towards him, finding it difficult to tolerate his company but at the same time distressed by her inability to care for him. Adam became exceptionally clingy and crying whenever separated from his mother. Individual weekly counselling provided Susan with a space to try and make sense of her feelings towards him. Over the year Susan came to understand that Adam represented in her mind all the abusive men from her childhood, namely her father and her uncles. At an unconscious level Susan had projected on to Adam feelings of anger, loathing, and disgust about her father, her uncles and herself. Adam also suffered from severe asthma and his vulnerability and helplessness reminded her of that part of herself that had to be hated and rejected. As she began to take back her projections and experience her own feelings she became able to relate to Adam as a separate and eventually even lovable child. A further year of counselling was still needed. After six months both Susan and Adam began a series of family play sessions with a family centre colleague which helped consolidate the internal changes and actively develop their relationship together.

The example of Susan highlights the potential flexibility offered by family centres. It was important that Susan had an opportunity to spend time working through her conflicting feelings and banish a few 'ghosts' before she could embark more directly on work on her relationship with her son.

Working therapeutically with parent and child

Although counselling work with a parent may change a parent's inner world, it often needs to be supplemented by work with the parent but focused on the child if there are to be rapid changes in parental behaviour (Cox *et al.* 1990; Trowell, Hodges and Leighton-Laing 1997). The parent–child game (see Chapters 3, 9 and 10) is one useful approach. Deco (1990) combines a systemic structural family therapy approach with art therapy. Mellow Parenting uses a range of methods in addition to experiential groupwork with parents, including parents' workshops using videotaping to draw a parent's attention to the child's point of view (Mills and Puckering 1995; Puckering *et al.* 1996; see also Chapter 13 on NEWPIN).

Relationship play

A similar pattern of work with the parent alongside work with parent and child together is involved in 'relationship play therapy' (Binney, McKnight and

Broughton 1994). This approach is designed to repair damaged attachment, helping mothers to relate better to their children through a structured programme of group games and play. Such programmes can work well, but seem to depend for success on being matched by parallel provision of a mother's group based on play or talking, where they can start to share the feelings involved in painful present and past experiences. As they discuss current difficulties with their children, their lack of support and powerlessness in relationships, mothers are helped too to reflect on their own childhood experiences and get in touch with some painful memories. Re-experiencing these feelings in an atmosphere of acceptance and containment can help put them in touch with their own child's present experience and allow them to re-edit their family scripts (Byng-Hall 1995) and change their 'inner working model'. While mothers have their group time their children are in a playgroup with separate staff. Group play sessions come after these separate groups. They are tightly structured to avoid both competition between mother and child for the worker's attention, and parental de-skilling and envy if mothers see staff engaging more successfully with their children, as can happen in unstructured play.

The content of the relationship play sessions is graded carefully to provide graduated steps to intimacy and physical contact between parent and child. Too much too soon is overwhelming and leads to aggression. Opening and closing rituals provide a clear boundary. Sessions start with group games such as *Ring-a-Roses* and *Pass the Parcel*, working up to games involved positive physical touch, with some parent–child paired back-to-back and fingertip games (such as *Incy Wincy Spider*), and traditional games such as *Grandmother's Footsteps* (the parents are grandmother in the first week, the children in the second) and *What's the Time Mr Wolf?* Later sessions use more close body contact paired play, based on the negotiation of power in an enjoyable way, such as mirroring, puppets, face painting, or taking turns to draw round one another on the floor. Close body contact and eye-to-eye singing games, such as *Rock-a-Bye-Baby* and *Row Your Boat* come even later, and are played first as group games and then in pairs, and may become 'homework' (McMahon 1992b, p.77). Then there is a turn-taking story-telling of a 'good' and 'bad' story, which must end on a 'good' note. The session ends with a song or nursery rhyme, with mother cradling the child, and a group 'yell' or action story to release any tension and prepare for leaving (Broughton, McKnight and Binney 1992).

Evidence suggests that relationship play therapy makes 'some impact on well established defensive styles of relating between mother and child' (see Chapter 9 for an example). Over time this benefit may fade unless it is 'part of a wider set of supportive services to vulnerable mothers and children' (Binney *et al.* 1994, p.58).

Parent–infant psychotherapy as a model for therapeutic practice

Among the more specific and formal therapeutic models for working with parents and young children, one which is particularly appropriate to work in family centres is parent–infant psychotherapy, where the parent is worked with in the presence of the child. There have been several case studies and much theoretical work (Brazelton and Cramer 1991; Fraiberg 1980; Hopkins 1992; Murray and Cooper 1994; Stern 1997); and currently the Anna Freud Centre Parent–Infant Project is developing this work. This model uses Kleinian object relations theory as well as Bowlby's attachment theory. It assumes that there is no such thing as individual psychopathology in infancy but that problems will be related to the parent–child relationship.

Parent–infant psychotherapy is based on work with damaging parental 'ghosts'. The child's presence ensures that the parent's feelings for the child can be noticed and thought about. Fraiberg combined this with interventions to support the parent emotionally, such as emphasising the parent's importance to the child. The worker helps the parent recall not only the events of the past but also the feelings associated with them. While the events may be remembered the feelings have often been deeply repressed because they are so painful. For example, abuse and desertion may be remembered but not the terror and helplessness, the sense of shame and worthlessness. The task is to help the parent connect how their child is responding with the parent's own repressed feelings. As the parent's pain is felt again but becomes bearable within the emotional containment provided by the worker, the parent may be able to start to see their child as the real person they are and to take back some of their own damaging projections. They may come to say 'I never want that to happen to my child'.

Experiences of food and feeding are often a potent demonstration of any lack of attunement in the parent–child relationship (Briggs 1995). There are numerous metaphors in everyday speech – 'fed up to the back teeth', or less intrusively 'needing time to digest', as well as starvation metaphors – 'feeling hollow', 'empty', 'hungry for something to get your teeth into' – which reveal the connection between food and feeling, usually going back to infancy. Meal-times in family centres are an important way of giving 'primary experience' through the provision of food, a potent symbol of caring. Yet they are often difficult occasions, arousing feelings in both parents and children about ways in which, for instance, they were 'starved', 'made to swallow' or had food 'stuffed down their throat'. The therapeutic management of these meal-times can involve a helpful attention to these 'ghosts in the nursery', as the following example[1] demonstrates.

Practice example – Food for thought

A mother became very frustrated and angry when her child refused to eat his dinner. The child became quiet and cried silently, but the mother continued to nag angrily. The worker felt concerned for the child and puzzled by the parent's reaction. Later talking it through with the mother, being careful not to be disapproving or accusing, she tried to convey empathy for the mother's concern that the child's physical well-being depended on his eating enough food, and how difficult she found it to provide food on a low budget. The child was healthy and not under-weight and the centre's meals were subsidised. This mother's perception seemed different from the reality of the situation. The worker wondered whether other things were at play and resisted her initial thoughts of reassuring the parent that all really was well and giving her a few encouraging ideas for making meal-times more pleasant. Instead she asked what meal-times were like when she was a child. The mother described a similar scenario to the one that had just taken place, and talked about the poverty her family had struggled with, her father's anger, and the guilt she had felt. She did not seem to make any connection with the scene that had just taken place. The worker talked about what it must have felt like for that child, fearful to eat a scarce resource and yet fearful not to eat and evoke her father's anger. As the mother got in touch with her own childhood self, both remembering and re-experiencing these feelings, she was able to work more freely on a resolution to the meal-time difficulty.

The 'ghost's' intrusion in the present revealed a vulnerability that corresponded with the parent's past. The child's problem indicated a problem needing to be solved with the parent. This seemed to be the key to helping the parent make the connection between her past experience and her present day behaviour, which in turn helped her to work with the centre staff in changing her responses, or as it were to banish the troublesome ghost.

Practice example – Holding on and letting go

Sally was at first unsure about the family centre and said that she might not stay. She said her son Mark, aged 18 months, was 'terribly naughty' but when asked how just said that he would not do as she asked. As we talked he sat wide awake in his pushchair. Sally did not want him to get out and run around in case he was naughty. Although I felt uncomfortable about this he did not appear distressed, and later she did sit him on her lap for a while. From our conversation I found out that Sally felt trapped by her responsibility for Mark. She lived with her parents after some years of independence and was often alone during the day when her parents were out. I had the impression that she saw herself as a 'naughty girl' because she was a single parent which her parents might disapprove of. I noted that her concern about the family centre was its structured day and the number of 'rules'.

The next time Sally came to the centre she allowed Mark to go and play, although she was anxious if he went too far away from her. When he did come back to her side she scolded him for being naughty and interrupting her by putting his head on her lap. I gently suggested that a little boy of Mark's age may well go off for a while and come back to his mum if he's a little uncertain about the world because going back to mum makes him feel secure. On her next visit Sally said that she found the centre too restrictive but she had found a local mother and toddlers group where she could meet people. I said that if this is what she wanted it was fine by me. She looked surprised briefly and then relieved. During the day both she and Mark were much more relaxed, Mark playing freely around the centre with his mother being readily available. Once Mark lost her and cried, and she came to cuddle and talk to him.

For the first two visits, keeping Mark restricted and under total parental control seemed to be enacting something from how she felt about her own relationship with her parents, that is, restricted and controlled because she was a 'bad girl'. Somehow by talking about these feelings, having attention drawn to Mark's stage of emotional development and her importance to him, and finally being able to make her own 'adult' decision without my 'parental' disapproval helped their relationship appear to move on, at least a little.

In the same way as a secure attachment enables exploration, the worker's emotional 'holding' helped the mother start to take her own decisions about staying at the family centre and moving on to another group. The worker's attention to the feelings of both mother and child helped the mother begin to provide a similar containment for her child, providing a more secure base out of which some autonomy becomes possible. These last two case studies provide further illustrations of the creative use of 'opportunity-led' work, which fits well with the idea of the family centre as a 'holding environment'.

Conclusion

We have covered a wide range of possible approaches to helping children and parents in family centres, from opportunity-led work in the public arena to planned and structured interventions with children, with parents and with parents and children together, sometimes in individual sessions, sometimes in groupwork. We have by no means covered all the forms which work can take, and some of these are discussed in later chapters. There is ample scope for creativity in finding ways of helping members of a family get in touch with their own inner worlds and change the way they relate to one another. As Fraiberg emphasizes, 'history is not destiny', and parents can be helped to change. Providing a holding environment with emotional containment for the parent can also lead to change for the child. The hope is that workers can provide enough good experiences and secondary attachment figures to sustain and support the child while at the same time help is being given to the parents to enable them to develop more satisfactory relationships with their children. Occasionally this hope is not realised and a substitute family may be the best way of helping a child towards a more secure attachment. While many parental 'ghosts' may not be easily banished we can at least draw hope that thoughtful early intervention has the best chance of making a difference.

We have drawn on the concepts of containment and the holding environment to show how workers' feelings and anxieties associated with the task can be worked with and contained, rather than defended against. The task calls for a high level of skills from workers and management, and an ongoing commitment from both to supporting reflective practice and providing strong support structures to enable this to happen. This in turn has implications for the provision of resources and training in which attention to reflection on the emotional processes involved in family centre work must take centre stage.

Acknowledgements

Practice examples based on work by Carol Taylor, Wendy Goddard, Nin Williams, Frances Fox, Janet Vale and Viv Dacre.

PART 2

Working Therapeutically in Family Centres

Chapter 5

Therapeutic Work, Play and Play Therapy with Children in Family Centres

Linnet McMahon, with case studies
by Rosemary Lilley and Denise Ledger

Therapeutic play work with children

The ultimate aim of family centre work is about helping children who are unhappy or anxious and insecure to feel better about themselves and to have some trust that adults will take care of them. Often the main task is seen as providing the holding environment for parents (or substitute carers) so that, like a set of Russian dolls, they may in turn come to provide a good enough emotional containment for their children. There is, however, a conflict between meeting a child's needs in the short and in the long term. If we work only with the parent it is a race against time to help the parent before it is too late for the child. So the child needs direct work in its own right.

We know that children benefit from sensitive responsive care with substitute attachment figures, and many family centres provide this, together with learning through play, which is widely understood by a range of pre-school workers. Some of this play is undoubtedly therapeutic in effect, even if it is not consciously planned as such. As we saw in Part 1 of this book, the value of a secure attachment is that, paradoxically, it provides a safe base which frees the child to *play* and explore. This makes play the key. We must meet the need for secure attachment and provide a holding environment to enable a child to find him or herself through play. However, a worker who understands the emotional meanings conveyed by a child's behaviour and play and who uses play as part of her planned therapeutic response has the possibility of reaching a deeper level of communication. Sometimes this may be opportunity-led work, with the worker responding to events as they arise, often in the 'public' setting of a family centre. At other times it may be planned play therapy in an individual session with a child.

Play for parents

Of course parents have their own needs for play. A group of parents playing can be helped to get in touch with the child within themselves and so acquire more empathy with the feelings of their own children. Many family centres run play sessions for parents while the children are looked after elsewhere, introducing activities such as sand and water, painting, play dough, 'junk' play, music and so on. Parents enjoy the groups, suggesting ideas to one another and are able to laugh at their actions, finding activities they are good at or do already with their children, and growing in self-assurance. This shared enjoyment can build a bond within the group and helps to reduce inhibitions when they later go on to play as a group of parents and children together.

The significance of play

But why does play help? We all know that when life is stressful we need time for rest and relaxation, sometimes alone and sometimes in good company. More than this we need a mental space for reflection in the absence of pressure, and this too is another version of play. When we are able to let our our minds wander freely without having to worry about the outcomes we often find that things start to slot into place, the world starts making sense again, new ideas pop into our heads, we feel more in control of our lives and we start to feel better about ourselves. If this is true for adults it is even more so for children who because of their immaturity have even less control over their lives. In play a child can exercise autonomy and try things out in a safe place without fear of the consequences, a creative and satisfying process. Winnicott (1971, p.54) said 'It is playing and only in playing that the individual child is able to be creative and to use the whole personality, and it is only in being creative that the individual discovers the self'.

Moreover, young children have not developed the cognitive and language skills to put their feelings into words. Their feelings are communicated through how they are and how they behave, and play is an important part of this. This unconscious expression of feelings in play may of itself enable a child to weather 'small storms'. However, when children have had much more troubled lives, play in the presence of an adult who thinks about what the play is communicating and who is able to bear the feelings expressed may ultimately help the child in turn to bear and think about his feelings. The integrated child who can hold on to good and bad feelings without the constant need to project or get rid of the bad feelings on to other people is better prepared to make sense of his world.

If we are to use play to help troubled children whose start to life has been complicated by difficulties we need to understand how play develops in families where the parent–child relationship is 'good enough'. Then we will be better able to identify the developmental stage a child has reached so that we can make appropriate play provision. If we remember that the securely attached child, who feels confident that any needs will be responded to, is free to explore and play, then we can understand that the child who is insecurely attached is likely to have missed out on play experiences because so much mental energy has had to be devoted to monitoring their parent and trying to get enough care.

How play develops[1]

Winnicott (1971) identified three stages in the development of play:

1. Primary experience: maternal preoccupation and sensory play

2. Symbolic play

3. Playing together.

1. Primary experience: maternal preoccupation and sensory play

Play begins in the space between the baby and the mother, the area of 'illusion'. Initially the mother's attunement enables her to make spaces for her infant to have a magical experience of feeling in control, as 'she makes actual what he is ready to find'. For example, when the baby is hungry food appears, and the infant's excitement is expressed in its whole body. The baby explores the world using all its senses – eyes, ears and mouth, finding its own hands and feet and using them in sensory-motor play, finding where his body ends and the mother's begins. The mother imitates and reflects the baby's sounds and facial expressions, and plays exciting games like Peepbo. Or she plays lap games, for example singing 'Pop goes the Weasel'; as she reaches the 'Pop' she pauses and the baby learns to wait for it, and in due course delightedly manages his own. These kinds of interactive and sensory or embodiment play with the parent are part of a baby's normal primary experience.

The child who has missed this good experience does not know what is 'me and not me', and so has little sense of being a real person in a world that is comprehensible and responsive. Children whose earliest experiences were damaging need sensitive responsive care of which sensory and embodiment play, and interactive turn-taking play, are a part.

2. Symbolic play

The next stage is the child 'being alone in the presence of someone', someone who is reliably there when needed and who at times reflects back what happens in the playing. As a child develops and becomes more aware of the difference between self, others, and the world around, she becomes more aware of her dependence on others. Symbolic or pretend play helps her to link the outside world (of people, objects, toys and other things) to inner experience (her own thoughts, feelings, fears and phantasies). This play is exciting and gives the child a sense of being able to manage her world, although it may involve activities as simple as feeding teddy and putting him to bed, or playing at going shopping or going off to work.

From around the age of one many children have a transitional object, a teddy, soft toy or cloth which is both a real object and one which has an emotional meaning to the child. Winnicott saw this as the child's first symbolic creation and the beginning of symbolic play, supporting the child 'engaged in the perpetual human task of keeping inner and outer reality separate yet interrelated' (Winnicott 1971, p.2). It is a symbolic way of managing the anxiety of separations, from the brief separation of going to sleep to the longer one of being looked after by someone else. That is why it matters for a child, at any age, who is entering substitute care or moving between places, to keep with them belongings which have symbolic value.

The child who can use symbolic play is developing a sense of self, with the capacity to hold on to experiences good and bad. Most children use play as a way of assimilating and coming to terms with the experiences of daily life, without adults being aware that this is happening. A child who has experienced damaging separations or losses can be helped by symbolic play with an adult who provides a mental space in which both can think about the child's painful experience.

3. Playing together

Winnicott's third stage is for the child to allow and enjoy the overlap of two play areas (child with parent, worker or other child), paving the way for playing together in a relationship. The peepbo game of infancy turns into hide-and-seek instigated by the child herself. Play with other children, often initially with siblings or older children, and later with peers, allows for the development of increasingly complex pretend play, co-operative role play and games with rules, as well as informal 'silly' games. Alongside this many children still preserve a space for solitary pretend play.

Help at this stage can include focused play or counselling approaches (often called 'direct work'). Having a play activity for both adult and child to focus on, Clare Winnicott's (1968) idea of a 'third thing', can make communication easier and more relaxed. It draws on the more integrated child's ability to think and be reflective. A series of pictures of houses the child has lived in, drawn with their worker, may help an older child keep in mind the story of her life. Even quite young children can be helped to understand what is happening, and distress made more manageable, if the comings and goings of family members, and their own moves, are enacted by the worker using toys such as dolls and cars and so on. Such play material needs to be chosen to reflect the child's race and culture, with thought given to supporting the child's identity. Brummer (1988, p.83) emphasizes that play materials for black children should include appropriate toys that, 'enable both child and worker to reflect on sameness and difference of colour'.

The role of the worker

Play is always a creative experience and playing itself is a therapy. Winnicott (1971, p.51) stresses that play must be spontaneous, and notes comfortingly: 'The significant moment is that at which *the child surprises himself or herself.* It is not the moment of my clever interpretation that is significant.' The role of the worker is then to provide containment for the child, until the child in turn becomes a container for his or her feelings, able to hold on to them and think about them (rather than get rid of them on to others), first through symbolic play and then by putting them into words that can be thought about. Dockar-Drysdale (1990, pp.98–9) summarises this: 'We are thinking in terms of a series of processes which must be gone through in order to reach integration. These are experience, realization, symbolization and conceptualization.'

Managing therapeutic work
and play therapy with children

If work takes place in the public arena of a play room or family room where there are other children, workers, and sometimes the child's and other children's parents or carers, much of the therapeutic interaction with a child is likely to be opportunity-led. For this to take place without interruption or impingement the staff need to work as a team, understanding and valuing what is happening through play, even if they are not aware of the significance of a particular interaction. While a worker is engaged with a child, others need to be ready to fend off intrusion from other children or parents. They may need to work at the sensitive task of supporting the parent whose response to their child may be very different, maintaining the parent's self-respect and at the same time showing or explaining the meaning of the child's play and offering an alternative model of how to respond.

If work takes place in individual play therapy sessions there is an equal need for the staff team to understand and support the work. A play therapy session needs clear boundaries of space and time. The room needs to be the same from session to session and to be arranged in the same way, with the same play materials. A session is for a fixed time and often has tight boundaries marking the beginning and end. It needs to be a regular and reliable provision, given priority and not to be abandoned at short notice because of an outing or other activity, or intruded on while it is taking place. Children often find the transition to and from a session difficult, and the support from other workers can often help a child to come, and after the session re-integrate back into ongoing activities or manage re-joining a parent. Sometimes children struggle with staying in the room for their session and may walk (or run) out, and so be loose in the building. The meaning of this needs to be thought about with the staff team and a way of managing it worked at, without the therapeutic worker being blamed for not coping.

If the play therapist is not part of the everyday family centre staff team such issues need particular attention before and during the work. In any case, workers' feelings need space for reflection. The hard-pressed centre worker may be envious of the protected space of the worker in play therapy and also feel that she has to deal with all the difficult behaviour while the therapy worker only gets the 'good' bits of the child. At the same time the latter may be feeling lonely and isolated, burdened by the child's expression of fear and despair. Whether individual sessions are provided by a centre worker or an external play therapist there is potential for role conflict, envy and splitting. The child may try to split the workers, treating one as all 'good' and another as 'bad', readily playing into a worker's doubts about herself and others. These projections are often best dealt with by reflection in the whole staff team, although individual supervision has a role to play too. Again, the child who has an individual play session may also have difficulty when that worker is part of the everyday staff team, and need help to manage feelings of jealousy and rivalry as she sees 'her' worker engaging with other children.

A parent too may feel jealous of a child's play session. 'A child offered play therapy without support being extended to the parents is at risk of having the therapy sabotaged and being scapegoated by the family as a trouble-maker, or having to resolve difficult emotions and experiences which the whole family needs help with. The task therefore is to engage the child's carers and provide a holistic package of support' (Nancy Secchi).

Another important issue concerns respect for the child's confidentiality, raising the question as to how far to disclose what takes place in an individual session. This is not easy to resolve but again needs working at, so that some personal aspects of the child's communication are respected but the risk of unhelpful 'private practice' is avoided. In the examples which follow, two of opportunity-led work and one of individual play therapy sessions, the attention given by the staff team to finding ways of reflecting on what was happening was a crucial component of effective work.

Case studies of opportunity-led work in the public arena
by Rosemary Lilley

Much family centre work takes place in groups, a public arena. This requires of staff considerable capacity to work effectively together, but nothing occurs by chance. Although intervention may appear spontaneous, considerable time and thought has to be given to planning interventions, as well as reflecting on what does and does not work. Staff's willingness and capacity to engage in this aspect of work is crucial. Successful group care work has all the demands of marriage but without the choice of partner. The necessity to expose oneself and one's work to colleagues is anxiety-provoking (Provence, Naylor and Patterson 1977).

Some therapeutic interventions are long-term approaches to a child's massive negative experiences (as in the case study of Karl). For other children (such as Joni) intervention may only need to be a one-off.

Joni

Joni was a blue-eyed angelic-looking little girl of two. She attended the centre with her mother and older sister because of their mother's depression. Although they were 'children in need' they were not known to have experienced abuse or neglect. Joni was an intelligent child, meeting her milestones, able to play with her peers and with a good capacity to relate to adults. Yet on occasions, and for no apparent reason, she would suddenly attack a child or adult – whoever was nearest – inflicting a serious bite on whatever part of their anatomy she could dig her teeth into. Biting is something that many parents find particularly difficult to understand and manage. Biting is primitive and brings out primitive responses. Other mothers advised Joni's mother to 'bite her back', which she knew was inappropriate but her desperation was so strong at times that she was heard to threaten Joni with 'I'll bite you if you do it again'.

It was equally difficult for staff to manage successfully. Behavioural management had no effect and yet nothing in Joni's play suggested why she was biting, and her mother could not identify any particularly difficult experiences. The attacks were random and no pattern of antecedents could be seen. Staff became more anxious and parents more hostile to Joni and her mother. Ultimately we started at the beginning and the keyworker was asked to sit down with Joni's mother and get Joni's history in detail. What emerged was that at four months Joni had been rushed to hospital and a multitude of tests conducted. It was her mother's account of a lumbar puncture that gave a possible clue, her distress on recalling the event indicating how it must have been for Joni.

With this knowledge the staff team planned how to approach the situation. Joni's mother was agreeable to the biting being openly discussed among the other parents. It was planned to approach Joni the day *after* the next attack. It was considered futile to intervene at the time of an attack as Joni would not be receptive. Thought also needed to be given to the impact of the discussion on the other children. It was recognised that several other children had been hospitalised and that they may have had painful experiences.

Is it not interesting that when there is some insight into a difficulty the opportunity to address it arises quickly? Joni duly tried to bite a child and her behaviour was managed with time out. The next day after lunch, a time of quiet play and parents and staff having a cup of tea, a member of staff took the lead:

'I've been thinking a lot about Joni and why she keeps biting people. We know she is a kind and clever girl; we know her mum and dad treat her kindly. It's very hard to understand why Joni bites people.'

A child pipes up, 'She's naughty'.

'Well we could just say that she is naughty but that is not going to help Joni stop biting. Whenever children hurt anyone I always think they are telling us that someone has hurt them. Sarah (the keyworker) has been having a long think with Joni's mummy and she has learnt something very sad about Joni.'

The story is then recounted. 'When Joni was a baby she was very ill and had to go to hospital. All the doctors and nurses were trying to make her better but to help her they had to do lots of tests and some of these were very very painful for Joni. Baby Joni cried and cried and the doctors would not let her mummy cuddle her until they had finished the test. Poor Joni, it must have been terrible for her.' As the story was being told a staff member was quietly getting out the doctors-and-nurses toys. For the next half hour children played doctors and nurses, having medicine, and so on, and parents talked about their experiences of taking children to surgeries and hospitals. Joni sat on her mother's lap being cuddled.

Six months later Joni has not bitten again.

Karl

When setting out the play activities in the family room each morning we think about the children's age and emotional level of need. Often there are sensory materials such as sand, water and dough which engage a child's sense of adventure and curiosity. Pouring water or sand into and out of containers gives the child a symbolic experience of the inner and outer world being explored, as well as the intellectual question of 'how much before it spills over'. Adults set boundaries as to what is acceptable mess. Cries of 'keep it in the sand pit' could be heard as Karl tipped buckets of sand on to the carpet. When he could not stop he was removed to play at another activity. The following piece of work is from Karl's special worker.

Three-year-old Karl had been severely neglected and abused and was now in care and living with his aunt who sometimes attended the family centre with him. He had limited speech, got himself into fights with other children and dictated and controlled everything and everyone around him, never completing a task or tolerating any boundary set. With a swipe of his arm he would clear a table, tread on others playing, and then vaguely chew a toy. If I insisted he help put right what he had done he would scream and throw himself in a ball on the floor. I felt that this was the panic reaction of an infant who did not feel contained, and I tried to act as a container. Karl found a small soft-bodied doll whom we named 'little Karl'. He began to carry this doll around alternately chewing and sucking its hands and feet, and it became his special toy for his own use. When he dissolved into panic and threw himself on the floor I spoke to him through the doll (a safe way to put into words his unspoken fears) saying 'You seem very upset, here let me hold you, no one's going to hurt you here'. I cuddled the doll and laid it by his side. At the end of the day he wanted to take the doll home and we explained he had to bring it back next morning. The doll became a 'transitional object', taking part of the family centre home with him. It also opened further doors, enabling talking and reasoning to become part of my relationship with Karl, and he grew in his ability to use talking creatively as a two-way process.

When Karl hurt other children he would be held on the lap of myself or a colleague, through immense rage, while we told him that he could not hurt people and we would keep him safe. He would also panic and scream at any transition, such as putting on his coat to go outside, and we needed to prepare for each change by talking to him to contain his fears. Progress was first seen when Karl began to do jigsaw puzzles, at first alone and then asking for help when he felt safe enough. He could not walk away from an unfinished puzzle. It was as if the puzzle represented having a 'whole' experience from start to finish, a compensation for his lack of nurture in infancy. His success gave him confidence and recognition when he could invite adults to share his world. He moved on to building large Duplo brick towers, guarding them from other children who would seek revenge in savage attacks. This required the worker's confidence in judging how far to let children's savagery come out and when to keep the lid on. Once the tower was higher than he was, Karl took great pleasure in carefully pushing it over, perhaps symbolising his struggle for autonomy and control.

Much staff time was put into thinking about Karl and his experiences, from formal staff meetings, group room meetings and end-of-day meetings to supervision and more informal one-to-one exchanges. Karl's capacity to create havoc and put adults against one another was immense. This 'splitting' became apparent when he was asked to do something. If I asked him he would say, 'No, Steven [a colleague] do it', or if his aunt was present 'No, Auntie do it'. As colleagues we worked together and Steven directed Karl back to me. Aunt was more likely to give in to him or use me as a threat, and was, it was felt, sabotaging what we were doing, although she probably felt better.

Concern for Karl's future ability to sustain himself was and is very great. Recommendations for child psychotherapy have been made. It is vital that Karl receives enough nurture and care so that he can come to terms with what has happened to him, rather than let it go underground to re-emerge in adolescence and early adulthood when he may well be facing the task of parenting himself.

A case study in play therapy with a child

by Denise Ledger

Ben, a large and lively white boy, was referred to the family centre by his health visitor when he was three. He was staying with his grandmother while his mother was in hospital. The family centre was asked to help him adjust to going home. The referral seemed straightforward. Ben's mother would attend family support sessions twice a week with Ben, so that she could begin to take over his parenting.

Drawing a genogram, or family tree (Dyng-Hall 1995) with her revealed that Ben was born prematurely and had spent his first three weeks in an incubator, during which time she had little physical contact with him, having another child at home to care for. It became clear that her relationship with Ben's father had been volatile, with Ben witnessing violence. She said that Ben had been very close to his father and had been difficult from the day his father left the home when Ben was 18 months old. She had removed all photographs of Ben's father and he was never talked about.

Ben continued to live with his grandmother but the contact with his mother increased until she was having some time with him every day. Both seemed reluctant to make the move to overnight stays for Ben. When this did happen it became clear that his grandmother was undermining his mother, telling her and Ben that she was unable to care for him properly. Not surprisingly Ben's behaviour became more difficult, and his mother became even more anxious and unable to manage him. Despite everyone's efforts, the next year saw Ben moving backwards and forwards between his mother's and his grandmother's home. The family centre focused on helping his mother regain her confidence in her capacity to parent, and to try to meet Ben's needs. It also worked on her own self-esteem and her ability to stand up to her mother.

Ben moved back home just after his fourth birthday. His behaviour was very difficult for his mother to manage even with support. He would want to be very close to her, and would then try to hurt her – an ambivalent attachment. He told her he hated her, and wanted to be back with his grandmother. The difficulties were compounded by his unclear speech and he became very frustrated when he was not understood. He would lash out at staff and other children at the family centre, and whenever he appeared very angry or anxious would hide away under a table. The individual work began with Ben at the point of his return home and continued until his transfer to school.

Play therapy with Ben

The hoped-for outcome of the work with Ben was ' …to repair or replicate the process of attachment and containment' (McMahon 1992, p.7). His mother was not able at the start of the work (as well as probably at the start of his life) to provide a secure base for him. She was anxious about managing his difficult behaviour and angry with his seemingly better behaviour for her mother. Her inability to contain Ben's child's feelings took the form of 'sieve' (Copley and Forryan 1987) where Ben's communication would either go straight through unnoticed, or would increase her own anxiety. Both mother and grandmother were still asking for more 'time out'. It felt as though Ben was getting a message that he was not really wanted anywhere.

It seemed important to establish some beginnings of a relationship with Ben by a consistent worker. In addition to Ben's place in the family centre's nursery unit, the family had an allocated family support worker. It was agreed that she and one of the nursery teachers (who had psychotherapy training) would focus on Ben's needs and the structure for working with him, so that together they could provide some degree of a temporary secure base for him. Two staff ensured that one of them was always likely to be available. John Byng-Hall (1997, p.27) defines the concept of a secure base as ' ...a shared family responsibility that ensures everyone that any member who is in need of help will be cared for, even when certain members are unavailable either temporarily or even permanently'. Ben's sessions with the family support worker were to include work with him and his mother together.

Further, Ben had one hour a week with the nursery teacher. Although this seemed like a great deal of time at the centre, it felt important that he knew that we wanted him, and were finding some 'special time' for him. Ben's individual sessions were planned to be non-directive. Axline (1969), as cited in Carroll (1998, p.65), defines non-directive play therapy as: 'a play experience that is therapeutic because it provides a secure relationship between the child and the adult, so that the child has the freedom and room to state himself in his own terms, exactly as he is at that moment in his own way and in his own time'. The room chosen for the work with Ben was used by parents with babies, where he could have an opportunity for the sensory and regressive baby play which he had missed in infancy. As well as the baby area the room was set out with a range of materials, including a soft play area, sand tray, home corner and puppets. As Ben was a very angry child the soft play area could allow him to be angry without hurting himself or the worker.

In his first session Ben was very quiet, rushing from one thing to another with furtive glances at his worker. Her notes state that: 'He was making quite a mess, he seemed to want to leave his mark on everything in the room. Towards the end of the session he said "Aren't you going to tell me to tidy up" (one of the nursery routines is tidy up time). When I started to reply he ran and hid under the table, and stayed there until I'd finished speaking. Did he think I was going to tell him off?' During supervision we looked at his need to make his mark on the session. It seemed as though he not only needed to touch everything in the room, but also leave part of him (the mess) behind. We thought that Ben might well have been checking that the session would still happen even if he made a mess and didn't do the things he had to do during nursery sessions. We wondered whether the mess was about how he felt he was, and there was something about leaving that behind for us to hold and manage for him.

After several similar sessions Ben began to focus more on one thing, with much less rushing around. He would play at being a baby, wanting the worker to wrap him in the blankets and bring him food. He talked about the smell of food. He liked to get into the bed that was really designed for dolls, but was just big enough for a small child to curl up in. These seemed to be important sensory experiences through which as Oaklander (1978, p.109) says 'we experience ourselves and make contact with the world'. In supervision the worker thought about her feeling of protectiveness and warmth towards Ben. He had felt like her own baby, a thought she had found a little worrying. Several subsequent sessions involved Ben being looked after like a baby. Reflecting together, we felt as though Ben had needed to evoke that level of care in order to feel well held and contained. The worker had not tried to interpret any of Ben's play by reflecting it back to him, but had become quite engrossed in watching and taking pleasure in his warmth. It seemed important that Ben was not being confronted with his emotions being passed back to him at this stage. He did not seem to be ready to manage them yet, and needed the worker to keep them safe for him.

These sessions seemed to be a turning point. Ben no longer headed for the home corner where the bed was. He played much more with the dough or sand. Animals would be 'monsters' crashing into things or burying themselves under piles of sand or dough. Ben would describe them as 'bad' and 'horrid', sometimes hitting them with a wooden hammer while they were buried. He would also play with other animals while the 'bad' ones were buried, saying he wanted to have the 'good' animals. Each session it was usually the same animals who were 'good' and 'bad', and at some point during every session where he played with them, the 'good' animals would become 'bad' too. Ben would say, ' Oh no! Why are you being bad. You'll have to go with the bad ones now', and he would bury the other animals.

The worker described how difficult she found this, wanting to tell Ben that the animals weren't bad and they didn't have to be buried. She felt angry with the adults who had let Ben down, causing him to be so distressed. Hoxter (1983, p.127) suggests, 'The feelings of injustice, frustration and the wish to blame someone seem to be endemic in this field of work. Although such feelings may be partially appropriate, the anger becomes disproportionate when it is also an expression of the ways in which we are carrying the children's own angry feelings of having been let down and the projection of our own guilt at being members of the adult society which has allowed this to happen.' In reflecting on the session we thought that Ben was using the animals to represent himself. There were disasters happening within the sand tray. Animals were making hills collapse, and digging up ordered areas where things were going on. Other objects and things he had made with dough were stabbed at in the sand tray. It seemed that Ben felt 'bad', and was often labelled as bad, but even when he tried to be good, and do what others wanted him to do, he still ended up being bad. Klein (1955) observed how a child's ability to use symbols enables him to transfer phantasies, anxieties and guilt to toys and other things. This expression through symbolic play encourages the conscious and the unconscious to work together, helping the child's inner world to be nourished.

A few weeks before Ben was due to move from the nursery to school, his behaviour became more violent. His mother was anxious about leaving the family centre, although work with her, based around the ideas of Fraiberg (1980) on the impact of the parent's own past on parent–child relationships, would continue when Ben started school. Ben too was to continue with his individual session, but his nursery sessions and family support session would cease. It was in a nursery session that Ben began to attack his nursery teacher. She had been working with a small group of children, and Ben had chosen another activity. She said 'He leapt up and just started kicking me. He seemed unable to say, or even know why he was doing it. I grabbed him and held him firmly on my lap, without thinking about whether it was the right thing to do. As I talked gently to him he seemed to relax into my body.' In supervision we explored her anxiety about managing the situation with Ben, his anxiety about his pending loss compounding his existing fears and his mother's anxiety. It seemed as though this was too much for Ben to attempt to manage for himself, and although it was not his individual time, he had sought out the one person who was able to contain things for him. He continued to need to be held physically. He was not able to ask for this and would usually kick or lash out in order to achieve it, although he seemed to hurt his worker less. Either he was using less force as he knew what the outcome would be, or the worker became less anxious about managing the situation. Ward (1990, p.349), although not advocating enforced holding of a child, comments 'Touching can give comfort to the distressed, reassurance to the fearful, and confirmation to those in doubt. It is a means of nurturing and cherishing children, as well as of healing hurt minds and bodies. It is perhaps the most basic and powerful means of communication…'

Ben found the transition to school very hard. His teachers said he was defiant, easily distracted, and violent. Several of the staff said he was a bully, and that he scared other children and staff. He is a large-framed boy, often seen as powerful and strong. Ward (1998, p.57) suggests that, 'These young people who themselves often feel very powerless come to be perceived as very powerful, by evoking strong emotional reactions in those who encounter them at an everyday level.' Staff were very anxious about managing Ben, despite the nursery teacher accompanying him on several visits and his school teacher trying to replicate her methods of working with him. The school had far higher levels of anxiety about physical contact and how it might be interpreted. For Ben there continue to be real difficulties in the disparity between his often violent behaviour, and his extreme vulnerability. However, the Ben we see now is able to show his sadness and pain.

It has been suggested by some of the adults who have come into contact with him that Ben cannot have been damaged by what has happened to him because he was too young to understand it, and that we are not being 'strict' enough with him. We do not agree. It seems likely that he was never offered clear explanations of what was happening, but what was really missing was emotional holding. In the work with Ben it has seemed crucial that he has been provided with the time and space in which to begin to develop a relationship that can contain his panic and anxiety, and begin to help him make sense of his world. He is now beginning to laugh and relax more during sessions, and rarely hides under the table. It feels as though he is making sense of his world at the family centre, and beginning to do this too at home, but he has continued to use violent behaviour to protect himself at school.

Ben was excluded from school within the first few weeks of term, and returned to the family centre for a further term. He is nearly six, and has just been excluded from his third school. The work with this family continues. Ben is about to start at a small 'Nurture Unit' within one of the city schools, where we hope the work being undertaken at the family centre can be built on.

Conclusion

Children like Ben who have experienced at best ambivalent mothering and repeated separation without adequate emotional containment will undoubtedly be hurt and troubled. Sadly they are not able always to know and understand why they hurt, nor where the pain comes from. Yet this internal pain is there, often crying out for attention, yet only visible through the child's behaviour.

For these children to begin to heal, they need to experience, and to feel some safety in, a special relationship. Play is the child's way of working, and is in Axline's (1947, p.16) words 'the child's natural medium for self expression'. We saw how Ben, through sensory and regressive 'baby' play was helped to make up for some of the primary experience he had missed. We saw him progress to using symbolic play to help him make sense of his world. The importance of the worker's ability to bear the real pain he was communicating was clear, as was the real emotional demand this made on the worker. Supervision was the key to containing the anxieties engendered.

The work with Joni, Karl and Ben emphasizes the importance of therapeutic work with a child not taking place in isolation but being part of a pattern of work with family and school, as well with the large group of family centre families and staff. The family centre has to manage a range of pressures and stresses arising out of the work. The centre leader has a significant task in enabling the staff team as a whole to think about how to provide a holding environment for the child and family and at the same time manage the stresses arising from the work. Further, this is often long-term work. Young children who have experienced severe difficulties in their early years will need to learn to trust the adult world that has let them down, and this may well take some time.

Acknowledgements

Thanks to Alison Sykes, Nancy Secchi and Nin Williams for some helpful ideas for this chapter. The case studies draw on the work of Mary Girdler and Suzanne Kraft.

Note

1   Another version of this section has appeared in Healing Play, Chapter 9 in Hardwick and Woodhead 1999.

Chapter 6

A Systemic Approach to Working with Black Families
Experience in Family Service Units
Yvonne Bailey-Smith

The term 'black' is used here to describe people who are of African and South East Asian ancestry. In using the term African, I do not in this instance separate people of African ancestry whose birthplace is outside of Africa from those whose birthplace is Africa. African and South East Asian are broad terms used here as acknowledgement of some shared experiences, and in particular both African and Asian people's continual struggles against racism and other oppressive behaviours. Mostly I will be using the term 'black'. The term 'Asian' will be used when making specific references to work with Asian families.

Introduction

Debate on how best to work therapeutically with black families is a continuing and necessary one. It is clear that workers need to become 'culturally competent' (Hardy 1997) in order to ensure the delivery of services which recognise the complex and diverse needs of Britain's black communities. Over the years, Family Service Units (FSU) have built a solid reputation for working constructively and creatively with black families, in ways which address their cultural and other experiences. The Queen's Park Unit has long been viewed as innovative in its approach to therapeutic work with this client group. A range of theoretical methods are drawn upon, and systemic thinking informs much of the practice. The systemic approach explores connections, networks of relationships and communication patterns between a person, couples or families, the people significant to them at any time, and the ideas and beliefs each of them holds which give meaning to their behaviour. It is a holistic way of working that recognises all experiences as valid, while allowing that some beliefs may be more desirable to one person's or family's framework of understanding than to another's.

The overall aim of systemic practice is to work with families to enable all involved to move forward from a named problem to its solution, and, it is hoped, with lasting benefits. To my mind, the systemic perspective offers individuals and families the flexibility to construct different ways of telling their stories. Stories that are related to cultural or other experiences do not have to be constraining but can be drawn upon in positive ways in order to enable families to change. It is a theory that does not have a pathological base; systemic practitioners are encouraged to work with what the client brings and from where the client is.

Working context

FSU (Family Service Units) was established in 1948 to work with families facing the most severe difficulties. It grew out of the work of the Pacifists' Service Units in the Second World War. FSU is a national voluntary social work charity with 20 units in England and 1 in Scotland. Each unit works within FSU's national values and its aims and objectives. The services provided reflect local needs and the expectations of the particular local authority within an overall national strategic framework. FSU exists to support families and children living in communities in the greatest need so that they can draw on their own strengths and take control of their lives. It strives to address the wider injustices and influences that prevent families from achieving their potential. This includes addressing where possible structural inequalities which are a primary reason why many of our families become clients in the first instance.

As a social work agency FSU finds itself in a unique position. The families with whom the agency works choose the agency. Referrals come from a variety of settings. It is, however, the family's decision whether or not to take up any offer of assistance. This fits well with FSU's belief that a family in difficulty or crisis needs to have their ability to make choices strengthened and enhanced, in order that they with other family members can take control of different aspects of their daily life. This kind of empowerment is one of the tenets of systemic therapy.

The systemic approach, working within the wider context

Within FSU we take the view that we cannot work therapeutically or ethically with black families without acknowledging and thinking about the wider context in which they live their lives. Racism and gender discrimination is a real issue for many of Britain's black population. Poverty and other structural injustices seriously disadvantage how many black people are able to live their lives. For some, this may mean: lack of educational opportunities; lack of job opportunities; poor diet; lack of necessary material possessions; poor housing; physical and mental ill-health; relationship difficulties; problematic behaviours from children within school and other contexts; lack of supportive friendship and family networks.

When these families come to us, part of the story they are likely to want to share will necessarily be around the impact of such issues on their lives. In FSU we find that black families come to us when they have sometimes failed to get the support that they require from other sources. Some have had years of statutory involvement but have seen little positive difference in their family system. Some have experienced what they described as over-reaction to a certain situation by some services, while others believe the definition of their problem was taken out of their hands and in some cases not taken seriously.

In working with these families FSU emphasizes the importance of working within a therapeutic context which is flexible, a context which does not hold on to rigid views of how therapy should be done. Widening our ideas of what is therapeutic has enabled us to provide a broad-based service to our black clients. It is a service which gives equal weight to therapeutic as well as practical input, where such practical input can be seen by the client and therapist as a useful way of enabling positive change. Situating therapy in a wider context can mean being prepared to connect to the individual or family's request for support with the different systems with which they are interacting. Examples may be schools, working contexts, health, housing, benefit agencies, private service providers and so on. The idea is that taking a holistic approach to the difficulties brought by the client of family can help to enable solutions. FSU takes the view that talking therapies alone can never be enough or even necessarily useful when clients are faced with real material hardships.

Many of the families we work with are refugees or asylum seekers. They come to us with powerful stories of uprooted lives and many traumatic experiences. Some now find themselves once again excluded at a number of levels from fully realising their potential within the country that they have chosen to live. Some families may have had no previous experiences of seeking external help in either practical or emotional issues. They may not find it easy to make sense of European concepts of therapy.

In working within the wider context we think it not only useful but also necessary to work with the ideas of *both/and* rather than *either/or*. In this way we can offer talking therapy alongside practical supports and vice versa.

Addressing issues of identity and culture through therapeutic work

The days are long gone when being able to show what Rogers described as empathic understanding was seen almost as a sufficient criterion for working with all clients, whatever their ethnic identity or cultural backgrounds. It is now well recognised that the Eurocentric bias in most psychotherapeutic training does not necessarily fit clients coming from non-European backgrounds. Black clients, particularly those born outside of Europe, are unlikely to feel comfortable with the European way of doing therapy.

Social constructionism is one of the theoretical approaches which informs the systemic way of working and has much to say on the issue of identity and culture in therapeutic work. One premise (Burr 1995; Pearce 1989 and 1994) is that reality is socially constructed in interaction between people. Social constructionists are interested in how stories about ourselves are derived, particularly focusing on language discourses and relationships. Language in all its forms is seen as the primary source through which people communicate and give meanings to their actions. Language therefore not only constructs and maintains our identities but can also be used to challenge, change or even create new identities.

This is an interesting notion to consider when working with black families who are living within the context of white-dominated Britain. The identities of black African-Caribbean peoples in particular have been invented and re-invented many times during the past 30 years. Many of the descriptions of black identities, as well as stories of cultural behaviours that have been ascribed, have been descriptions which have been constructed *for* black people rather than *with* them. This has coupled with a history of not having their voices heard on many levels. In the context of therapy, culture should be viewed as an essential discourse where people are able to construct their identity and sense of belonging in co-ordination with others. 'It is within culture that we construct our sense of the "we" and what it means to live within one culture rather than another' (Hannah 1992, p.70). Questions which can be asked for example are: How does something make sense in a particular culture? What is the context that the worker is trying to understand? How can we as workers make sense so that we can understand that a particular way of being is coherent to that culture?

Those of us who engage in therapeutic work with black families can play a key role in their empowerment. We are in positions where we can give voice to families who may not be feeling heard in any other context. However, effective therapeutic work cannot be done without preparation on our part to examine some of the information that is stored about black and Asian people. We must begin by examining and assessing the component parts of the work we do with these individuals and families, particularly those parts that foster, maintain, and fail to monitor and expose racism within our work. It may be useful for workers to spend some time reflecting on some of the stories that we have heard about a particular client's culture. How old were you when you first heard these stories? From whom did you hear them? What was the context in which such stories were being told? How did you make sense of them? Did you take them on board as objective truths? How did you verify them? If such stories are written down or claimed as historical, from whose perspective are they written? How did you question stories which appeared to have a cultural context?

It is notable that for many years the language and descriptions used within the therapeutic fields in respect of black clients was often the language of negativism and in many cases the language of racism. Workers were not encouraged to be curious about where these clients may have been coming from. They often had their own ideas about what was informing a particular behaviour or ways of doing things. The question of how the ethnic identities of worker and client might impact upon the therapeutic conversation was not seen as significant. More often than not workers saw themselves as the expert with all the answers. Black clients were viewed as pathological and solely responsible for their problems, particularly where a fit could not be found between the client's way of seeing things and the worker's.

The view of the black family as pathological is one that has been challenged by a number of writers. Smith takes the view that culture is very important when working therapeutically with people from a different ethnic group to the therapist's own. She is critical of those who 'bury their heads in the sand' and protest that the only essential attitude required in the therapeutic relationship is one that contains empathy. She asserts that all counsellors have historically held attitudes and expectations about their own culture which are inevitably biased, and states that the 'attitudes and expectations of the counsellor can be as much a "problem" as those of the client from another culture' (Smith 1985a, pp.537–79).

Boyd-Franklin, looking specifically at some of the issues for black people in therapy, suggests that black people see the world predominantly through the lens of racism. She has this to say: 'Black people, because of the often extremely subtle ways in which racism manifests itself socially, are particularly attuned to very fine distinctions among such variables in all interactions with other blacks, with white people, and with white institutions. Because of this, many black people have been socialised to pay attention to all of the nuances of behaviour and not just to the verbal message' (Boyd-Franklin 1989, p.96).

In the context of living in Great Britain it can be argued that racist behaviours predominate on many levels, the therapeutic field notwithstanding. It could equally be argued that whites also use the lens of racism in their perception of blacks. This may have informed the idea, put forward by some black professionals, that it might be useful in some cases for the worker to come from the same or a similar ethnic background to the client. Of course such similarities may not mean the sharing of a culture. It does however point to a necessity for cultural differences and issues of race to be acknowledged as important within the therapeutic relationship.

I take the view that workers need sufficient understanding of the client's cultural and other belief systems in order to be curious and make sense of the client's world. Such understanding can only come from an exploration and co-creating of ideas with the client. The systemic way of thinking is to see the client as the 'expert' and the therapist as in a 'not knowing position' (Anderson and Goolishian 1988, p.29). This is a position which allows client and worker the possibility of co-creating new narratives about their experiences 'lived' and 'told' (Pearce 1994, p.63) rather than clients having to cope with the imposition of the therapist's description. It is a position which encourages therapist curiosity, and does not suggest any preconceived opinions or expectations of the client, or of the difficulty the client is bringing. Neither should there be any presumptions about if, when, or how, change might happen. In this way the worker puts her or himself in a position of being informed by the client.

In keeping in mind respect for cultural differences which may exist between worker and client, workers may sometimes fail to ask questions which could be highly relevant to a particular client or family's situation. One fear is that cultural misunderstandings will be brought forth. An example of this may be a reluctance to ask questions about other people within the family system. When for instance only the mother presents for a family session, fathers of African-Caribbean children might not get asked about, because of general assumptions of how African-Caribbean families are organised. By neglecting to ask certain questions, the worker may be inadvertently closing opportunities for family members present to talk about some of the issues that are important to them. Workers must bear in mind that the issue may not be about the father's lack of interest in the family, but may be more about cultural antipathy and unfamiliarity with the idea of sitting in front of strangers talking about your deepest worries. For many reasons, including reasons of gender, the women in these families may find it easier to make that first contact.

When we join a culture, because we are not free of our own assumptions, one question that we must ask of ourselves is, what makes a difference? Differences in cultural behaviours can become obvious when we make comparisons, so we can get into the world of the other by asking questions of comparison and difference.

The use of circular questions (Burnham 1986) can prove a very useful tool when trying to make sense of how a family system with which the worker is not familiar may be structured. For example, the worker may want to find out from the family member who has named the problem, who else in the family he or she has spoken to? Who else agrees that there is a problem? Who else wants to do something about the problem? Once it is established who else in the system is concerned and is invested in creating change, then the worker can invite as many of those people as possible to a session or sessions to work at a solution. Peter Lang, a systemic therapist, suggested in his workshop 'Philosophers for Therapists' (11.12.99) that workers try not to describe clients as being resistant to change, because often people see the world in the only way that they can see the world. It may not be our way of seeing things, and may not be acceptable to us; however, it may be useful to start from the premise that it is we who do not know enough about their structure.

Rack (1982) makes the point that we sometimes shy away from dealing with issues which relate to culture because of the possible underlying values systems which may go against our own beliefs of what is right or moral. Being open to clients' descriptions of their identity and culture is not about necessarily sharing values. It is about trying to find solutions to the difficulties being experienced.

Burr (1995) invites us to take a 'critical stance towards taken-for-granted knowledge'. This is the knowledge that we have learnt over time and which we may go on to believe represents unbiased and/or objective reality. It is the knowledge that as therapists we must guard against taking into the therapeutic relationship with our clients, since it is not knowledge that is co-created or co-constructed with them. She went on to make the salient comment: 'If our experience of ourselves in our different cultures is only given structure and meaning by language, if these meanings are not fixed, but constantly changing, sought after and struggled for, then our experiences are potentially open to an infinite number of possible meanings or constructions, what it means to be "a woman" "a child" "to be black" could be transformed, reconstructed' (Burr 1995, p.43).

Pearce's (1994) idea that we not only create but are created by culture suggests that as individuals we both contribute to the construction of cultural practices and are recursively shaped by them. In terms of the therapeutic conversation, then, opportunities are opened up for the worker to co-construct with clients new self-narratives and stories lived in the context of relevant issues such as differential power and social differences, which may be based on race, culture, religious or other belief systems. The social constructionist position is one that privileges the idea of cultural discourses and how these connect to the issues brought to therapy by clients and worker. It is a position which values relationships between people and their differing contexts and one which values the notion of change for those who are seeking change.

Practice example 1 – Helping a family in evolving and changing its cultural story

An 18-year-old East African woman whom I will call Halimo informed me that she was pregnant for the fourth time. Having worked with her for two years, I had gained some understanding of the importance of her religious and cultural belief systems with regard to having children. She believed herself to be blessed, but at the same time she also expressed feelings of depression and complained about the family's living environment (a small two-bedroom house). She spoke of her unhappiness at her partner's lack of support in caring for their children or in taking general responsibility for the family.

While working with Halimo some child-protection concerns arose. The child-protection conference recommended that the parents be offered nursery places for the elder children. Accepting that her children would benefit from attending a nursery was a difficult concept for the client. She explained that sending children off to such institutions was not an acceptable practice within her culture. However, once she became aware that other community members were making use of nurseries she became more comfortable with the decision. She was able to make sense of this in terms of changing context and differences in the support which extended family members are able to offer in their new environment.

As the social worker in this case, I believed I had a duty to offer assistance around the family's housing needs as a part of the therapeutic process. Halimo's partner did not agree to join any of the sessions. Instead use was made of her knowledge of her partner to ascertain some of his views around parenting. My understanding from her was that the support provided by FSU represented a practical manifestation of Allah's help. The next question was to get her to consider what Allah's expectation of them as parents might be. Questions were asked to get the couple to think about how they might manage a similar situation in their country of origin. The role of the extended family was looked at. How will they know when they have been sufficiently blessed with children? What are the different cultural expectations of them in their role as mother and father? I was also curious to know their thoughts about how they think their children's futures might look.

Halimo often compared her situation to that of her own mother who was struggling to care for Halimo's eight siblings on her own with the help of state benefits. Halimo felt that we were not being sufficiently helpful to her. Rather than join her in the belief that her mother was on to a good thing, we looked together at the different circumstances that her mother was having to cope with, which included having to parent alone following the death of her husband. She was able to reflect on the differences between herself and her mother and see that her mother's decision to seek state benefit was more out of necessity and lack of other options at that time rather than any kind of life choice. She also began to think about herself as a separate entity from her children, husband and mother, reflecting on the aspirations she had when she first arrived in Britain at age 14.

By being curious about the client's family and cultural system I was able to challenge without being critical. The questions asked were intended to go beyond what was initially presented. It was recognised that it was not necessarily irresponsibility on Halimo's part that brought her to the situation in which she found herself. At the same time I was able to positively connote her strength in doing a remarkable job with very meagre resources.

Halimo and I continue to work on how to include her partner in a supportive role with his family. Some of our sessions could be perceived as unusual within the world of therapy, for instance taking her to a local park and discussing with her the different play activities with which she and her partner could involve their children; and again looking with her at what would be considered an acceptable level of adult involvement in children's play within her cultural context. In terms of planning her family she began to have ideas that she does not want to have another child for the time being. She has spoken of requesting the support of elders in her community to talk with her husband about his responsibility.

In the case of Halimo what was observed is an evolving and changing cultural story. There is for her a developing understanding that she is living within a different contextual situation from the one she knew as a younger person. At the same time she is respectful of many of her cultural traditions and works very hard to preserve those aspects of her culture that are important to her, her family and her community. This family have not resolved all the issues that are present for them, but have made a start.

The notion of systemic curiosity

The techniques of circular questioning and hypothesising which are used in systemic therapy are nurtured by curiosity. Circular questioning enables an interactive process between client and worker. It puts new information into the system and, it is hoped, new understandings. It can help clients to invent or find solutions to the problem or problems being presented. However, the curious stance which circular questions and the creation of hypotheses brings forth can undermine family belief systems that are based on 'truths'. For example, in Halimo's situation the story is that her husband is unhelpful. Using the language of relationship, questions which could be asked of Halimo could be: 'If you decide to be less helpful to everyone in your family, do you think your husband might then use the opportunity to show how helpful he can be?'; 'Who is more likely to bring up the subject of the family's lack of living space, you or your husband?'; 'I was having the idea that you and your husband talked about and made the decision that it may be more useful for you to come and talk to us about the difficulties being experienced by the family. I was wondering in what other ways your husband supports you in making important decisions for the family?'; 'If your husband was present here for this session and was asked the same questions, would his answers be the same, similar or very different to yours?' The idea here is to help the client in thinking more about her context and how she might be able draw on the resources of significant others in her family. The problem is thus located within the set up and organisation of the family system rather than in individuals within the system. Another aim is to move the client away from 'problem talk' to 'solution talk'.

Circular questioning can be used as a multi-faceted tool. For a problem definition: 'If you could give this problem a name, what would it be called?' To highlight the origins of the problem: 'When was the problem first noticed?'; 'Who was the first person to notice that that there was a problem?' To get different family members perceptions of the problem, to look at differences and change and to look at future possibilities: 'Who agrees that this is the problem?'; 'What are some of the changes that have happened in the family since the problem started?'; 'What has remained the same?'; 'If you all woke up tomorrow and the problem had completely disappeared, how would things look in the family, how would things be different?' It can also be used to compare and contrast and rank difficulties in the system: 'If you were measuring this problem in terms of other difficulties which have been experienced in the family, how would you grade it, say between one and ten?' Challenge dominant stories by asking questions about helpfulness rather than concentrating on questions about the problem: 'When was there a time when your husband was more helpful?' To assist in the problem solution, encourage individuals within the system to generate ideas for solving the problem.

Practice example 2 – Helping a family with a 'stuck' belief system

Over the years practical assistance has often been viewed as the primary way in which black families could be enabled. A widely held view was that blacks could not use nor necessarily benefit from talking therapies. A concern for me has been how such views have sometimes served to keep black clients in positions of dependence, where black clients become professional clients.

Mr and Mrs B, an African-Caribbean couple with six children, had been supported by social services through the late 1960s and 1970s. Mr B, an alcoholic, had taken to street drinking close to the family home resulting in a great deal of embarrassment for the family. Mrs B felt unable to cope without the support of her husband and turned to social services for help. She made the decision to leave the family home and the children were placed in care. When she eventually returned home, the children also returned home and social services agreed a level of financial support which was eagerly taken up by the family. At the time there was little exploration of Mrs B or her children's feelings about the events that had overtaken their family. Their hopes, dreams and expectations for the future were not discussed. Mr B was not considered to be part of the equation. Little attention was paid to any skills or resources the family may have had or may have needed to develop which may have one day enabled them to take charge of their lives. Therapeutic interventions were not considered as an option which may have helped the family think through the changes and maybe look at ways of managing similar or other difficulties in the future. Little had changed for Mrs B, and she once again left the family home and the responsibility for her children this time went permanently to social services.

When Mr and Mrs B's children began having their own children some 20 years ago each of them in turn found themselves approaching social services and asking for support. Two generations later when one of the siblings and her six children was referred to FSU little had changed. The family's story of lack of finance had become the dominant script. The story which unfolded over a period of time was that Ms B the younger had her first child when she was aged 18. Following the birth she presented at social services requesting financial support. Five more children followed in quick succession and with each child's birth Ms B requested social services assistance in much the same way. Each time she was given financial help. The money was used to purchase essential household effects. When items needed replacing Ms B would return to social services. Like her parents before her Ms B also came to the conclusion that she could not cope with her children. In her case she was taken with her children to a live in a family centre where the idea was to teach her good-enough parenting skills. Ms B interestingly described this period as the most helpful social services had ever been. On talking with Ms B, my sense was that various family support workers carried out the parenting of Ms B's children, which pretty much freed her up from any parenting tasks. After several months of living in the family centre, the family returned to their home and the requests to social services continued.

The family was referred to FSU with no clear brief of what we should or could do. The story of the family being a nuisance, very aggressive and demanding was strongly put across in the referral, and as an agency we initially bought the story and decided it would be more appropriate to assign two workers to the case. At the time of the referral, I was half way into my training as a systemic practitioner and was beginning to have some different ideas about how we might work with families where belief systems on the part of family members as well as workers had become entrenched creating a 'stuckness' all round.

Our first point of curiosity was to try and make sense of the family system. The origins of the family. Who was in the family? We looked at the possible impact of Ms B's experiences in her birth family. We heard of some of the difficulties Ms B's parents had experienced as first generation black immigrants to this country, and how profoundly these had impacted on their sense of identity, pride, confidence and self-worth. We heard stories of loss and change. We heard clearly that the family did not receive the kind of support or understanding which might have enabled them to be good enough parents to their children and perhaps help them to a more positive start. Once we began to make sense of the experiences the family had lived to date, then it was not difficult to see why the pattern of dependency was continuing with Ms B and her siblings.

As a starting point for the work we wanted to know from Ms B whether she saw the difficulties being experienced by herself and her children as similar or different from those experienced by her parents in the parenting of herself and her siblings. What areas of her own upbringing was she most pleased about? What aspects of the family's involvement with social services did she recall to be most helpful? What was less helpful? Ms B did see differences. She and her children's father were not drinkers. She did not abandon her children. She had made the choice to parent alone. She was in a sense proud of her mother for making the decision to leave as it meant that she and her siblings were kept together and had some stability. She felt that her parents had tried their best in what were very difficult times and circumstances for them.

There were now at least three teenagers in Ms B's family. They were asked in turn about the family's strength. We began by asking each child their ideas of why we were there? How they thought we could be helpful to the family? What help each of them had most valued in the past? We asked questions of difference and what might be described as miracle questions, e.g. if you woke up in the morning and a miracle had happened overnight to this family, what would the miracle look like?

We were interested to know who apart from social workers they believed could offer the family support. We wanted to know whether the children's view of the problem was the same as their mother's and whether any one in the extended family shared similar views of the problem? Getting the children's view of the problem proved useful. It meant that the mother no longer had a monopoly on the problem definition. The different responses of the children to the same questions expanded the definition of the problem and in doing so also expanded on possible solutions. They were given the time and space to talk about their different needs within the family which often went beyond how much money or even material possessions was available to them.

The client made it patently clear in our first meeting that questions about the father of her children were off limits. My colleague and I discussed Ms B's insistence that questions were not to be asked about her children's father and decided that to allow the client to restrict the questions we could ask would be tantamount to allowing ourselves to be recruited into her way of seeing things. The question for us was how to question in ways which were not disrespectful to the family stories, but at the same time not join the system and maintain the status quo. We wanted to challenge in ways which could help to create some different stories. We began by creating different hypotheses about why some parents might make the decision to parent alone. We looked at some of the ways in which historical, cultural, family, and gender stories can at times help to maintain patterns which might suit individuals, but are not necessarily the most useful in the role of parenting.

Since we could not ask direct questions about the role of the father in this family, we asked questions such as: 'If Mr B was listening in to this conversation, how do you think that he might understand him not being mentioned or included as part of the family? Would he have different explanations from you about his lack of involvement in this family? You are all mostly saying it is his choice not to be involved, how would you have liked him to be involved?' Questions to the girls were: 'Would his relationship with your sisters be the same or different to that with your brothers?' Questions were also asked to ascertain the different children's feelings about their absent father. An important aspect of working systemically is to always look for strengths and positively connote them. On very many levels we were able to see that Ms B had worked enormously hard to hold her family together and had been very successful in doing so.

The systemic notion of 'curiosity' allows the therapist to ask a variety of circular questions, which in turn invites the client to take an observer position on their situation, and in doing so to think about creative ways of changing dominant stories about themselves, the idea being to enable the bringing forth of solutions which are more than short term. Questions such as: 'Who else in your family agrees that this is the problem?' Observer perspective questions: 'If you were in a position to advise someone else about how to deal with a dilemma in ways which might have a more lasting outcome, what advice would you give?' With such questions, the clients can be enabled to become experts on their situation: 'When have there been times in your family when you feel you have been able to sort out a problem or difficulty without the help of outsiders?'; 'Who in your family, friendship or other networks would you say was best placed to help your family come up with a solution to this dilemma?' Acknowledging that families have strengths: 'How did you manage to do that certain thing in a way which was so helpful to a family member?'; 'How will things look for you and your family, say in one year's time? Will you want to be asking for the same kinds of assistance?'; 'Your family has had social workers for some three generations, what are your ideas about how this has been helpful/not helpful.' These types of questions can be asked of all family members who feel able to give a view. This kind of circularity will give a clear sense of how different family members are thinking as well as highlighting some ideas of what may be organising the family's way of managing things.

When some of these questions were asked of the above family, the initial responses were somewhat hostile. The questions nevertheless appeared to have led the family to begin to give some thought to how they organised themselves. We found that the present generation of young people in the family have very different ideas from their parents and grandparents about how they want to live their lives. Living on benefits is not seen as an option. Instead the older children have involved themselves in further education and do not see a future dependent on social welfare.

I believe that with this family the systemic approach had served to create a significant shift in their thinking. When, for example, Ms B finally moved with her family to a larger home and requested help in furnishing it, I felt confident in saying to her that on a practical level she had been enabled enough and that she now had to take some responsibility for managing her family's affairs. Had I said the same things to her two years earlier, her response would almost certainly be angry and defiant. Ms B actually gave me a very nice smile and told me confidently that the family could now manage without social workers. However, since that conversation took place the family have been referred back to the unit but to date have not taken up a service.

Practice example 3 – The cultural context of marital break-up

The third practice example involved working with an Asian/Iranian family. This was in a cultural context very different from my own and one with which I had little experience of doing family therapy work. In this case some of the questions asked were aimed at orientating me to some of the ways in which the dilemma of separation and divorce can be managed in a culture where the break-up of a marriage is not only the business of the couple, but can have far-reaching consequences for the wider family structure and community. When it is the woman who is wishing to end the marriage the process can be fraught with difficulties. One risk of separation is that she might end up losing the support of both sides of her family. A young Asian family born in this country may therefore need to have conversations with elders in the family or community in order to seek guidance on managing or sorting out particular difficulties.

A 37-year-old Pakistani mother of two came for help fearing the break-up of her ten-year-old marriage. A Christian married to an Iranian Moslem, they both had very strong and set beliefs about the sanctity of marriage. The client explained that her husband, a handsome and charming man, treated her like a queen at the beginning of their relationship, but three weeks into their marriage he hit her for the first time. She was understandably shocked but did not believe such a situation could happen again, but it did, over and over again.

The client came to FSU with a dilemma. How to survive in a marriage where it was clear that she and her children were in danger from her husband's violence. She did not come with separation or divorce as a choice. She explained that to leave the marriage would be to let herself down, as well as let her husband, children, family members, friends and their respective communities down. She used the old adage of 'having made her bed so must lie on it'. Her confusion was great and for the first six or so sessions her response to questions aimed at getting some ideas about what she wanted from the work was, 'I don't know'. Exploration of her situation found that not only was she feeling bound by what she believed to be cultural expectations of her as a wife and mother, a more significant bind was a complete lack of belief in herself as in any way an able person. Her husband had not treated her as an equal partner in the marriage. She found that her self-esteem and self-confidence had eroded to the point where she believed that even if she were able to make the decision to leave she would not be able to manage her life on her own.

Again in working with this client, I was aware that I was working with beliefs at the higher level of culture and religion. The work could not progress unless these organising principles were talked about and their significance in the client's thinking and decision-making addressed. She was able to explain to me that elders within her husband's community would be the people best placed to advise her. Her reason for coming into therapy first was to explore the best way to put her concerns to them. It was important to her that the elders did not take the view that she was a 'bad wife or mother'. She wanted a continued relationship with her husband, but not one that continued to oppress her. Putting aside her own needs, what she wanted most of all was his continued and consistent presence in their children's lives.

This client's Christian belief system was used as the basis for the work. Through this I was able to explore with her the meaning she gave to marriage, her views on violence in marriage, what she saw as the impact on herself and her children. Given that her determination to be a good wife had not had the desired effect of her husband stopping or lessening his violent behaviour, how was the future looking to her? She chose not to bring her children to the sessions, conscious that it might distress them. I therefore had to find ways of ascertaining the children's views as well as any ideas they had for a solution. To do this I made use of the client's excellent relationship with her children. Ideas were shared about different ways in which she could have conversations with the children in order to hear their thoughts and views.

The work lasted two years during which time she felt able to take her case to the elders. She commented that the connections which were made to her cultural and religious beliefs enabled the creation of a certain clarity for her, which she was able to make use of in her conversations with the elders. She is now divorced, a decision which was supported by the elders and her children. She has emerged as an extraordinarily capable woman who has grown beyond any of her own expectations. As she had wished, her children's father continues to maintain a consistent and supportive relationship with them. There is no longer physical violence. She is working on maintaining a relationship with her ex-husband, which is not oppressive in other ways. She has spoken publicly of how she experienced the therapeutic support she received from FSU; her positive feedback has included her belief that FSU offers a culturally sensitive service.

Practice example 4 – Using a cultural genogram with a family

A 35-year-old African-Caribbean woman sought the unit's support several months after her husband of 13 years made the decision to leave her and their 2 small children. She said that she had little warning of her husband's intention and he offered no explanation to either her or the children. A middle-class family, with both parents in professional jobs, she explained that she believed that as a family they were leading a comfortable and relatively happy existence. Prior to coming to the unit she had sought the advice and support of her GP, but was disappointed that the support offered was a prescription of anti-depressants.

Along with my co-worker we constructed a cultural genogram with the client and her children. A cultural genogram not only maps the family systems but maps belief systems located in culture, that is, history, ways of doing things, processes of communication. Most of our experiences are given meaning through our culture; therefore, in order to fully appreciate or make sense of behaviours or actions which are not familiar to us, we may need to examine cultural belief systems. More importantly a cultural genogram can be used to map patterns of behaviour in families. It may, for example, highlight marital patterns; it may dictate whether problems are managed at an individual level or in more family-orientated ways. It may even go as far as providing information on how a particular family system is organised. It might explain what is considered acceptable or accepted behaviour in a family system. For example, a family story may be, 'we do not talk to outsiders about our difficulties'. Or equally the belief could be that only outsiders can see what is going on inside the family.

When the genogram was completed, the client pointed to the lack of information about her husband's family system as opposed to her own which gave extensive information. The genogram provided a catalyst for the telling of many stories. The couple originated from different islands, and despite starting out in their relationship with what appeared to be many shared understandings, they in fact had very different belief systems around a number of areas. There was the question of the client's sister-in-law and teenage nephew who lived next door, but of whom she had no knowledge prior to hearing the boy referring to her husband as 'uncle' as they passed in the street one day. She was surprised too, following the death of her mother-in-law, at hearing that her husband had an elder brother.

We found it useful to explore with the client her ideas about the gaps in her knowledge of her husband's background. We were interested to know about some of the subject areas she and her husband believed it important to discuss in their marriage. We were also curious to know her hypotheses of why she thought he had chosen to keep what appeared significant information from her. We quickly found that we had got into unexplored stories which she had felt uncomfortable about thinking through on her own. We were led to creating some interesting hypotheses about family secrets and the need for them. She was enabled to connect back to conversations with her husband when he had tried to give her some indication of certain situations in his family connected to his family's belief in 'obeah' and its possible powers. (The dictionary definition is that 'obeah' is a kind of sorcery practised in West Africa. However, my understanding from talking with West Africans in Ghana is that the practice of 'obeah' is linked to religious practices. It is true to say, however, that in the Caribbean the meaning ascribed to the word is that its practice is connected with 'evil doings'.) We were then able to hypothesise with her about the possibility of her husband wanting to protect her and their children from things he believed could harm them. His lack of communication appeared to fit with the notion of the less one knows, the less the harm that can be done.

Instead of continuing to see her husband's behaviour as negative and emotionally distant, she began instead to realise that whatever it was that led him to leave his family must feel very real for him. She is therefore now more interested in what kinds of questions she may need to ask him in order to show her support for him, as well as hoping to open up conversations about if or how they might go on as a family. She also moved from a 'fixed story' that she had to know why her husband left and hoped she could make him change, to the notion that life could go on whether or not she knew his reasons and that the only person she can change is herself. Here a little bit of cultural knowledge created the opportunity to ask questions which can so easily be missed within the therapeutic context. She was enabled to talk about a subject which as a middle-class black woman she did not feel particularly comfortable about discussing in other contexts for fear of being labelled 'mad' or 'superstitious'. She was able to share with the therapeutic team her immense relief at not being thought of as 'mad'. Part of the process of therapy must be to provide a space where what might be being experienced as unexpressible can be expressed without the fear of being judged. For too many black clients the opposite is often the case. This may offer one explanation of why so many shy away from making use of therapy.

Conclusion

As a black woman working with black and Asian families, I am aware that common assumptions which I may hold about clients because they are black do not necessarily fit their cultural context. How we as black people identify ourselves is connected to a whole host of lived experiences and stories that we have come to know over time. Depending on our origins, whether we are Africans in the Diaspora, whether our birthplace is Africa, or Asia, or wherever else on this planet we have found ourselves, we will come with our different ideas and expectations of how we want to live our lives. Black and Asian clients who have reason to call upon therapeutic services expect a service which will be respectful and challenging and which can take on the different contextual situations in which they are living their lives. They expect a service which will neither gloss over their at times difficult existence with rigid therapeutic talk, nor do they expect a service which negates their many strengths and strategies for surviving in often hostile environments. Family Service Units as an organisation is leading the way in the development of culturally sensitive therapeutic services which are inclusive of the needs of black and Asian families.

There are a number of points that I believe may be useful in guiding agencies and workers who want to provide a service that is meaningful for black families. The first is to be aware of the assumptions that a worker whose lived experiences may be located within Western or other cultures can so easily take into the work with a client whose culture is dissimilar to their own. It is important to remember that meanings originate in culture, so as not to rush to conclusions which in any case may only be based on old stories mistakenly believed to fit certain ethnic or racial groups. Be prepared to be flexible – the way therapeutic approaches are taught and worked with in this society is largely Eurocentric and does not necessarily fit with the experiences of some black individuals or families. A white worker needs also to be aware of the language she uses when working with black families; language carries with it ideologies and it is an important tool in the continued discrimination and oppression of black people. Many social work clients find themselves locked into unhelpful positions by societal and institutional structures which do not see equitability of lifestyles or accessibility to services as desirable. It is important not to continue simply colluding with the system in keeping such positions fixed.

Black practitioners working with black clients must take care not to put themselves forward as experts or take the position of rescuers. They need to be aware of the stories they as a black person may have internalised and how they can unconsciously or consciously use these to further oppress their black client, for example using their position to place the client in a them-and-us situation.

It goes without question that white practitioners cannot get into the experience of their black clients, so must be prepared to accept the validity of the black clients' experiences as expressed by them. They need to be aware of power dynamics and be careful not to patronise their black clients. They must recognise that like anyone else black clients are multi-faceted, multi-dimensional people, and not reduce them to a colour. Finally, they need to work with the stories and meanings that the individual or family brings, question their own assumptions, refrain from imposing descriptions, avoid the assignation of pathology and be transparent in language and actions. It is important not to negate the struggles faced by many black families, and it is vital to be aware that too often it is these very struggles which bring them to the service being offered.

Chapter 7

Working with Men in Family Centres

Paul Collett

Superhero or 'quiet desperation'

Henry David Thoreau, in his nineteenth-century classic *Walden* (1854), said that 'the mass of men lead lives of quiet desperation'. I believe that this was true when he wrote it and it is true now. In the film *The Full Monty* a group of men explore many of the issues facing masculinity in 1990s Britain to comic effect. They had been excluded from the traditional role of 'breadwinner' with the closure of their steel works and were forced to search for a new identity. The film touches on themes of impotence, homosexuality, divorce, depression, suicide and the relationships between the sexes and fathers and sons. Their new identity is of course forged through the striptease group, Hot Metal. The moment of fame and fortune they briefly enjoy lies outside the aspiration of most and beyond the attainment of the majority. The success of the film is evidence of the chord that it struck in the popular imagination. While many men might hope to be a superhero such as a character portrayed by Arnold Schwarzenegger most feel more like Mr Bean, remaining, in Thoreau's definition, quiet and desperate.

This chapter explores some ideas about men's issues in general before thinking about men in family centres and therapeutic work with men in particular. It considers the importance of engaging in work with men and looks at some general difficulties. It goes on to think about the use of groupwork in meeting the needs of this client group within a family centre setting. I draw upon my experience in working with men in groups and one-to-one, in social services-run family centres.

Why working with men matters

Working with men has been a long-neglected issue, which in recent years there have been significant moves to redress. Classically, 'parenting' has been equated with mothering. Family centres, when not viewed by male social services clients with suspicion and hostility, have been perceived as a service run by and for women. There are few men who become primary or sole carer of children when a relationship breaks down. Indeed at the end of a relationship many of them lose contact entirely with any children that they fathered, lying to themselves and their children that this is for the best. Often blame is in some way imputed to men when their families come to social services attention; they may be perceived as having been violent, abusive or simply irresponsible, leaving their partners shouldering the consequences of their behaviour. Consequently, the majority of services are reserved for their 'victims'. Child abuse literature has repeatedly emphasized the fact that children referred to child-protection services are predominantly cared for by their mothers, according to Kieran O'Hagan (1997, p.27) in his article 'The problem of engaging men in child protection'. For this reason it is easy to understand why more state assistance is directed towards mothering rather than fathering. Pragmatically this has to be the case. Men might have been seen as the undeserving poor, rather than equally powerless players in a system that has disenfranchised them. However, it would be wrong to deduce from this that men are insignificant in child-protection social work. It would also be wrong to infer that men require less support with their parenting than women; the reverse would appear to be true. Given that more mothers remain caring for their children following a relationship breakdown, more fathers find themselves, through new relationships, involved in the arduous role of step-parenting.

Government to a very limited extent recognised and sought to address the social problem caused by 'feckless fathers' by setting up the Child Support Agency (CSA). This agency merely sought to confront men with their continuing financial responsibility for their children and did not try to address the emotional or other practical implications. A major criticism of the CSA has been its inability to recognise and balance the needs of second and step-families against those of first families. The task of reintegrating men into family life is more subtle and complex than its approach would suggest. A generation of fatherless children is growing up for whom the word 'Dad' has been cheapened by a succession of short-term father figures. Remarriages are more likely to end in divorce than first marriages. Many men have no ongoing relationship with their biological children and carry a resultant burden of unresolved and at times unacknowledged grief. This can only impede their ability to fulfil the role of step-father. Child-protection research would indicate that step-fathers can pose a particularly high risk to children, and numerous enquiry reports following the death of a child have highlighted this. For example Maurice Beckford was responsible for the death of his step-daughter Jasmin Beckford.

Although society has undergone many changes it certainly remains true that mothers provide the majority of parenting. We do now have 'parent' and toddler groups in place of the mother and toddler groups as a statement of willingness to include fathers. Men who frequent such groups are likely to appear something of an oddity and to experience difficulties breaking into conversations. What is more, 30 per cent of family centres employ no men whilst 75 per cent employ 1 or less (Ruxton 1992). This can compound the perception of men that they are superfluous to family life. Without an equivalent change in attitude, recent changes in family centre practice in recruiting men will appear merely a token. The reasons for male non-participation in child care would appear to be economic, social and psychological rather than biological. This being the case, social work agencies could promote greater gender equality by the simple expediency of employing more men in family centres (Hanlon 1995; Ruxton 1992).

Indeed, prior to exploring these issues it is important to acknowledge the legitimate concerns of those who would assert that the male role in sexual abuse specifically should justify men's exclusion from both family settings, and any work place that allows access to vulnerable children. As Pringle (in Bates *et al.* 1992, pp.213–25) noted in 'Danger! Men at (Social) Work':

> the gender role in the occurrence of sexual abuse calls into question the safety of children in any welfare setting where males are present as carers and/or therapists, not merely the residential sector. The implications for such an analysis in terms of policy and practice may be dramatic as regards the future role of men in welfare systems.

These genuine concerns need to be confronted rather than avoided and the lessons from the scandals in children's homes such as Clwyd and Leicestershire should be incorporated into practice. However, social work's denial of the male contribution as well denying them a service has been to the detriment of women and children (Gutridge 1995). It may be theoretically possible, if questionable, to exclude men from every work base allowing them access to children, but it would appear impossible to remove men entirely from family life. Risks that cannot be removed need to be addressed.

O'Hagan (1997), drawing attention to the importance of working with men, cites numerous enquiry reports where the ignoring or avoidance of working with men resulted in the death of a child. He offers four principal reasons why social workers avoid engaging men. Although the social work profession is female-dominated he points out that male workers are equally likely to behave in this way. First, it is due to public and professional perceptions of the roles of men and women; child-rearing is perceived as 'woman's work'. Second, it is the product of a hostility and distrust of men reinforced by some feminist theory. According to this view all men are, if not rapists, then potentially so, a view which of course has some validity. Third, it happens because of a simple lack of training. Women with more developed social skills are generally easier to engage. It can be hard to know how to speak to certain men. Fourth, it is because of an often justified fear of men. Men are physically more powerful than women and are often heralded by a deserved reputation for violence. Ironically, however, the principal source of violence against child-protection social workers is not men but women, perhaps because their male partners have been so effectively avoided. Although male workers might be thrust into potentially difficult situations they might not necessarily be the best to diffuse them. Indeed research would indicate that they are more frequently assaulted than their female colleagues. Through avoidance

> the man is marginalized beyond agency influence, yet remains highly influential in respect of the quality of care and protection afforded to the child…avoiding men is not usually in the child's interests. (O'Hagan 1997, p.36)

A look at society gives some clues to the male image problem. Figures from the Home Office indicate that crime is a predominantly male activity. In 1985 one third of men in the United Kingdom had been convicted of a serious offence by the time they were 31. Of the 58,500 offenders in 1993 who received a custodial sentence 96 per cent were men (Home Office 1993). Taking into account remands into custody, some 97 per cent of the prison population is male. For many men crime might be deemed a passing phase that begins and ends with teenage spots while for others it becomes a career. It is true that males have a higher basal metabolism than females, contributing to their reputation for being the generally more active sex. The impact of the hormone testosterone, although not exclusively masculine, may also influence male behaviour. However, what individual histories of emotional, physical and sexual abuse and neglect might contribute to these appalling figures can only be guessed at. What is known is that men tend to act out in criminal behaviour, feelings or problems that women might express in other ways. While men have historically been over represented within the prison system, women have disproportionately used psychiatric institutions. Interestingly research into suicide would indicate that while more women attempt suicide more men succeed and while the female suicide rate has fallen steadily since the 1970s the male rate has continued to rise.

The media provides some very mixed messages about male sexual conduct, and responses to women. For example, in its editorials in September 1998 the *Sun* newspaper was surprisingly the loudest in its condemnation of the notorious sexual proclivities of the American President Bill Clinton, while other parts of the paper appeared specifically to cater for the voyeuristic tastes of its male readers.

Given the profile that these statistics represent of men, as well as the personal experiences of too many women, of violence, harassment and intimidation, it is hardly surprising that many women have misgivings about working with men. Yet, while sometimes rightly viewed as 'oppressors' in their own world, many of the males who are social services' clients fail to be 'macho' and do not even attempt to be 'new men'. They might appear big fish to the women and children whose lives they dominate, but if they do they swim in a tiny pond. To begin to understand and help these men, many of whom turn out to be care leavers themselves, it is therefore necessary to begin to see them as being equally oppressed by a system that has disenfranchised them.

The task of the worker

Family centre staff, of whatever gender, wishing to work with men, will of necessity need to confront their own stereotypes and prejudices before they can help men to face theirs. Male workers, for example, will require sensitivity and good supervisory support if they are to avoid collusion or 'mateyness'. To achieve this it will be necessary for the worker to keep a female perspective in his mind through regular discussions with female colleagues or a female supervisor. Female workers on the other hand may need specific support in working through their anger against men.

Beth Erickson (1993) highlights a number of issues that women working with men need to be aware of. Although specifically addressing female therapists many of the points that she raises might equally apply to male therapists. She emphasizes the need to be aware of different gender socialisations. She says that the female therapist should be comfortable about being a woman, as well as being comfortable around men and talking about male issues. The male therapist should equally be comfortable about his own gender. To achieve this it is necessary to like men, to be confident about dealing with male power and anger and to use both the feminine and masculine sides of the personality. She asserts that 'communicating with competency' is essential as well as finding a way to acknowledge and deal with misogyny. Both male and female workers are likely to require assistance in helping any man whose reputation for violence they find intimidating.

A study of 13 family centres (Ghate *et al.* 2000; Joseph Rowntree Foundation Findings 2000) highlights the need for gender-differentiated practice – emphasizing the different and sometimes conflicting needs of men and women, rather than gender blind practice where the same activities are open to all (see also NCVCCO 2000). Yet having *some* identifiable strategy for working with men mattered more in engaging fathers than what the strategy was.

A men's group in a family centre: a case study

There are a number of reasons accounting for inequality in the groupwork provision for men and women. Perhaps foremost among these are the psycho-social differences between the two sexes. Research indicates that men focus more easily upon tasks, goals and activity than upon communication; they appear to find it easier to talk about almost anything other than their feelings, which is in marked contrast to women. In addition, subtle social pressures on men contribute to making it difficult for them to 'appear' vulnerable to their peers and partners. An example of this would appear to be the reluctance of men to see their family doctor. In 1990 women made some 143 million visits to the GP compared with 75 million visits made by men. The blatant message 'big boys don't cry' may now be rarely heard but it is still given covertly. Although these issues tend to be stereotyped and should not be over emphasized they reinforce the impression that women should fare better in therapeutic groups than men.

Men may be put off by the term 'group'. One family centre (Platt 1999), aware of numerous fathers who were sole carers or the head of a household struggling to meet their children's needs, but unable to attract them to a group, realised that men were contacting the family centre by telephone. Centre staff decided to develop a support and information line for fathers, but first explored the legal and ethical issues which could arise from working in this way. The helpline was a success, fathers telephoning to seek advice on benefits, on relationships, on managing children's behaviour and on using other local services. Staff then hosted three evenings where fathers were invited to visit the centre with their children. Out of these a successful fathers' group was established.

In the discussion which follows I draw upon my experience in working with men in groups and one-to-one in social services-run family centres in Southampton. I had been recruited to work in what was then an exclusively female family centre, in recognition of the gender imbalance in the centre and the potential effect of this upon the families that utilised its services. The Forest View Family Centre, set up as the first of its kind within Hampshire in 1986, had a long established tradition of providing a wide variety of groupwork to girls and women. Although the need was recognised the centre had not succeeded in providing this resource to boys and men. Staff from the Derby Road and Forest View Family Centres, and the child and family guidance clinic, ran two men's groups. Supervision and consultancy was provided by a psychiatrist (who was also trained as a psychotherapist) for the first group and by a clinical psychologist for the second group. I was involved, during the second half of the 1990s, in pioneering one group with boys and the two groups with men, and in providing consultations with those seeking to establish a further men's group.

The early identification of a consultant familiar with the centre and the client group helped with the discussion and agreement of roles and boundaries, including how to talk about the group to other workers. Consultancy enabled workers to develop and reflect upon practice and grow in knowledge and awareness, and hone groupwork skills. It helped us explore co-working, including its impact on the group relationships and functioning. On a personal level the consultant was very valuing of the workers, offering personal support and a keen interest in the course of the group. Prior to the group there were two planning and supervisory sessions, with fortnightly supervision backed up by telephone contact through the life of the group.

These groups primarily operated as support groups for men who had either primary or shared care of children. The aims and objectives of the two men's groups that I was directly involved with were as follows:

- to assist men to understand and meet the needs of their children
- to help men improve the quality of their adult relationships
- to create a safe and supportive environment that might facilitate the exploration of parenting and relationship issues
- to look at society's expectations of men as individuals in their own right, as parents and partners
- to look at being assertive without being aggressive.

It was the unanimous decision of the workers and management not to run a group that catered primarily for paedophiles. It was recognised that other groups, usually probation and health run, were more specifically geared to addressing the needs of this client group. A mixed group of perpetrators and non-abusing fathers was also thought inappropriate in potentially making the children of non-abusing fathers vulnerable to abuse. Establishing this criteria with referrers was difficult from the outset because of the demand for a social services-run group for paedophiles and the lack of this particular resource.

The ages and backgrounds of the men referred to the groups varied considerably. Ages ranged from late teens to a man in his 50s but the majority were in their early to mid-20s. Most had had a job, such as labourer, taxi-driver and night-club bouncer, but were currently unemployed, while a few had never worked. About half had been in residential care and more had experienced some sort of social-work intervention during their childhood. A number had been in prison. Most had experienced the divorce or separation of their parents. All of the men had some involvement with children either as fathers or step-fathers, and at least two were seeking to raise their children as single parents. They had been referred to the men's group by either a social worker or a health visitor. The men's motivation for wishing to attend varied from wanting to talk to men in similar circumstances to their own, to attending only under a certain amount of pressure or in a bid to impress those who were working with their family.

The two men's groups sought to cover a number of serious, sensitive and at times painful issues. The group co-ordinators sought to encourage the men to look critically at the role of men within society in general and families in particular. To do so time was allowed, in preparing to run the groups, for honest sharing between the groups' facilitators about their backgrounds, beliefs and family histories. Humour was integral to the success of the groups. After commencing with the usual ice-breaking exercises a discussion was held on male icons and role models. A paradoxical examination of the weaknesses of an Arnold Schwarzenegger character and the strengths of Mr Bean introduced this. It was recognised that these characters represented stereotyped images of masculinity and not a reality that anyone could fully identify with.

Some of the men's past institutional experiences had given them a clearer understanding of the use of rules rather than the building of relationships. Although they were able to discuss their feelings in the group they acknowledged some difficulties in understanding the feelings of partners and children. This led to difficulty in being able to meet the needs of others, which in turn left their own needs unmet. The group exposed the difficulty experienced by some men in living up to male stereotypes of being strong and the breadwinner. Men felt belittled and socially unacceptable if they displayed weakness or vulnerability. Expectations of men being available for work, even if they had responsibility for the care of children, were much stronger than for women in a similar position, and were perpetuated by different treatment from Social Security. The men reported a lack of support in the community for fathers and felt that they were greeted with the expectation that they would be aggressive and potentially violent. In a self-fulfilling prophecy the frustration that was created when they encountered these attitudes was more likely to release this potential.

In subsequent weeks the group explored influences upon men while growing up, and sought to identify who were the men's strongest role models, sporting and movie heroes, and so on. This linked with a discussion about contemporary society and their children's role models. We explored how the men felt that others perceived them and the image that they sought to convey. Issues of self-esteem and personal presentation came up. Discussion about children, discipline, child protection and child development arose every week in various forms. The group also examined what the men looked for in a partner and what a partner might look for from them and why relationships often ended in disappointment. The men impressed us with their honesty in exploring issues of unfaithfulness, jealousy and betrayal.

One of the men who made particularly strong use of the first group was a man in his late 30s, whom I will call Simon. He was struggling to bring up his four daughters as a single parent following the break-up of his second marriage. His wife had a severe alcohol problem and he had gained residency of the children following their separation. As he tried to undertake occasional night work as a security guard to support his family he had little chance to develop relationships outside of his family or respite from his caring role. Having some familiarity with groupwork through his experience of adult mental health services he had a head start on most of the men. Simon was articulate, plainspoken and gained the immediate respect of the other men because of his tough, witty and forthright manner.

Simon's commitment to the group was as total as his need for it was self-evident. He acted at times as the go-between between the college or university-educated professionals and the men in the group. He would help translate when we lapsed into professional jargon or when he had grasped a concept ahead of others, although he was also able to keep quiet and encourage the contributions of others. At the end of the group he confessed to feeling somewhat bereft. For him 12 weeks was far too short a period and he would have preferred the group to have been far longer. He offered to come to the first session of the second group in order to 'sell' the group to a new clientele, an offer that was accepted.

Both groups ran for 12 weeks. The numbers attending varied from week to week but in both groups a committed core of between four and six developed. There were some who for various reasons did not remain with the group. Others had attended under a certain amount of duress and appeared to have derived limited benefit.

Despite our good intentions it was not possible to entirely eliminate the risk posed by undiscovered paedophiles participating in the group. The mixture of group members became difficult when a group member was suspected of perpetrating sexual abuse upon children. This became the subject of a child-protection investigation. This individual was to an extent ostracised and ultimately withdrew from the group. While this may not have been the best outcome from the man's prespective it did appear to be satisfactory for the safety of the group.

Pitching discussions at the right level, avoiding being too simplistic on the one hand and sufficiently challenging on the other, was a constant challenge. A specific issue was recognising the difficulty for both clients and workers when working with group members who have disabilities, which affected communication within the group. In the first group one of the group members suffered a hearing impairment which affected his ability to participate in discussions. The group co-leaders recognised the poignancy of this issue. The man eventually left the group, his frustration at not being able to hear fully or participate in discussions contributing to this decision. Greater planning and consultation with colleagues specialising in hearing impairment might have circumvented this problem.

At the conclusion of each group its success was evaluated, with feedback being requested from the men who attended. They valued realising that they were not alone in finding caring for children a struggle. One of the men wrote that he found the group 'very helpful with dealing with different kinds of issues'. This man particularly valued the understanding that he found in the group that he had not always experienced from his female social worker.

One suggestion from the men was for an informal social occasion before the start of the group, to give them an opportunity to mix and get some idea of the aims of the group. They thought that this would help in creating a 'group identity' at an earlier stage. The group's co-leaders, while acknowledging the need of establishing relationships within the group, felt that this might have set too informal a tone. It was agreed that providing food and drinks was essential to setting men at ease and creating a nurturing environment. Those who persevered to the end of the group felt that there should be a greater incentive to attend and a greater reward for doing so. But the group's budget was finite and we had to prioritise spending accordingly.

The men said that they would have appreciated more assistance and information on practical issues such as finances, clothing and benefit advice. They also expressed the view that more time could have been beneficially spent on exploring issues of stress and means of coping with it. All agreed that a longer group would have been of great benefit. Twelve weeks seemed a long time at the outset but we were fairly ambitious regarding the ground that we wished to cover in the time allotted. However, it appeared that whatever the length of group some would have found it difficult to end. The men also expressed the view that there should have been more post-group support. Following the conclusion of the group they had no one to unload to and nothing to replace the group.

Groupwork may not be a solution for all types of men. It may not appeal to some men who are new to family support services who may prefer more masculine practical activities such as 'fixing things' and sports (Ghate *et al.* 2000). However, our experience was that it was highly valued by a few. The quality of referral and the process of selection are crucial to success. This type of work with men has its detractors, mainly because of the infamous masculine characteristic of 'emotional illiteracy'. Our experience was that when the macho facade was overcome a nurturing environment could develop. Initially men would swagger and size each other up but when they realised that they were all equally vulnerable many were more willing to co-operate rather than compete. When combined with individual counselling, groupwork can be highly effective in facilitating the exploration of male issues and challenging entrenched ideologies. Our experience was, however, that while we could see that the majority of the men would benefit from some sort of individual work very few chose it for themselves.

Conclusion

For men to work effectively in family centres it is necessary for them to face a number of uncomfortable facts about themselves and their gender. Before seeking to challenge others it is necessary to challenge yourself. It has long been the rule that all psychotherapists will undergo psychotherapy as part of their ongoing training. It is to be regretted that there is no equivalent requirement upon social workers and social work students. As already alluded to, the majority of abuse on women and children is inflicted by men and the guidelines for preventing this abuse in schools and welfare organisations, despite recent revisions, are probably inadequate. Although 'ordinary' men might like to believe that rapists, sexual murderers and paedophiles are a species different from themselves, research would indicate that such individuals hold views about women that do not differ from that of the general male population. Family centres clearly have a crucial role to play in challenging masculine attitudes of misogyny and promoting positive involvement of fathers and step-fathers within family life. Openness by female workers to men trespassing on their traditional domain has to be a first step.

For a long time it has been recognised that men are part of the problem as far as families are concerned. Clearly this is the case. However it must be recognised that men are also potentially part of the solution. Fathers who 'fail' in their parenting of their own children are likely to become step-fathers to someone else's. They are unlikely to absent themselves entirely from what we term family life. How much better that this involvement should be positive rather than negative. It is essential that men should learn the skills that their fathers never taught them and perhaps never possessed. To achieve this family centres must welcome fathers and be deliberately welcoming. For men to feel welcome in family centres may require some changes in both family centre workers' attitudes and in family centre ethos. The debate between the sexes needs to be opened up. In the same way that applications are welcomed from minority groups the appointment of appropriately skilled men to family centres needs to be encouraged. A positive response from men is far more likely to proceed from a positive approach.

Chapter 8

'Holding' as a Way of Enabling Change in a Statutory Family Centre

Sarah Musgrave

Introduction

What is 'holding' and how does a mother hold her child? Can a term used to describe a stage in early maternal care relate, in practice, to work with children and their parents in a statutory family centre? Is it a useful concept to keep in mind and can it enable family centre workers to improve their practice? Does a 'holding environment' enable the staff to offer the users the environment most conducive to personal development and growth and is it possible to offer this within the confines of statutory work?

In this chapter, I aim to explore the meaning of holding by considering D. W. Winnicott's views on how a mother holds a child physically as well as emotionally, relating this to the way in which family centres' staff can hold their clients. I will consider how the centre itself can be a 'holding environment', containing the work within it and offering a safe and consistent working space.

I will also consider Winnicott and others' views on holding within the therapeutic relationship. I will relate these to how I attempt to hold three of my clients, two adults and a child, and how I believe this is experienced by these individuals.

Gladstone Street Children's Resource Centre

Gladstone Street C.R.C. is a local authority family centre type resource, for children aged 11 years and under, their siblings, parents and carers. As part of a child protection agency, it holds certain statutory duties and powers in relation to the children and families with whom we work. These impose a responsibility to investigate reports of children at risk, to act to protect the child and to promote the welfare of the child. In addition, the social services department has specific procedures to inform practice relating to the disclosure of alleged abuse, whether by a child or an adult and all other aspects of child protection and welfare.

Service-users are referred by social workers, for the purpose of addressing serious child welfare and child protection issues. Some service-users have referred themselves to the fieldwork teams, while others are referred by GPs, health visitors, schools, hospitals, police etc. In most cases, substantial change is necessary if families are to be able to stay together safely. Change can feel threatening and dangerous, even if it means moving on from a situation of great unhappiness and uncertainty. If families are to take the risk of working through difficult and painful areas, they need to do so within a safe, secure environment. Parents or carers may need to look at their own personal issues, which due to their enormity or severity may be preventing them from offering good-enough care. Some parents have organised their whole lives in such a way that these painful issues are well guarded against and it is a major step to trust anyone at all. Children also attend groups, sessions with siblings and/or carers and alone, in order to have the opportunity to talk and act out areas of chaos, confusion or trauma.

The centre has a manager and six family resource centre workers, five of whom are qualified social workers and one whose background is in education. In addition, there are five sessional workers, who have a range of duties, including working directly with families, primarily in support but sometimes in more demanding roles; working in groups; providing childcare; supervising contact and staffing playschemes. The centre, which was originally a school, has three large rooms with kitchens and play areas. These rooms are used for work with parents and children i.e. groupwork, individual work and contacts. There is another smaller room that is used for family work and individual sessions.

My own role within the centre is as a family resource centre worker. My training was originally in social work, followed by five years in an area team. I moved to the family centre in 1991, following a reorganisation, while also studying for an MA in Therapeutic Child Care at Reading University. The main area of my work is individual work with adults and children, as well as seeing parents and children together. This may focus on assessing need or safety, or to enable the individual or family the time and space to explore issues such as loss, abuse and so on.

It is in this context, that a concept such as 'holding', as proposed by Winnicott, can inform the method by which we both enable and encourage individuals and families to make changes and progress to a more integrated state.

The 'holding' function in infant care

Winnicott developed ideas about holding and the role of holding in the mother–infant relationship and its parallels in the analytic situation. He considered that Freud had never developed this as a theme, possibly because Freud had experienced good-enough mothering and was therefore able to provide the same reliability to his patients (Hopkins 1987). Winnicott (1965a, p.18) refers to holding as one of the stages of maternal care, i.e. (i) holding, (ii) handling and (iii) object presenting. Holding refers to the actual physical holding of the infant as well as the total 'environmental provision indispensable to emotional development in earliest infancy' (Davis and Wallbridge 1981, p.21).

During the holding phase the infant is at his most dependent. Winnicott describes his understanding of the stages of development as 'absolute dependence', 'relative dependence' and 'towards independence'. He considers that holding includes the whole routine of care throughout the day and night and also follows the minute changes related to the infant's growth and development, both physical and psychological. In particular Winnicott describes holding as a physical holding of the infant. The mother meets the baby's needs as they arise, she expresses love in terms of 'physical management and in the giving of physical satisfaction'. Through holding a child, the mother also 'integrates the various feelings, sensations, excitements, angers, griefs etc., that go to make up an infant's life but which the infant cannot hold…the infant is not yet an infant, the mother is holding the infant, the human being in the making…she understands'. (Winnicott 1964, p.183). As Davis and Wallbridge (1981, p.35) say, through being held by the mother the infant gains a sense of trust in the mother and in the environment, and hence develops into a well integrated individual.

'Holding' in therapeutic work and how this experience can be provided within a family centre

Winnicott regarded psychoanalytic treatment as interpretative but also as 'the provision of a congenial milieu, a holding environment, analogous to maternal care' (Phillips 1988, p.11). Stamm (1985) adds that the holding environment is a catalyst that allows normal developmental tendencies and strivings within the patient to unfold and to assume their proper course of growth.

So, taking Winnicott's view that holding is central to the emotional health of the infant and also central to the therapeutic process, how do or can the family centre staff provide this holding experience? For purposes of this chapter I will give short theoretical examples of how clients can be held, followed by examples of my own clinical practice.

'Psychotherapeutic space', 'attention' and 'acceptance'

Lanyado (1991, p.32–3) suggests a powerful means of holding a client is by making available to the client a psychotherapeutic space in the therapist's mind, 'here is an adult who believes it is important to concentrate just on them, to the exclusion of all others, for the length of their session'. She relates this to the way in which an 'ordinary devoted mother' spends much of her time with her baby in 'primary maternal devotion'. Through this the client may feel securely held by their therapist's mind and by the external therapeutic environment the therapist provides. Lanyado continues by saying that the therapist's mind should be 'genuinely free of anything that will dilute the intensity of attentiveness'. The therapist also holds the client by receiving whatever is told, calmly, and by having the capacity to tolerate the intense emotional pain communicated by the patient. However, of particular importance is that the worker (and the mother in normal development) has to survive.

Practice example 1 – Laura, an 11-year-old girl

I should like to relate these particular ideas to an example of my work with Laura, an 11-year-old girl.

Laura was referred to me as a 7-year-old who had been severely neglected by her parents. She had been placed with foster parents at age three and since then had had numerous placement breakdowns. Her present foster placement was also breaking down. The referral from the area team suggested that Laura needed time to explore her life with her family of origin and her subsequent placement moves. It was also an opportunity to gain a greater understanding of how Laura had experienced the various families with whom she had lived, with a view to finding a placement that would meet her needs more fully. I was also asked to meet with

Laura's foster parents on a regular basis, to support her carers in understanding and working with Laura's behaviour, and in order to meet her emotional and physical needs.

I planned to meet with Laura weekly, with a view to allowing her to use the time in whatever way she chose, within the boundaries of time, space and no one being hurt. The room I work in with children has comfy chairs, floor cushions, dressing-up clothes, dolls and soft toys and a few toys on shelves. In addition, I have a box, that is specific to the child, containing drawings the child may have done, art materials, figures and anything else that becomes particularly important to the child.

When I first met Laura, she presented as confident and chatty but also very superficial in all that she said. She looked around the room and quickly tipped everything on to the floor by sweeping her hands along the shelves. This took a matter of seconds, while the mess we picked up together took the rest of the session.

She continued to start our sessions by exploring the room and then sitting under the table crying in a tiny voice, calling out 'mamma', 'drink', and so on. She quickly showed me how her needs should be met by becoming mute, by pointing to a baby blanket until I wrapped her in it and then by asking for a feeder beaker when she needed a drink. I felt like the mother of a tiny child, and felt she needed to be held physically, in her blanket, as well as emotionally.

During these early sessions she always shut the blinds, closed the curtains and turned off the lights. From this evolved her need for 'a nest' (a womb or possibly very early primary care?), where she curled up on a small rug and I wrapped her in blankets feeding her from a feeder beaker and with small pieces of biscuit. I experienced this as holding Laura physically and psychologically. She wanted me to integrate and hold the feelings she did not understand and to offer her, in our sessions, a whole routine of care.

After I had seen Laura for about six sessions, she brought with her an enormous hard doll, who had no name. She asked me to look after the doll for her, when she was not with me. As such I would bring the doll to each session and together Laura and I would check the baby was clean, put on a clean nappy, offer her milk from a feeder beaker, check she was safe and so on. At the end I would wrap the doll in blankets and assure Laura I would look after her baby until we met again. Each week I felt exhausted after Laura had left me. I felt that she had needed me to offer her the primary maternal preoccupation that she had never received as a baby. Similarly she needed me to hold her inner child, through the doll, even when we were apart.

Several months later, Laura's father had a heart attack. Instead of our usual sessions, Laura and I spent our next two sessions sitting beside her father in hospital, while he was on a life-support machine. Laura was able to talk to her father, to give him small gifts and drawings she had done and to say goodbye. Laura's father died on the morning of our next meeting. After breaking the news to her, Laura danced around the room frantically. When at last she stopped, she dressed up in a black cape and lay on the floor, telling me she was dead. She asked me to be her daughter, telling me to say how I felt. Through this we explored her fear of what would happen to her father's body, her worries about what people would be saying about her and the overwhelming fear of not knowing what she should be doing or feeling.

At this stage I worked with Laura for nearly two years. During this time she disclosed abuse by a cousin and another carer. She had also had a further placement breakdown before a long-term placement was found. For various reasons our work together stopped; however this placement broke down too and after six months we re-started our weekly sessions.

As our sessions continued, Laura's need to regress lessened. Instead, she explored the role of her natural parents, by putting me into the role of herself, as a much younger child. As soon as she arrived in the room, she would announce our roles, as well as advising me of the sort of things I ought to say. She would tell me I had been left alone and was crying and that no one cared about me. I would then be told to call out, but that no one would come. Meanwhile, she would take various roles, sometimes a relation, sometimes one of her parents. Each person would walk past me, however loudly I tried to attract their attention. Through sessions such as these she has explored her anger, frustration and sadness about feeling unloved and unwanted. Each time we had a break the hopelessness and desperation returned.

I continue to see Laura weekly and she is now 11. She has grown considerably and can now talk to me, as well as act out her inner world purely symbolically. While I can only offer her the space to work and grow, it feels as if she would fall apart, if there were no one holding her. By being held and contained, she is able to experience 'primary maternal care', with the view to breaking down the cycle of placement breakdowns, hopelessness and helplessness. In turn, my need to be held in order to hold her is met through supervision and consultation with a child psychoanalyst. By sharing my own feelings and being held myself, I am able to hold Laura, by tolerating and containing her conflicts and pain, by responding to her calmly and, as Lanyado says, by surviving.

'Understanding' and 'holding feelings and anxieties'

Hopkins (1987, p.5) comments on Winnicott and adds another element to the process of symbolically holding. She suggests:

this often takes the form of conveying in words at the appropriate moment something that shows that the analyst knows and understands the deepest anxiety which has been experienced or that is waiting to be experienced.

She considers that this implies that the function of holding, in addition to conveying love, is to relieve anxiety and hence a client who is not adequately held must feel both unloved and anxious.

Monson and Bayliss (1997) develop the idea of holding anxiety in relating to the inner child.

When (these) childhood experiences have been unhappy ones, parents can find themselves feeling again like the child they used to be. Aspects of this childhood self may be projected onto their own, present-day child, who comes to represent usually a bad or unwanted part of the parents' self... Sometimes these childhood feelings are so strong that they take over and dominate the adult part of the parent and parents are too identified with the child inside to be able to properly parent ... This is when *parents, too, need parenting, someone who will listen to, take in and hold for them the feelings and anxieties of the inner child and by so doing, make those feelings more bearable.* If there can be some holding of these child feelings, then the adult within the parent is free to function again and a space created in which new ideas can be taken in and thought about. (My italics.)

Perhaps the following example illustrates these ideas.

Practice example 2 – Linda, a mother

Linda was referred to me after she had asked for her child to be accommodated. The referral from the area team described a woman who was feeling low and lethargic, and who was feeling unable to care for her child. She had recently left her child's father and was now in a relationship with a Schedule One Offender (child sex offender). She was known to have had several violent partners and the police had recently been called to a domestic dispute between her and her new partner. While she did not consider any of her childhood or recent experiences had contributed to how she was feeling now, she had asked for counselling to 'sort herself out'. In addition, the social services department were seriously concerned that she did not recognise the risk her partner posed to her child and were carrying out a risk assessment on her partner. In response, I met with Linda and contracted to meet with her weekly to meet her own needs, as well as looking at the needs of her child and how these might best be met.

She presented as a young mother struggling with the demands of a young child who had been severely neglected. Although Linda had chosen to have counselling she found it very difficult. However, over the weeks Linda spoke of her mother dying when she was a child, the subsequent physical and sexual abuse by her father and her partners who had gone on to hurt and abuse her. Initially she gave me an unemotional and superficial account of her own childhood, assuring me that she could manage and that she did not need any sympathy. As she became more aware of her own pain, the outer, confident facade disappeared and I felt as if I was sitting with a young, vulnerable child. Her flippant, derogatory comments became fewer and in their place were expressions of fear, loneliness and loss. She talked at length of being an adult from the time her mother died, and through this she started to mourn her mother and the childhood that had been snatched away from her. Her 'acceptance' of her upbringing disappeared, and in its place she started questioning all the norms as she understood them.

In the early weeks, she occasionally missed appointments but as she began to explore and stay with her experiences her dependence on me grew. She started telephoning me between sessions and turning up half an hour early. She talked of needing the link with Gladstone Street C.R.C. in order to manage the flashbacks and nightmares that seemed, to her, to fill the space between sessions. She found both these and the growing recognition of her feelings to be painful and sometimes overwhelming. It was at this point that Linda almost drained me with her neediness. However, by enabling her to stay with and explore this pain and anxiety, Linda realised that she could face it and work through it. She also realised that others could have some understanding of her experience and that she was no longer 'alone'.

After many sessions, Linda was able to see beyond her own experiences and to relate her own thoughts, feelings and fears, to those her own child might be experiencing. Until then her own denial of pain or loss had overwhelmed any possibility of recognising her child's needs. From this point onwards, Linda gradually seemed to grow into an adult who could consider the role of parenting again. She found pleasure in the time she spent with her child and, as this contact was increased, she expressed confidence in herself and in her ability to look after her child.

Our work together has ended and Linda's child has been rehabilitated into her care. Through helping her to face her own anxieties and holding her through this process, I believe I have enabled her get in touch with her childhood and recognise the impact it has had on her. I also feel that through this process of being held and heard I have enabled her to recognise her own child as an individual with individual needs, separate from her own and separate from herself. While being held in a therapeutic setting, Linda has been able to be the uncared-for child and to grow into becoming a caring mother to her children. By holding Linda's anxieties, however repellent they were to her or me, and by staying with her while she explored the depth of her anxieties, has meant that she has grown into the person her child so badly needed.

'Doing what is best' and 'boundaries'

Holding is further discussed by Modell (1978, p.221) who suggests that:

> the symbolic holding is conveyed not only through the analyst's affective response to empathy but also in its capacity to do what it thinks best for the patient irrespective of a need to win the patient's love or approval…this is directly analogous to the parent who judges what is in the best interests of the child.

A holding environment also means setting limits, analogous to holding a child who is having a temper tantrum: in the adult it is the message that we will not be destroyed by the patient's sadism. Modell also suggests holding implies accepting the obnoxious, similarly to a mother who accepts her child's soiling.

Lanyado (1991) describes the use of boundaries as a further means of creating a therapeutic space and hence holding the client. She describes how important it is to be clear on the timing of sessions with a regular and fixed start and ending time.

These aspects of 'holding' are illustrated in the following example.

Practice example 3 – Tony, a father

Tony is a 25-year-old father of three children, two sons and a daughter. He was referred to me by his social worker after he had 'admitted' to dropping his daughter down the stairs, causing rib and arm fractures. He had requested counselling to help himself become a better parent and to make some sense out of the previous few months. During this period, he and his wife had drifted apart, although they remained living together, and his daughter had received her injuries. The social worker also expressed a generalised concern about Tony, although nothing specific was mentioned. Tony came to meet me and we agreed to meet weekly, initially for six weeks. If he found these sessions useful, I agreed to offer further appointments.

Initially, Tony talked of regret and remorse and feeling generally hopeless and overwhelmed. He presented as intelligent but detached, repeatedly saying how sorry he was, although this was never supported by his mood or attitude towards his daughter. Instead, he talked about his irritation at the involvement of the social services department, talking at great length about how badly he was being treated, how no one understood him or was bothered to find out about his needs. His real regret seemed to be that he had been inconvenienced by the injuries suffered by his child.

As our work together progressed, Tony talked of carrying a burden that was impossible to share and asked for further sessions. He described his need to keep people at arm's length and the enormous energy he put into doing this. He felt unsupported by his family and friends and continued to appear to focus all real regret on the recent impingements to his own life. After several weeks Tony arrived looking anxious and exhausted. He was finding it difficult to sleep, had difficulty concentrating at work and was having trouble relating to his family and colleagues. During this session he described the sadistic fantasies he had had about his daughter and admitted he was responsible for the fractures. He gave an emotional account of how his feelings of jealousy and hatred towards this child had finally overwhelmed him and how he had acted in such a way that the child had suffered horrendous injuries. He went on to tell me how this had happened.

As he spoke, I was aware of feelings of horror, but also the necessity not to show, at this point, how shocked or appalled I felt. I was aware of the need to accept the 'obnoxious', however difficult that might be, and also of my statutory duty as a social worker working in a family centre. My duty was to consider the welfare of his children as paramount and to ensure that they were protected from further harm. This inevitably meant I could not keep this information confidential. Instead, I explained that I would need to talk to my manager and that the police and the social services department worked together when there was any fear of risk to children. Tony responded angrily to this, but also talked of knowing this might happen.

My own impression was that he was feeling out of control and no longer able to maintain his cover story, feeling as trapped by this as by the threat of professionals finding out the truth. I was also aware of the need to accept what he said, recognising the difficulty he had had in telling me. I reassured him that I believed it was important that he had been able to talk about it. We ended the session with Tony saying he felt tearful and drained and needed time away from his family. He also felt very worried about what might happen. I offered him a further appointment that week, in order to contain some of his anxieties and also in order that we could work on any action that might have taken place. Tony presented as emotional and child-like, barely able to make decisions and needing me to hold the situation for him.

Throughout this session, I was aware of the need to pass this information on. First, to protect the children from further assault, but also to stop a situation that had become out of control and potentially lethal. As a statutory worker, it was my duty to ensure that my own department and the police had access to this information. I was also aware that I was acting in a way that I thought was best for Tony, 'irrespective of a need to win the patient's love and approval'. He himself at that time did not have the ability to manage his behaviour.

Tony continues to attend sessions at Gladstone Street C.R.C., while living separately from his family and with limited and supervised contact to his children. His insight into his own thought processes, childhood experiences and behaviour is growing and he has acknowledged full responsibility. He has looked at the ways in which he relates to all members of his family, particularly concentrating on his own childhood experiences at the hands of women and his present-day relationships. His psychiatrist considers the risk he poses is lessening.

In Tony's view it was the clear boundaries, the regularity, the consistency, and the belief that I would accept whatever he said that allowed him to speak honestly and reveal more of himself. By being held through this he felt able to talk. Could the authority of my position itself have played an important part? I wonder whether Tony chose not to tell other professionals who had worked with him and assessed him, because he did not feel sufficiently held. Could my authority have acted as as a mechanism in which he felt contained and secure? He knew that I would act on his disclosure. Did this in itself give him the security to know that he could finally allow others to manage a situation that he could not?

Gladstone Street C.R.C. as a holding environment

Mawson (1994, p.69) suggests, 'it is necessary to provide conditions of safety, respect and tolerance, so that anxiety and insecurity can be contained and examined productively'. At Gladstone Street C.R.C. we recognise these issues, as well as respecting and valuing the health of team members and the building itself, in order that individual, family and group sessions can be 'held' within the wider holding environment.

Family centre workers work in close proximity but also meet together for two hours each week to discuss team issues. This is a time for case discussions, administrative issues and discussions about service-users' needs and the ways we can meet these. In addition, there is time in which each member has the opportunity to share personal issues, concerns, feelings of pressure, etc. Through this, the group is aware of each individual's needs, of occasions when more support is needed and of how the team is functioning as a whole.

Each member also has individual supervision fortnightly, and again this is an opportunity to discuss case material in depth but also areas of personal growth and development. Team members also offer support to each other less formally and rely to a large extent on the administrative staff, who not only welcome service-users but also hold the centre together as a whole.

Overall, I would support Stamm's (1985, p.222) view that 'the holding environment is not a therapeutic technique or process done to the patients by the staff. Rather it is an ambiance or climate that the unit seeks to maintain.' At Gladstone Street C.R.C. this involves attempting to offer our clients the time and attention they need, through working to keep the centre itself a facilitating place for staff and service-users.

Conclusion

Winnicott describes many elements of holding but in particular he considers it as a total environmental provision, which includes physical holding, the management of experiences, empathy, the reduction of impingement, the opportunity for the infant to gain trust and to be understood and hence grow and develop.

Similarly Winnicott and others have considered the holding of service-users within a therapeutic relationship. The examples I have given have included setting clear boundaries, enabling the client to feel safe, the accept-ance of what is obnoxious, a catalyst that allows for development and growth to unfold, and a concentration similar to primary maternal preoccupation. In addition as a mother does, the family centre worker has the capacity to contain conflict and relieve anxiety, to remain calm and to act in the service-users' best interests without the need to gain their love or approval. The worker similarly needs to survive. Certainly in many ways this mirrors the way the mother holds the child.

The examples of my clinical practice show the attempts I have made to offer a safe and boundaried space in which to enable each individual to explore and understand. I have given examples of my work with a child and with two adults in a statutory setting, to show that while each is an individual with individual needs to be met, their need to be held and the need for me to offer a holding environment is similar. I hope also to have shown how 'holding' can be incorporated into many aspects of practice in a statutory setting. If we hold each individual, value them, respect them and through working with them recognise and understand their needs, we will be offering the 'holding environment' described by Winnicott that is such an essential part of growth and change. If not, we may be failing those people who have sought or who need to be held.

> In the context of good enough holding and handling, the new individual now comes to realise some of his or her potential. Somehow we have silently communicated reliability and the patient has responded with the growth that might have taken place, in the very early stages, in the context of human care. (Winnicott 1988, p.102)

Chapter 9

A Family Centre Approach to Early Therapeutic Intervention for Young Children and their Families

Denise Ledger

Recent research studies, commissioned by the Government following child abuse enquiries during the 1980s, call for a rebalancing of child-protection work, stating that for vulnerable children:

> There would be efforts to work alongside families rather than disempower them, to raise self-esteem rather than reproach families, to promote family relationships where children have their needs met, rather than leave untreated families with an unsatisfactory parenting style. (DOH 1995, p.55)

My interest is in how both parents and children can be empowered and supported to promote and safeguard the longer-term welfare of the children. I have been in my present post of Family Services Manager for nine years, managing Buddle Lane Family Centre, a busy city-based resource, and community-based workers. The centre provides a large range of services to 'children in need' and their parents. Many of the parents have themselves been in local authority care at some point in their life. This has highlighted for me the potential generational cycle of poor parenting, and its ultimate cost both to children emotionally and to the local authority financially.

Barnett undertook a piece of work at Buddle Lane Family Centre in the 1980s (Bain and Barnett 1986) as the centre was changing from a day nursery to a family centre. This work was based on an application of the principles of a similar project in London in the 1970s, overseen by Isabel Menzies-Lyth (Bain and Barnett 1986). These two projects focused on the improvements necessary within day nurseries to provide both a therapeutic and educational environment for pre-school children. Clear ideas were put forward about how nursery settings could shift their culture from undifferentiated group care, which focused on physical well being, to more individualised care which incorporated the psychological care of the children. Changes were made within Buddle Lane Family Centre following this report which included the start of work with parents, with assessment and planning to help children with their individual needs. Bain (Bain and Barnett 1986, p.84) noted in her conclusion:

> The change in the Devon day nursery is profound and encouraging. However there are still many unsolved problems…the process of change has not been easy, and is still going on with some major questions not yet answered…how best to deal with highly disturbed parents…what additional training and professional help do the Family Centre staff need to best help them and their often equally disturbed children?

This chapter looks at the way in which services have developed since the 1980s, focusing on the early therapeutic interventions with young children and their parents. I refer to the parent 'she', as the particular case used to illustrate the work involves a mother and her children. Although the case is obviously individual, it is indicative of the range of difficulties that many families bring with them to the centre.

The framework for therapeutic work

Family centres tend to have wide-ranging remits. It is crucial therefore for the service to be clear about what they are doing and why, that is, to have a good understanding of the 'primary task' (McMahon, Dacre and Vale 1997). The primary task within Buddle Lane Family Centre is to help families experiencing difficulties to improve the way in which they care for their children. 'If the mother's own feelings of need as an infant were unmet, and there is not a "good enough" memory to call upon, the mother is vulnerable, feels she cannot cope, then blames herself for failing' (Pritchard 1999, p.249). The therapeutic work within Buddle Lane is grounded in the concepts of 'holding' and 'containment' for both children and their carers (see Chapters 1 and 2). There is a continuum of support whereby parents are helped to provide a degree of containment for their children, while staff are supported and held in their work.

Bower (1995, p.75) describes how some parents, on being offered purely practical solutions to problems, may say they 'have tried it but it doesn't work'. She suggests that the parents' own childhood impinges on their ability to parent. Although behaviour can be adapted quickly in the short term, if long-term results are to be sustained parents are likely to need much more support to develop an insight into why they have been responding to their children as they have. This involves helping parents to understand, and to change, their feelings towards their children. Stern (1985) stresses the need for 'attunement' within the parent–child relationship for the child to feel held and safe. A low warmth and high criticism environment has been shown to be a predictor of disturbance in children (DOH 1995; Pound *et al.* 1989). Changing this environment for children necessitates changing how parents feel, both about themselves and about their children.

The following case study demonstrates the therapeutic work that is taking place with one family. It is an ongoing, rather than a finished piece of work, which I hope will highlight the complexities of therapeutic family centre work. Many families have benefited from this therapeutic approach, which is focused on early intervention with young children and their families. Changes have occurred, and have been sustained, within families that have taken part in this work.

The referral

The family was referred to the family centre by the duty social worker. There had been a duty visit to the home following concerns by the school that the two children appeared neglected and the older child was presenting behavioural difficulties in the classroom. The mother appeared to be very depressed and unable to manage her lively children. The referral requested parenting skills support to help her.

The following information was gained at this stage. Judy, a white woman in her mid-20s, lives on her own in temporary housing with her two children. She is separated from her most recent partner (the father of her younger child). She finds the children difficult to manage, often losing her temper and shouting. She herself spent several years in local authority care. She is being treated for depression. Tina is five years old and attends the local school where her behaviour is described as disruptive and difficult to manage. Both her mother and school report that she is very bossy, and likes to get her own way. She has more than the average number of bumps and bruises. She is a loud, vocal girl who shies away from physical contact. Joe is three years old. He was born prematurely and his development was slightly delayed, although there are now no medical concerns. He is lively, with poor communication skills, and prone to biting and screaming when frustrated. He does not attend any pre-school.

An initial assessment by the family centre took place in the home, with the purpose of clarifying both the information about the family, and the parent's understanding of the referral. Two workers were used so that the children could be given individual attention by one worker while the other focused on the parent. This generally avoids the children hearing, on the home visit at least, information about themselves or their parent that is distressing. During this home visit and the first few sessions at the family centre, observations, questions, an ecomap (to highlight the existing support network) and genogram helped to reveal the picture of this family. Burnham (1986) suggests that the genogram can be used to explore the family of origin, as a planning tool and as a therapeutic tool in a session with a family. It has certainly been useful in my work in helping parents to understand the inter-generational complexities of family difficulties, thus removing some of the 'blame' that parents deal themselves for not doing well enough.

The next stage involved a meeting between the parent, the referring social worker, one of the family support workers involved in the initial assessment, and myself as centre manager. The purpose of the meeting was to discuss what support the family centre could offer, and to look at how Judy could be involved in the decision-making about these services. While the meeting took place Tina and Joe played in an nearby room with the other family support worker who had visited them at home. While Judy was finding parenthood very difficult, she wanted to improve her relationship with her children. In response to the initial assessment question, 'What do you want to change for your children?' Judy had replied, 'I'd like the children to have a better childhood than me. I'd like them to enjoy it and have fun.' Her response to 'What would you like to change for yourself?' was, 'I'd like to enjoy the children more. They're hell to live with. I do like them really, but it's so tiring and they're so difficult. I'd like to really like it. I want people to like me and to like my children too. I don't want to be angry with the kids all the time. I don't want them to go through what I had to.'

This seemed to be a positive starting point.

> Children can generate and offer a reparative hope in their parents who wish to parent in a better way than they feel they were parented. Whilst this may, of course, produce the opposite effect, it does seem important that the wish to be a good-enough parent is there and feeds into the therapeutic alliance. (Green 2000, p.26)

Judy seemed keen to begin work at the family centre. It was agreed that she and both children would attend sessions with their allocated family support worker during the coming school holidays. We hoped this transitional period would enable the family to feel more comfortable in attending the centre, and provide some instant practical support during the school break. Judy and the children attended as planned for the six weeks of the school holidays. Tina and Joe had places in the two-week playscheme at the end of the holiday. Although they were lively they managed the sessions well. Meanwhile Judy had begun to talk with her family support worker about her worries. During these sessions the following programme of work was agreed:

1. Judy would have a weekly counselling session to help her, both in her own right and as a parent, explore her own past and the dysfunctional impingement on her present capacity to cope.

2. Joe would attend three nursery sessions each week at the family centre nursery. During this time he would have a weekly individual play session to help him make sense of what had been happening, and to find ways of communicating his feelings. A referral was also made for speech and language therapy.

3. Tina would have a weekly individual play session. It was agreed with the school that this would happen during the school day in a suitable room at school.

4. After some initial individual work Judy and Joe would attend a group at the family centre, focusing on improving the relationship between parent and child.

Within this programme, the family support worker would continue to provide weekly support to Judy to help her manage the practicalities of two small children. The sessions were primarily for Judy to be able to offload the difficulties of the week, and to help her to manage the children's behaviour. Material from the Parent–Child Game, developed by Forehand and McMahon (1981) and adapted by Jenner (1992) was used. This approach focuses on the reduction of child-directive behaviour by the parent, and the increasing of child-centred parenting. Judy was encouraged to decrease the amount of attention that she was giving to her children when they were doing things that annoyed her, and increase her attention when the children were compliant. This work aimed to give Judy more tools for the job of parenting while she looked at the underlying issues that were affecting her capacity to parent. The family support worker's role, through supervision, was to take a co-ordinating role to ensure that crucial information was shared and that Tina and Joe were held in mind throughout the work.

Work with the parent

Work with Judy was undertaken by the family support worker in conjunction with the centre counsellor. The counselling sessions are, as in other counselling contexts, confidential. However there is a clear agreement within counselling sessions that any matters relating to a child's welfare or the parent's capacity to protect their child remain of paramount importance. Within the agreement parents are encouraged to pass on any of this crucial information themselves, but are clear that the counsellor will share any such information with the family support worker. Parents are also encouraged to share with their worker any issues that arise during counselling that they (the parent) and the counsellor feel could be helpful in the broader picture of effecting change within the family. My role was to provide supervision for both workers.

The purpose of her individual time was to help Judy make some sense of her own past and the impact it was having on her parenting.

> ...it is not necessarily what happened in the parent's own childhood, but what they made of that experience which influences whether or not they can provide a secure base for their own children... It suggests that to help parents achieve a coherent picture of their past may enable them to provide a better parenting experience for their own children. (Byng-Hall 1995, p.120)

Initially, Judy found it difficult to talk about herself. She would say, 'this is about sorting the kids out', suggesting that there was some 'treatment' the children could have that would make them better behaved, and therefore she would like them more. She spent much of her time complaining about their behaviour. One of the first things the family support worker suggested was making a time for this at the beginning of the session out of the children's hearing. The worker was keen to give Judy an opportunity to express her feelings about the children but wanted to avoid further reinforcement of the negative comments that they seemed to hear so often. Judy was reminded to try to restrain her comments while they were with her.

Although Judy had clearly said that she wanted to make changes and improve things for her children, she seemed reluctant to be involved in anything herself that might begin that process. She would arrive late for her counselling sessions, arrange doctor's appointments in the middle of family support sessions, and generally be dismissive of the centre staff. The feelings evoked in the workers by Judy's apparent lack of commitment were discussed in supervision. Workers felt both saddened and cross that they had not been able to engage with Judy as quickly as they had hoped. One of them had been involved in the holiday playscheme where Judy had been given a break from the children. As she talked openly about the feeling of not being 'good enough' to manage to engage with Judy as she would have liked to, feeling cross with her that she had provided some respite, and was now being pushed away, we made the connection back to Judy. Her unavailability seemed to link clearly to her inability to form a trusting relationship rather than her reluctance to embark on the work. The workers' feelings seemed so similar to the emotions Judy had expressed. 'For many parents, the sense of shame with which they come to our services acts as a powerful reminder of the sense of "bad" or "imperfect" parent…' (Horne 2000, p.49). Understanding this helped in persevering in building a relationship with Judy. Truax and Carkhuff (1967) identified three key features of effective therapy or counselling as 'active empathy', 'non-possessive warmth' and 'genuineness'. Throughout the following sessions staff tried to give Judy some positive and accepting experiences that might help her feel more contained herself. She was warmly welcomed by all staff, even if she arrived late. If she did not arrive she was contacted to see how things were. She was always given ten minutes at the start of the session, which was her time to talk and to be listened to.

Judy began slowly to talk about her past. She told her story in a very matter of fact way, saying that although her time in care had not been good it had made her what she was today. She added, 'No one's going to tell me what to do any more. I don't care what people think of me. They take me as they find me.' This appeared to be in stark contrast to what Judy had said at the time of referral. In looking at this in supervision we realised that Judy's words also described how Tina presented at school. It seemed likely that Judy was projecting her feelings on to Tina. Tina had initially been quiet at school, being very much on her own, and compliant. At the point of referral the school were saying she was disruptive and bossy, not caring if the other children liked her or not. It became more and more clear as sessions with Judy progressed that her early childhood experiences had been traumatic, and there had been an absence of any consistent holding environment for her. Its absence had caused her to feel unsafe and extremely wary of making and sustaining relationships. Modell (1975, cited in Shapiro and Carr 1991) comments that if the holding environment is absent the child is forced into a premature maturation, an 'illusion of self-sufficiency', which seemed to be what Judy was demonstrating.

As Judy became more trusting of the workers, she began to talk about her feelings towards the children, always beginning with, 'I'd never hurt them, but…'. What became clear was that Judy had on occasions hurt the children, and seemed to be very anxious that she might do this again. She would fluctuate between being outwardly confident, saying everything was fine, to being 'at the end of her tether' with the children, and wanting them 'out of her sight'. This reminded me of the concept of the 'false self'. 'The False Self, if successful in its function, hides The True Self' (Winnicott 1965, p.150). Judy seemed to have developed part of herself to present as a confident mother who was able to manage things, which protected the vulnerable, scared and fragile person who was actually very frightened both for herself and for her children.

The children too were obviously anxious around Judy. They kept a watchful eye on her, not moving an inch if she raised her voice to them. This and the information from Judy increased our concern. The family support worker explained to Judy that we were very concerned both about her and about her ability to manage the children, and that we would be referring the case back to the duty social worker, suggesting that a child protection conference needed to be called. Judy was very angry with all the staff at the centre, and continued to show the 'capable' Judy whenever she could. During the period leading up to the conference, there was more evidence of Judy not protecting the children, leaving them in dangerous situations. Joe also had several minor injuries, which Judy found difficult to explain. Judy had made no attempt to hide these from us, and had continued to attend regularly.

Following a lengthy child protection conference, the children's names were both placed on the child protection register. Judy had been very upset and cross during the meeting and staff were anxious that she would not want to return to the family centre, as she seemed particularly cross with us for instigating the process. However, she returned the following day, appearing more relaxed and prepared to work with staff. She seemed to be relieved that we had really listened to what she was trying but was frightened to say. She had not been able to contain and manage her own feelings towards her children, nor had she been able to provide a holding environment for them. Her own early experiences of being held, physically and emotionally, had been poor and interrupted. It seemed important that we, the family centre, could begin to give her some security and containment that she was not able to do for herself. By holding her anxiety, and taking steps to minimise the risks to the children, I believe we made a huge step forward in the work with this family.

Hay, Leheup and Almudevar (1995) discuss a model of therapy for families where the workers become the 'transitional family' for the family in therapy. The role of the family centre could be described in a similar way. Not only is there consistency of approach from all the staff involved with the family, but the team offer persistent support and emotional holding for both parents and children. Britton (1983), looking at therapy for the child, suggests the 'transitional family' can provide a helpful, potentially corrective, emotional experience for the child. The work with Judy too is focused on providing her with a similar experience in order that she can begin to make sense of her past experiences, and use this understanding to make changes in the way in which she manages the children.

Groupwork with the parent and child – relationship play

In addition to the work undertaken during family support sessions, where parent and child or children attend together and an individual plan of work is drawn up, the family centre provides groupwork focused on parent–child relationships. This work is based on the idea of infant–parent psychotherapy, described by Fraiberg (1980), that symptoms in the infant are best dealt with by working with the parent and infant together rather than separately. The child's presence not only ensures that the child is held in mind, but also allows for observation, and exploration of the parent's feelings here and now. Hopkins (1992) advocates this approach with very young children, suggesting that the capacity for rapid change in the relationship is a reflection of the combined flexibility of the infant and his parents. She explores the notion that the parent's feelings from a past relationship can sometimes be transferred to the child, preventing the parent from responding to the child's needs. Coulter and Loughlin (1999, p.58) say that, 'These past experiences may cast shadows on the relationship a mother has with her own baby and can act like a fairground mirror, reflecting back not the real baby but a distorted image of the baby.'

Within this framework the family centre regularly runs a group for parents and children, focused on communication and relationships. Parents are invited to join this group, which takes place for 2 hours each week for 12 weeks. A home visit is made to explain the group and to listen to any fears. As the group is about improving the relationship and communication between parent and child, each parent attends with one of their children, usually the pre-school child that they find the most difficult. Alternative childcare arrangements are made for any other children in the family. Many of the ideas for this group have been taken from the work undertaken by Broughton, McKnight and Binney (1992) about 'relationship play'. Additional material and exercises have been used from Manolson's work (1992 and 1995) about the Hanen Approach, which promotes communication and connection between parent and child. The structure of the 12-week course is planned in advance. The group comprises eight parents, eight children and four staff. All children attending are known to the staff involved and are able to leave their parent without distress. Each session begins with the parents and children in separate rooms, joining together for the last 30 minutes of each session.

The parents' group and children's group

IN THE PARENTS' GROUP

The parents and staff together set the ground rules for the group, which are displayed in the room for every session. Each session has a clear format, with opening and closing rituals. Time is firmly adhered to, with the group commencing and finishing promptly, so that no parent is given more time than another in the group. The content of each week's group is planned in detail by staff following the previous week's session, so any adjustments can be made in response to issues that have arisen. The parents' sessions begin with exploring why they have come to the group, building on the initial home visit. During the subsequent weeks they look at what, and how, they communicate with their child, and their memories of communication and relationships from their own childhood. This is often painful and very difficult, but being within a group where the feelings, if not the experiences, are usually similar is in itself helpful. Parents no longer feel they are the only person feeling or behaving towards their children as they do. Practical exercises are included – for practice for when the parents and children join together, for experiencing in a safe setting some of the feeling evoked in them by their children, and lastly to play and have some fun themselves! This does not happen instantly within the group, and many of the parents are very anxious about playing for themselves. Some have never really had this opportunity before, and need to feel well contained before they can engage in this new activity.

THE CHILDREN'S GROUP

The children's group too has a clear format. Each of the two staff has four children who they focus on, with each child being given as much individual attention as possible. Activities within the group focus on improving the children's communication skills, hopefully enabling them to help their parent tune into them more easily. Many of the children have an established pattern of gaining attention from their parent by inappropriate behaviour. Whilst the parent is busy within the group trying to discover how to communicate and relate to their child, the child too is discovering other ways of communicating.

Then *parents and children* join together for relationship and contact games. Again these are graded, with very little physical contact such as *Pass-the-Parcel* and *Ring-a-Roses*, through to paired close contact games such as *Row Your Boat*.

Judy and Joe

Joe left Judy happily on their first session to join the children's group. Judy played an active role in setting the adult group ground rules, and in sharing why she had come to the group. During the children's session some video film was taken of each of the children for a few minutes, and the parents (whose permission had been gained beforehand) were looking forward to seeing it the following week. Joining the children at the end of the first session, parents were asked to sit wherever their child was, and just watch them play. Judy found this very difficult, wanting to talk to the staff or another parent in the room.

When the video was shown, parents were asked to watch their own child at play, and try to describe what he was doing. Some of the group were able to do this, saying things like 'He's playing with the tractor. He's getting cross with it...' Judy and some of the other parents found this much harder. Judy was able to comment positively on what other people's children were doing but found it hard to focus on Joe without being negative, 'He's made a dreadful mess with the paint. Why can't he do it properly like the other children?' This seemed to link closely to her thoughts about herself; she often said she'd made a mess of things, and she just wanted to be like other parents. As the sessions moved on, Judy talked more and more about her own childhood. There had been very little physical touch, cuddles or affection. She felt she had got close to one member of staff in the children's home, but she had left. She said how hard it was to touch or hold her child, but she hadn't really thought about why before. Judy really enjoyed some of the practical communication exercises within the group, which were intended to demonstrate how hard it is to be on the receiving end of something you don't understand.

One exercise during the session involved parents being in pairs, sat back to back. Each had 20 coloured building blocks. Judy was asked to build something, and then to explain what she'd done so that her partner could build the same construction with her bricks. This had to be carried out by word only; the construction could not be seen by the partner. The frustration that Judy began to show when her partner could not understand her instructions, and her partners ensuing despair at not being given clear enough instructions was very evident. Only one of the pairs managed to copy the construction accurately, and this afforded plenty of discussion about the feelings that were evoked through one small example of miscommunication. Judy was able to make links between this and her expectations of Joe. She had felt very cross with her partner during the exercise, and she said that she often felt like that with Joe. She had assumed he was always 'playing her up', but commented 'He might not always understand what I'm on about. I do shout at him a lot.'

As the group progressed, Judy became more and more confident in getting close to Joe, and joining his play. He too began to tap her arm when he needed her attention, rather than screaming or throwing something. Judy and some of the other parents thought that some of the contact games were babyish, and that the children wouldn't like them. However, the children loved them, and the parents too seemed to take pleasure from the experience they had not been able to enjoy when their child was younger. Photographs were taken during some of the relationship games, so that Judy had some tangible evidence that she could hold and get close to Joe. The group provided a secure base for Judy to begin to instigate and enjoy physical contact with Joe. The next stage is to help her provide that contact when Joe needs it, rather than when she is being encouraged to do it. Main (1986, cited in Hopkins 1987) suggests that what has most meaning for an infant is not the amount of contact he has with his mother but her physical accessibility in response to his initiative.

Work with the children

In addition to work with parents, and work on family relationships, the children too need work in their own right.

> Distressed children have the right to have their unhappiness acknowledged and their stories heard. They need someone who will listen to them, who can accept and contain the reality of the past, and free them to discover optimism in the present. Without this help they remain locked into feelings and behaviours from earlier events or circumstances, which they continue to carry into adult relationships and experiences. (Carroll 1998, p.153)

Many of the children who attend the family centre, including Tina and Joe, have not had good early experiences. Many have had limited opportunities to develop secure attachments with consistent carers. Fraiberg (1968, p.293) suggests that troubled children, who have not had sufficient opportunity to develop affectional bonds, are likely to experience further difficulties as they grow older.

> These children who have never experienced love, who have never belonged to anyone, and were never attached to anyone except on the most primitive basis of food and survival, were unable in later years to bind themselves to other people, to love deeply, to experience tenderness, grief or shame to the measure that gives dimension to the human personality.

Using therapeutic play

This work at the family centre focuses on play, which is widely understood in terms of young children's learning as a child's 'work'. Play is the medium through which children begin to make sense of their world, and which helps a child's inner world to develop. While the work with children that is undertaken at the family centre is not formal psychotherapy, it is providing therapeutic support to children experiencing difficulties, and as such aims to help children to manage and make some sense of the painful things in their lives.

> Some children have too much happening in their lives, separations, losses, abuse, repeated disruptions, changes of family membership and abode, changes of caretaker and attachment figures. Such events can be too great to cope with unaided. (McMahon 1992, p.25)

The family centre approach to work with children is based primarily on the principles of child-centred play therapy with the basic premise that play itself is both creative and therapeutic. West (1992); McMahon (1992); Wilson, Hendrick and Ryan (1992) and Carroll (1998) all discuss Axline's model of client-centred, non-directive play therapy (1969, 1982). As Dasgupta (1999, p.179) says:

> Non-directive play therapy allows the child to be him or herself without facing evaluation or pressure to change. The child is the source of his or her own growth and therapeutic change... During non-directive play therapy, a child can experience growth under the most favourable conditions: by playing out feelings, the child faces them, learns to control them or abandon them.

The role of the worker is to attend to the child's feelings.

> It does not matter that we do not understand all that a child's play may mean. The task in play therapy is not to interpret it to the child but to stay with children as they find it out for themselves. (McMahon 1992, p.54)

Therapeutic play work with Tina and Joe was to help them to make better sense of what has already happened in their lives and, ' ... to repair or replicate the process of attachment and containment.' (McMahon 1992, p.7). The work with Joe was undertaken by a family support worker in a room at the family centre, booked for the same time every week. The work with Tina took place with me, within her school. It was harder for the school to find a regular time with use of the same room. It seemed important for Tina that the structure of the session was clear – that she knew which room she would be going to, on which day, and how long the session was. The school understood the importance of this, and managed to find a small room that we could use. Structure and consistency in the setting up of the sessions is a prerequisite to building up a trusting relationship. It gives the child a clear message that he is important and valued.

For both children the sessions needed clear boundaries with no interruptions and with play materials available. Sand and water play, small world play (animals, small play people, cars etc.), home corner, dolls, puppets, paints and other resources are readily available at the family centre. (These are chosen to match a child's culture and race to foster the child's recognition of and confidence and pride in their identity. Ahmed, Cheetham and Small (1986) discuss further ways in which work on identity for black children can be incorporated into practice.) A check was made with the school about what resources could be provided and what needed to be taken to the room each week.

Joe

Joe's first session was very busy, as the family support worker's account illustrates. 'Joe rushed through the door, straight to the sand pit. There was barely time to say hello to him and goodbye to Judy. I told him he could do whatever he liked as long as it was not dangerous. He seemed to have taken that for granted; within seconds the sand was flying everywhere. He kept turning towards me and smiling. I continued to watch. He ran to the box of animals, tipping them out on the floor, and banging them fiercely. One by one he took the animals over to the open window and hurled them outside.' During supervision Joe's arrival into his first session was discussed. It seemed as though Joe was giving a very clear symbolic picture of what life was like for him. Things were all over the place, like the sand, and adults had left his life suddenly. It felt as though Joe had done the same to the animals, making them leave suddenly and violently.

After two or three sessions Joe became less frantic and was no longer throwing the animals. He made animals and cars disappear under furniture and shouted at them before he hid them away. As sessions continued he began to look to his worker to 'find' the hidden toys, suggesting that he was beginning to trust and develop a therapeutic relationship with her.

Tina

Tina, by contrast, came into her first session very quietly. She sat down on the bean bag while I explained that she could do what she wanted in the session, as long as it was not dangerous, and did not disturb other classes in the school (the proviso the school had made). She continued to look at me, her face expressionless, so I asked if she had understood what I had said. 'Yep' was her reply, followed by nothing. She sat very still, just looking at me. I resisted my instinctive feeling to fill the silence, and sat mirroring Tina's position on the bean bag. After what seemed to me like an eternity, but was in reality a few minutes Tina spoke, 'Tell me what I've got to do then.' Tina seemed to expect, as in all other areas of her life, to be told what to do rather than make any choice of her own. I quietly reminded her that she could do whatever she liked.

She continued to sit quietly, picking up a book and flicking through the pages. I was feeling very anxious about whether Tina would settle in to these sessions, should I be more directive at this stage? I could sense Tina's anxiety – was this a safe place to be, could she really do what she wanted?

I began to play quietly with the small farm animals near me. It felt important not to pressure her verbally into beginning to play, but she seemed so powerless. I felt that turning my focus to the toys, rather than Tina, might help her to join in. After a few minutes she began to play quietly beside me. I continued to play until she started to become engrossed in her own play. Just before the end of the session, Tina picked up a small panda. She turned her back to me and said, 'Well then, you'll just have to come home with me. I don't care if she says you can't.' She turned back towards me, stuffing the panda into her pocket. I told her that it was fine to take the panda home with her, and I would look forward to seeing her, and the panda, again the following week. As I said this I was wondering whether the panda, or indeed Tina, would return. I had found the session very difficult. Tina's quietness and inactivity had been hard for me to manage. The hour seemed to last for ever, yet when it was time to go I felt that Tina was expressing a real feeling. Maybe she needed to take some of the calmness from the session out with her, perhaps the panda was symbolic, and she wanted to take me out with her. I thought carefully about what I would do if she lost the panda, or worse still, if it were destroyed. To my great relief Tina arrived the following week, clutching the panda!

Tina was quiet during her second session but did explore the play room, using the panda in her play. As the session drew to a close I suggested that I could keep the panda safely in a special place until next time. This was not solely to prevent my anxiety about whether the panda would return, but also to give Tina a clear message. The panda had been integral to her play; it had been the child in the home corner, and the 'naughty' panda at the farm. It felt important for me to tell Tina that I would hold the panda, which was starting to represent Tina, safely until our next session.

Tina's anger has begun to emerge through her play, with traumatic scenes of road crashes and houses being demolished. We have reached the point where, as I comment on the hurt and pain of the toys injured in Tina's accidents, she begins to rescue one toy from the debris. I am hopeful that this will continue, and that together we may be able to repair some of the early hurt to Tina.

Therapeutic play work continues with these children. It has been important for me, and the family support worker, to listen to what Tina and Joe have been saying, to observe their symbolic play and communication, and to take heed of the feelings evoked in us by the children's projections. Holding and containing these feelings until the child is ready and able to manage them for himself can be exhausting work. Copley and Foryan (1997, p.167) recognise this stating, 'The needs of staff who are the recipients of many felt-to-be unbearable feelings in the service of a containing approach also have to be considered.'

Therapeutic play work with children may appear simple, playing with the children or watching them play. Enabling children to explore and repair early damage is, however, very complex work. All staff undertaking this work at the family centre receive, as well as their regular supervision, additional support to help them untangle their thoughts from a play session. This play work is recognised as a crucial ingredient in the work with distressed families.

Conclusion

Although Barnett's work (Bain and Barnett 1986) recognised that improvements in working practice had taken place at Buddle Lane Family Centre, there were also questions raised about what further developments were needed for staff to be able to work effectively with disturbed parents and their equally disturbed children. I hope the account of the current therapeutic work within the centre might highlight some of these developments, and the value of work with both parents and their children.

The work discussed takes place within a busy setting, with staff undertaking several roles within their working day in their quest to empower both children and their parents. This demands flexibility from workers with an ability to hold the children in mind, while working with the often conflicting needs of the children and their parents. Staff too need support in exploring the issues of transference and counter-transference in the therapeutic relationship. There is an expectation that staff try to hold or contain feelings for both parents and their children until they are more ready to manage this themselves. For staff to manage this responsibility the holding environment needs to be mirrored in the way in which staff are treated. The support systems for staff aim to provide some of this containment. The continuum of holding is vital for this work: the managers provide this environment for staff, who in turn provide it for parents (and their children) until they themselves are able to hold and contain painful feelings. It is important that the child too is held safely during the process, while the parent is not able to do this adequately.

I hope the work with Judy may have demonstrated the need to involve, empower and work in partnership with parents, recognising the 'enormous influence which parent's own emotions and childhood experiences have on their capacity to cope with their children' (Bower 1995, p.75). If this work is not undertaken it is much more difficult to make and sustain significant improvements for the children. I would suggest that work which provides parents with a secure holding environment for themselves is likely to be beneficial in helping them to provide better experiences for their children.

Work with Judy and Joe has focused on the parent–child relationship. This too is a crucial part of the work within the family centre, providing a secure base for the parent to build or repair their relationship with their child. As work with the parent takes place it is often easy for her to lose sight of the child, as she focuses on her own issues. This relationship work helps the parent tune in to her child, increasing physical holding and intimacy, thus providing a stepping-stone in repairing insecure attachments.

I hope the work to date with Tina and Joe will have demonstrated that children are able to communicate through their play. As staff working with these children, who have experienced often repeated and damaging separations or traumas, we need to be able to listen to this communication. Examples of the work with Tina and Joe indicate the beginning of a relationship with the worker through which the child is 'given the opportunity to play out his accumulated feelings of tension, frustration, insecurity, aggression, fear, bewilderment, confusion'. (Axline 1969, p.16). Therapeutic play work is an effective way of helping children to both understand themselves, and to be understood by others.

Early therapeutic intervention with young children and their families can be an effective tool in diversionary planning for children, preventing the child's transition into substitute care. Preventive models of work as described by Widerstrom et al. (1997, p.290) are often viewed as difficult to describe and to justify as 'they seek to avert a problem that has not yet occurred'. However early intervention has been researched (DOH 1998, 1999) and found to be effective. Early intervention, with therapeutic work for both parents and children, has the potential to make a real difference to children's lives, which ultimately must contribute to more sustained positive outcomes for children.

Chapter 10

Developing and Auditing a Local Family Centre Feeding to Thrive Service

Anton Green

This chapter describes the origins and development of a local project offered from the Penn Crescent Family Centre in Haywards Heath, West Sussex. It also describes how the project was audited for clinical effectiveness and outcomes. The project's aim was to provide a supportive service for families with young children where there was a high level of anxiety about weight-gain or eating.

The project was locally developed, largely from within existing resources, in order to extend support to an area of previously unmet need. The impetus came from a presentation by The Children's Society on their pioneering project, The Infant Support Group, in Wiltshire. Their project team included staff from a number of different disciplines including nursing, social work, and early years work with children. Their focus was on the family pattern of parent–child interaction around meal-times and eating. Crucial to their approach was the team evaluation of information from direct observation, used to maximise helpful feedback for the family. This fitted well with our existing family centre practice.

Penn Crescent Family Centre offers a positive parenting support service. Staff work collectively to offer a variety of day programmes for parents and children built around a community lunch. In accordance with the social services department's threshold criteria, the service is open to all with either high priority need (such as children's names on the child protection register) or medium priority need (having some significant difficulties with parenting). The centre offers good quality childcare, adult group work, individual counselling, or couple work time, and supported time in the play setting for parents with their own children. Parents can opt to use the Maudsley derived Parent Child Game using the centre's video suite (see Chapter 3). A key feature of the centre's working model is flexibility. Some families attend the day programme and receive all of the above provision. Other families have a specific provision, either by appointment at the centre or through home visiting (Green 1998).

The skills of family centre workers draw on person-centred psycho-dynamic and cognitive strands of thinking, while social learning theory underpins many of the ideas about day-to-day positive parenting tactics. Staff develop child-observation skills in order to carry out focused assessments and use collective evaluation in developing constructive feedback for parents. In small groupwork and counselling they support parents through a progression from self-related issues, to reconnecting to the world of the child, exploring children's feelings and emotional needs, and then looking at behaviour as part of parent–child interaction. Parents look at their parenting in the 'here and now' but may also reconnect with and resolve significant and potentially traumatic or disturbing issues from their own past. For family centre workers the ability to offer perceptive facilitation, and appropriate timing and pacing, are key skills. This particular balance, and indeed tension, is at the heart of much of the therapeutic work in family centres.

In developing our family centre service we have sought to apply principles of empowerment and partnership. In a child and user friendly setting the idea is to give parents from diverse backgrounds the best possible opportunity to reflect, share and participate. This may be in personal growth and self-awareness, and in the consolidation of real gains in positive parenting. We use a task-centred framework, with regular opportunities to choose goals and review progress, giving parents maximum choice and inclusion. Planned user feedback (through satisfaction questionnaires) and continuous evaluation are part of the culture of empowerment. All these ingredients readily transferred to the new Feeding to Thrive Project.

The new project itself was rooted in the rapidly growing knowledge and practice base in respect of infant nutrition and feeding. The causes of non-organic failure to thrive are many and a range of professional disciplines have a contribution to make, from paediatric medicine, to clinical pyschology, dietetics, speech and language therapy, health visiting, and social work. The challenge was to see how family centre workers could use this knowledge in the context of their existing skills. A training package was provided by The Children's Society, with particular attention given to understanding of infant nutrition. It was useful to be able to build in the clinical outcomes audit from the outset, drawing on the skills-sharing ethos of the local hospital-based clinical effectiveness team at the Princess Royal Hospital, Haywards Heath.

The background to the Feeding to Thrive Project

It became apparent by the early 1990s that existing hospital-based and community services were not tailored to deal effectively with non organic failure to thrive in young children. From the many pioneering research and practice initiatives, parallel work in two innovatory centres was particularly significant. The Children's Society, before setting up their community based Infant Support Group commissioned research by Jane Batchelor and Andrew Kerslake (1990). In the Newcastle area, work was begun by Michael Parkin and carried on by Charlotte Wright and colleagues as the Parkin Project. This was a paediatrically led service located within Health, but again directing support back into the community rather than concentrating it in the traditional hospital setting. Similar findings in demographically diverse parts of England suggested that the true incidence of non-organic failure to thrive was spread quite evenly across socio-economic groups, cultures, and across urban and rural areas.

It became apparent that existing services were primarily only able to respond to failure to thrive with a medical cause. Professionals were not always recognising, identifying or necessarily understanding non-organic failure to thrive (Hampton 1995). Parental concerns and anxieties were not always being understood or taken seriously. The traditional screening model was allowing one third of children with non-organic failure to thrive to remain undetected.

Worryingly the social class of a family might influence professional response. Children diagnostically described as 'small' were more likely to be from two-parent, home-owning households, with at least one parent in employment (Batchelor and Kerslake 1990). However, there might not be a full medical consideration of whether family history and percentile-derived weight or height indicators suggested genetically predisposed or innate smallness. Children from a deprived socio-economic background would be more likely to have the label non-organic failure to thrive applied, but carrying with it the inference of concerns, and the suggestion of either neglectful or even abusive parenting. In no more than five per cent of children with non-organic failure to thrive would there be a need to use a child-protection process to overcome parental resistance to change or to combat clear-cut neglect, or emotional abuse through wilful omission or parental psychological disturbance (Wright and Talbot 1996). The use of a child-protection framework would still only be beneficial if the appropriate support services also existed to contribute to the assessment and treatment process.

The reasons for non-organic failure to thrive are numerous. On the one hand we have a fuller understanding of the child's physiological development towards independent feeding and acquiring the preference for a balanced adult diet, within the child's own family and cultural norms. On the other hand we better understand the interactive process between parents and children, and how a child's progress with eating and nourishment can be either facilitated or blocked by more or less appropriate parental responses (Harris and Booth 1992; Hampton 1996).

As a core human activity eating is central to the human experience, and significant within family life. Psycho-dynamic thinking focuses on the early symbiosis between a parent and breast- or bottle-fed infant which potentially meets all the baby's physiological and emotional security needs. The infant goes on to develop self-awareness and explores the distinction between self and carer. The subtleties around mouth, eye and hand sensation and grip, plus object-relatedness and internalisation within the carer–child attachment, are significant. An emotionally distant, unaffirming or critically directive parenting style may have major consequences for the developing infant. We need to recognise the power of the past in conditioning parental responses in the present. In social learning terms we can see how a cycle of tension or rejection may develop between child and carer. If early bonding and attachment are impaired then there may be a greater likelihood of this happening. The positive rapport between child and carer can be undermined if feeding becomes unrewarding. The focus on parent–child interaction enables one to draw from a whole body of work which assesses the nature of parent–child attachment and relationship patterns, through careful and methodical observation and analysis. The work of Iwaniec (1983) in developing formats for this has been significant. The work of Briggs (1997) is also notable in its use of psycho-dynamic child-observation methods.

Human evolution has left infants physiologically both self-regulating (having a natural appetite for the calories they need for both energy and growth) but also neophobic (by nature wary of new food) (Harris and Johnson 1997). There appear to be two significant 'windows of opportunity', one for flavours at between 16 and 24 weeks, and a second for textures at around one year. The human feeding cycle is complex and depends on an integrated sequence of events requiring considerable nervous and muscular co-ordination. If acceptance of texture after one year is a problem together with slow ingestion, an oral-motor dysfunction may be present (Moores 1997). In respect of the developing chewing reflex, parents need to be aware that spitting out food is normal until their babies learn to control the tongue to enable chewing rather than sucking to take place (Harris and Johnson 1997). Weaning is a messy business and parental ability to tolerate this is significant in the introduction of finger foods, and in encouragement of exploration and self-feeding.

The Infant Support Group checklist (derived from Iwaniec, cited in Hampton 1995; Iwaniec, Herbert and McNeish 1985) is a useful guide to assessment. If feeding is to be encouraged we need to ask: How far is the carer aware in early infancy of the baby's internal body rhythms? How far is the carer able to recognise and respond to cues being given by the child? Is verbal or non-verbal pressure put on the child to eat? Is the food age-appropriate and what size portion is offered? How much or how little does the child eat? Is food held in the mouth and then repudiated? Is the child comfortably upright? Is the carer well placed to positively reinforce eating without creating pressure? Does the child eat with the rest of the family, and what are the seating arrangements? Is there any conversation during the meal (other than about food or eating)? Are there 'markers' to distinguish that meal-times are different from other times? How often is the child praised? (Hampton 1995).

Certain patterns characteristic of some children with non-organic failure to thrive have emerged from observation. Muted appetite may indicate prolonged use of milk feeds, which have diminishing nutritional appropriateness after six months, and avoidance of weaning. It may also result from too little variety of food being offered over time, perhaps with a lack of associated routine. Boys, rather than girls, tend to be selective eaters, and while a chocolate and chips-only diet may provide sufficient calories, it may still be seen as a social or pyschological problem. The media's emphasis on healthy eating has led to some parents lowering the essential fat content in their young children's diets with detrimental consequences. Depression may undermine a parent's capacity to encourage healthy eating. Not all studies detect a link with parental eating habits but the work of Russell et al. (1998) does indicate a specific link between some parents with anorexia and the under-feeding of their children.

In seeking to correct parents' misperceptions we need to avoid attributing blame. The priority is to work with what is maintaining the negative pattern. The search for a point of breakthrough may well involve giving the child due autonomy. Crucially it will also involve building parents' self-confidence and enhancing their problem-solving capability. The biggest challenge in helping parents to change is to find a link between their worldview and yours, so that they may become empowered to try out some new ideas. Parents' hopes, acknowledged as goals by the worker, can be realised through a series of agreements. A small initial breakthrough may pave the way for gains which may progressively transform the picture.

Developing the Feeding to Thrive Service in mid-Sussex

The project was born out of creative discussion between the Penn Crescent family centre staff group and the local health visiting team, via the co-ordinating community nurse advisor. Drawing from the relevant research and pioneering working models it was clear that existing local services to children failing to thrive and their parents/carers were inadequate, having been based on the traditional medical model of excluding physical illness, but failing to offer nutritional, behavioural, social or psychological insights to deal with feeding problems. The previous service was hospital-based, involving the expensive referral route to consultant paediatricians, often leading to tests which would be intrusive and traumatic for the child and the family. Poor overall outcomes resulted in only five per cent of children having specific physical problems. It was estimated that at least one child on each health visitor caseload per year would present with non-organic failure to thrive, resulting in 34 children per year locally not receiving adequate support or treatment. A range of short-, medium- and longer-term consequences can be cited if failure to thrive is not responded to quickly and some recovery growth achieved at the earliest possible time (Batchelor and Kerslake 1990).

Staff at the family centre already had an excellent track record of partnership with the local health visitor team as well as the locality social work office, leading to significant cross-fertilisation of ideas and skills. The appointment of a health visitor designated as a feeding specialist and with experience of offering a specialist infant nutrition support service, paved the way for the Feeding to Thrive Project to move ahead. We wanted to enhance the capacity of local health visiting colleagues to operate a fully effective screen for non-organically failing to thrive children, and to be able to offer the relevant supportive guidance to both families and GPs. Social workers locally also needed to think about their preconceived ideas from working with some very deprived families with a non-organic failure to thrive component, and to review this in the wider context of knowledge and thinking, in particular how to create a supportive climate for change.

A project development steering group drew in a locality social work manager, the community nursing advisor, the family centre manager, the health visitor with the feeding specialism, the community paediatrician and, in an advisory capacity, a senior clinical psychologist and a senior dietician. Speech and language therapists were progressively consulted. The project's service group consisted of the six family centre staff members together with the specialist health visitor. The service would be offered as a home visiting outreach service, but it was also expected that the skills and insights gained would be applied beyond the project, to work taking place in the family centre. Some families would avail themselves of both. Collective evaluation by the project team of the observed data or video recordings of meal-times would be a central feature of the approach. The service was provided on a part-time basis from existing staffing resources. The only additional costs were in year one, associated with start-up and funding the audit.

Working practices and evaluation objectives

The criteria for referral by GPs and health visitors for the Mid-Sussex Feeding to Thrive Project were for children between six months and three and a half years for whom:

- weight is below second centile
- weight has fallen through two or more centiles
- weight has fallen steadily over three months
- there are feeding and behavioural problems associated with falling percentiles.

It was felt important to ensure that those children whose weight was tracking below the second centile, but who may be genetically and innately predisposed for it to do so should not become a focus of unnecessary concern. Weight centiles alone are therefore insufficient. Amplified percentile charts (Wright 1996) help to determine whether failure to thrive is moderate or severe. 'Thrive lines' (Cole 1998) assist in determining true failure to thrive, in particular in the first year of life where weighing intervals have been spaced at one month apart. All local health visitors were given training in recognising and responding to failure to thrive so that only children with significant non-organic failure to thrive would be referred to the service.

In developing the approach it was important to match standards to working practices. Each child needed to meet the referral criteria and the referral to be consented to by parents. Copies of the percentile information from birth for weight, length and head circumference were made available for the project prime worker and team. The initial engagement between the prime worker, child and family initiated assessment on a partnership basis and the range of feeding problems could be identified and acknowledged.

A series of tools were used to assist the family in identifying and making changes to the feeding problems including discussion, observations of meal-times, and parent–child interaction using both checklists and, by consent, video. Weekly review meetings were undertaken by the wider team so that members could reflect on meanings and exchange ideas, and consider possible alternative approaches the family might agree to. These informal meetings also provided invaluable support for the prime workers.

A three-day food diary was obtained from the family at the outset by the prime worker so that the dietician could undertake a nutritional analysis and make recommendations. Where helpful a catch-up weight-gain target was recommended. The nutritional analysis was repeated at the end of the work.

Regular reviews were undertaken by the prime worker with the family to assess improvements and changes in the child's feeding patterns. These were recorded and included the continuing centile track of the child. The option to include another team member in the review process could be taken up, particularly in more complex situations.

The Children's Society's 'key indicators of improvement' checklist were incorporated so as to demonstrate the range of changes in the child's feeding and associated behaviour. This was supported by an evaluation of parents' satisfaction at six months and at the end of work. The approach tried from the start to enter into a genuine partnership with parents, recognising their anxieties, hopes and aims. It aimed to view the child holistically. It sought to seek and to measure specific concrete, observable change. It recognised that beyond mere improved nutrition and growth, and potential improvements in behaviour around eating or meal-times, there could be a major reduction in overall stress and trauma for child and family.

The service group worked with 21 families in its first year. While this represented a relatively small audit sample in one local neighbourhood, the outcomes were encouraging. The results of the audit reflect trends noted in early infancy nutrition support work elsewhere. The model of operation therefore seems valid. The benefits for the members of the service group acting as prime workers were considerable in developing their confidence in the validity of the approach. This saw the consolidation of new knowledge and skills and the cross-fertilisation of ideas and perceptions. This was evident from a multi-disciplinary perspective between the family centre workers, health visitor feeding specialist and dietician, who most regularly participated in the vital collective evaluation.

Audit and outcomes

During the audit period, 20 referrals were received and allocated within a week to a named outreach worker. This was fewer than expected and may be explained by the training received by every health visitor and social worker at the beginning of the audit, resulting in earlier recognition and treatment of failure to thrive. In consequence, those children referred had true failure to thrive complex disorders. Nine completed the programme, ten cases are still ongoing, and one child withdrawn by parents has since been fostered. Five months was the average contact time and the longest time was one year.

The following results are based on the nine children who completed the programme.

Every child's weight graph showed a halt to the falling weight pattern. Eight out of the nine children showed an improvement of weight on the centile. Calorie intake and number of different foods taken increased. Four children and their parents had exhibited behavioural problems and anxiety around meal-times at referral. These were all resolved. Four children had all their feeding problems resolved, while four had reduced their problems between 30 and 75 per cent, with one remaining unchanged. Of all nine families, at the end of work only one parent still had feeding problem behaviour but this had decreased by 80 per cent. None of the children was referred to hospital for physical testing.

Parental satisfaction questionnaires were given to the families at the end of work. They showed that all nine families were satisfied with all aspects of the prime worker's care, though two parents were unsure of the necessity of the service at the beginning. By the end they said that they were grateful for their prime worker's help, and any anxiety at the outset had been allayed by the quick response of the service. Benefits were greater parental confidence, reassurance, lessening of anxiety, new nutritional information, neutrality, a realisation of how cultural differences can affect growth charts, and pleasure at their children's weight gain. Things parents had found hard in working with the service included 'sticking with it', 'taking on board new advice' and 'dealing with initial guilt feelings'. All the parents recommended the service.

Failure to thrive remains undoubtedly a complex disorder. The new service has been able to improve the nutrition and growth of the children and reduce the levels of anxiety around meal-times. The project has proved rewarding to families and the Feeding to Thrive team, both of whom enjoyed the partnership approach. The service has been successfully integrated into existing caseloads with the desired addition of support from a dietician whose accurate calculation of calorie intake proved invaluable in assessing outcomes. This audit has demonstrated that a co-ordinated multi-disciplinary and multi-skilled approach to the management of failure to thrive is clearly beneficial to the children and families and is effective with the minimum amount of medical intervention.

Case study

This case history concerns a family with more complex problems than most of the users of the early Feeding to Thrive Project. It is given with the consent of both parents and names have been changed. The feeding input was a major part of a range of complementary initiatives to support and enhance the parenting of two-year-old Anita whose name was put on the child protection register under neglect, following a police protection order.

The circumstances of Anita's birth could not have been more adverse. The parents of her mother, Lesley, both died separately and suddenly while Lesley was in hospital for bed rest because of concern about poor placental nourishment. The next day Anita was born by caesarian section five weeks early and transferred to special care. Lesley attended the double funeral of her parents just a few days later.

Lesley was reflective and open about both her family background and her parenting of Anita. As a child, Lesley suffered from severe asthma and she felt her mother was over-protective and limiting of her activities. Her mother would blame her over any disagreement and would emotionally disconnect and retreat to watch TV. Lesley had a warmer relationship with her father. She remembers him making her a beautiful dolls' house, and feeling warm and safe while he read to her. He would not challenge her mother. The overall emotional tone in the family was rather flat. When she was ten Lesley spent some years at a residential school for delicate children, a bleak experience. Lesley's older brother, in common with some other members of the maternal family, became alcoholic in later life. Lesley was a heavy cannabis user, and some months after Anita's birth started to use heroin.

Anita's father, Brett, also a heroin user, had an unhappy childhood. His older sister died when he was three. Another sister died at one week old. Brett's mother had a major breakdown after losing two daughters and he spent some months with his grandparents. Another sister was born later. Brett feels he was always treated differently and his sister was spoilt while he was rejected. He was scared of his father's violence and he remembers a time when his father smashed up the house. His mother tried to reassure him by saying that his father was doing this so he would not hit her, which showed that he really loved her. As Brett had already been hit by his father, he thought this meant that his father did not love him and that he was 'just like a piece of furniture'.

By seven months, the health visitor was becoming increasingly concerned at Anita's progressively tailing off weight profile. Lesley began seeing a community psychiatric nurse and was prescribed sleeping tablets and anti-depressants. There was also involvement with the substance misuse team. The material condition of the home was giving concern. At eight months a paediatrician said Anita was small but healthy, indicating no readily observable organic problem, but the weight recorded in the paediatric clinic was aberrantly high compared with the health visitor record. Precisely the same scenario recurred at 14 months.

At this time the family started at the family centre on the day programme, although the father managed only spasmodic attendance. On Anita's first visit it was observed that she was not appropriately dressed for a cold day. Her hair was very sparse, and her nose, hands and feet were red. Her skin was in part mottled with a bluish tone, and in part had a translucent look. Her body was very thin and her stomach markedly protruding. She was unused to a feeder cup, having only been used to taking fluids through a bottle with a teat. She ate very little, although she was offered finger food as an alternative to being fed. Anita was mobile and actively climbed. She did not vocalise very much. Her arms were outstretched to all adults. She often assumed a curious fixed grin expression when in eye contact with adults. The attachment between mother and child seemed on first impression to be quite weak.

In looking at Anita's growth record it was recognised that she had suffered poor placental nourishment and was born about one month premature. Nevertheless she achieved a recovery weight gain trend in the early weeks in special care and when first bottle-fed at home, at eight weeks, to half way between the second and ninth centiles. It is legitimate to recognise this is a significant baseline figure, reinforced by there being a length over weight correlation. Thereafter Anita's weight had tailed away progressively throughout her first year of life to a position worryingly well below 0.4 centile. All weight plots in the first year took into account her prematurity.

Had the Feeding to Thrive Service been in operation earlier the health visitor would have received the extra training input which would have enhanced her ability to be confident in viewing Anita as clearly failing to thrive. When the family centre discussed its concerns with field social work colleagues, the paediatric diagnosis remained a powerful influence. Nevertheless it was decided to begin a comprehensive assessment. Coincidentally the police intervention precipitated a child-protection process, giving a very clear framework in which to work. This meant establishing an enduring partnership between parents, senior social work practitioner (child protection keyworker), family heath visitor and Feeding to Thrive/family centre prime worker. Encouragingly both parents accepted the need to make changes and work at things and this contributed to a viable long-term partnership which was able to surmount variations in mood and inevitable setbacks.

Lesley had not seen herself as becoming a parent prior to her pregnancy with Anita. She lacked contact with family or friends with young children, and faced with her own huge loss, she struggled to understand Anita's needs. After the early months it became even harder. She was aware of her own lack of knowledge about child development, which undermined her confidence. Alongside heroin use she herself developed an eating disorder. She acknowledged her feeling of inertia, with a tendency to stay in bed, not to be able to maintain tidiness, and a huge lack of energy. Lesley felt that Brett was more experienced in parenting. It seemed that Brett could deliver some good parental input for Anita, but only in short bursts, needing space for his own preoccupations and pursuits.

Anita's referral to the Feeding to Thrive Service met its main criteria. Her progressive weight decline was over two centiles and was accompanied by many concerns about her physical appearance, as well as feeding problems. The Feeding to Thrive Support programme went through three stages. After the police protection order, Anita was initially, by agreement, in foster care. The first step was to help the foster carer establish a meal-time routine for Anita whom she saw as 'difficult to feed'. This involved an initial burst of nutrient-rich and high-energy milk feeds, followed by more emphasis on solid foods. We were prepared for Anita to suffer an initial further weight drop but this did not happen, and gradually some gain began to be made. Anita had contact time with her parents at the family centre and showed some distress on being returned to foster care. She began to come home for weekends, and then returned home.

Lesley's task was then to maintain and develop what the foster carer had begun. She was supported by her programme at the family centre and she also had the specialist Feeding to Thrive support at home. Anita had clearly been held on milk for too long and had a characteristically muted appetite. Also there was a very clear association between eating at home and having been in an understimulated and haphazard environment. When Lesley resumed feeding Anita at home a video was made and collectively analysed by the Feeding to Thrive Service team, and constructive feedback and encouragement given. Although Lesley might have been discouraged by Anita's wilful food-throwing and lack of interest in food, she was showing considerable patience in finding the right balance between praise and encouragement, and in seeking to reduce less desirable behaviour through planned ignoring and firmness. Despite her own lack of interest in food, she managed to prepare more appetising, high-calorie food in small incremental offerings and to tolerate mess. Her struggle was exemplified by a moment when Anita wanted to feed her with the finger food, and Lesley had to wrestle with her own feelings of distate, and continue to tolerate mess and allow Anita's exploration of food and self-feeding. It was for Lesley to decide which tactical suggestions, such as where best to position herself versus the high chair, or whether or not to have the TV on as a distraction, to use.

The Feeding to Thrive assessment summary produced by the prime worker at this time presented the interpretation of the history around Anita, her pattern of nutrition, and the results of the period of observation after work had begun. It included a baseline calculation of the average number of different foods Anita would accept at the start, and the calorie intake catch-up target set at between 30 per cent and 50 per cent above the normal requirement of a child of that age, to be used as a general yardstick (1300–1500 calories). The assessment summary led into a simple agreement, with Lesley and Brett's own goals set out, including their hopes that Anita would ultimately achieve recovery weight-gain to around the second centile, and that meal-times would become more rewarding.

When Lesley decided to detoxify and took Anita with her to a residential rehabilitation unit, the feeding programe, including use of video, was continued in partnership with unit staff. Lesley made a significant breakthrough, achieving an amazing transition from apparent anorexia, to having a good appetite, interest in food and in her own appearance, although sometimes finding it hard to put Anita's needs before her own. She was open about her struggles to give Anita sustained stimulation, positive attention, and a consistent response. Anita benefited from the social setting at the unit, making strides with speech and language, and with a more spontaneous response to adults. Then Lesley left the unit abruptly and returned to Brett, resuming heroin use. However, she persevered with the positive feeding approach for Anita, with Brett's support. Gradually Anita eased up towards the second centile, eating well and behaving well at meal-times.

Nevertheless Lesley was troubled when Anita was wilful and attention seeking. It was decided to use the Parent–Child Game approach (see Chapter 3) alongside the final stage of the Feeding to Thrive support. Lesley showed commitment to the weekly Parent–Child Game. It demanded high concentration in the controlled conditions of the family centre's video suite, with supportive prompting through an earpiece. Lesley's parenting style was not overtly critical, but was somewhat passive, and sometimes directive. She crucially needed to learn the skill of attending verbally to show Anita she was interested, and to use more praise and encouragement for play, as she had for meal-times. Lesley saw for herself that Anita's concentration and imaginative play increased with positive attention. She went on to achieve a really positive rapport with her daughter.

Feeding to Thrive work on behalf of Anita came to a formal end when Anita had maintained her position at just below the second centile for a consistent six weeks, a successful outcome. In terms of enduring gains, the picture is encouraging. Anita's name remains on the child protection register, but this was directly related to a temporary dip in weight during Lesley's second pregnancy. When challenged, the couple's positive response and Anita's recovery was swift. Anita became more difficult and demanding when the baby was born needing special care and her mother went off to the hospital daily. Lesley asked for some video refresher sessions in relating to both children at once, and these seemed helpful.

It is clear that both Feeding to Thrive and the Parent–Child Game paid off for Lesley and Anita. This happened within the containing framework of the child-protection process. The partnership between the family, social work keyworker, health visitor and family centre worker (who remained a constant throughout) gave reliable and consistent support, providing the concerned and containing 'mothering' which both parents had missed in their childhood. As Lesley herself said, what helped most was her worker's support in 'sticking with it at times when it all seemed so hopeless'. The outcome for Anita in nutritional and emotional terms was positive, and Lesley's gains in insight were continuing.

Acknowledgements

To the contribution of Anne Kyle, health visitor and feeding specialist, Haywards Heath, and Madeleine St. Clair, manager of the clinical evaluation team at the princess Royal Hospital, Haywards Heath.

Further Reading

Douglas, J. (1989) *Behaviour Problems in Young Children*. London: Routledge.

PART 3

Managing the Work
of a Family Centre

Chapter 11

Management Issues in Creating a Therapeutic Environment

Christine Stones

Introduction

Family centres have been categorised in a number of different ways. The various attempts are a response to the diversity found among centres. Most classification systems distinguish between centres with a community development orientation and those with a therapeutic focus. For example Downie and Forshaw (1987) suggest a twofold classification:

1. neighbourhood-based community centres with an open, community work orientation

2. centres for selected families, not open to all, with specific 'treatment' plans for individual families.

Holman (1988) provides three groupings:

1. client-focused model

2. neighbourhood model

3. community development model.

Some neighbourhood-based centres seek to combine both therapeutic and community development work. Although this chapter is written from the perspective of managing such a neighbourhood centre, many of the issues will apply to all centres concerned with therapeutic work.

Description of the centre

New Fulford Family Centre serves two outer city estates in Bristol. The population is in the region of 22,000 and thus the size of a small town, but the area enjoys few of the resources that a small town would enjoy. Barnardo's established the family centre in 1984 with the aid of central government start-up funding. The centre is now financed by Barnardo's with a proportion of funding being provided by the local authority, Bristol City Council.

The aim of the centre is to facilitate opportunities for growth and development for children under five and their parents, and where appropriate to prevent children needing to be looked after by the local authority. This aim leads to a number of detailed objectives which include:

- challenging abuse and violence in families
- promoting children's rights
- aiding the functioning of families
- enhancing individual strengths
- promoting self-help
- increasing community strength and development
- relieving isolation and stress.

As the list indicates, the focus of the family centre's work encompasses the individual, the family and the community. In order to achieve its aim the centre provides a range of services. Some would be clearly categorised as therapeutic, e.g. play therapy and individual counselling. Other activities do not directly involve a therapeutic approach, e.g. drop-ins, holidays and outings.

Implications of context

There are a number of potential advantages of a neighbourhood centre base for therapeutic approaches. These include:

- Acceptability – a neighbourhood family centre with an open-door policy can reduce stigmatisation.
- Accessibility – a neighbourhood base can make therapeutic services to families more easily accessible. Counselling services are often scarce and those provided are often based in the centre of a town or city.

- Addressing a family's varied needs – parents and children in need of therapeutic help are frequently struggling with other issues such as financial or housing difficulties, lack of safe play space or isolation.

- Sources of support – open-door centres are in a good position for engaging families with a range of strengths and vulnerabilities and this can enhance the possibility of support from within the neighbourhood for families experiencing the most difficulties.

These potential advantages are not automatically realised. A neighbourhood-based centre with an open-door policy can be more complex than a context solely devoted to a therapeutic approach. Neighbourhood family centres with their multi-faceted composition offer the possibility of synergy, i.e. the combination of the multiple elements creating more than a simple sum of the parts. But, it could be argued that there is also a possibility that the differing elements detract from the efficacy of each other with the risk that the combination is less than the sum of the parts. The management challenge is to maximise the therapeutic opportunities of the whole centre and recognise the treatment potential of the total establishment rather than just specific interventions.

Significant elements in a family centre setting

The elements I would like to examine are:

- the staff team
- the families using the centre and relationships within the centre
- the physical resources
- the programme of services/activities
- competing needs
- the wider organisation
- the external environment.

The staff team

The staff team is the most central influence on the therapeutic nature of a family centre. It can by the effectiveness of its functioning either facilitate or impede therapeutic processes. Brown and Clough (1989, p.197), reflecting on their collection of papers on life and work in day and residential centres, comment on how the contributions make it clear

> that the quality, style and composition of the staff group (race and gender balance, range of skills and personal attributes) is the main determinant of centre climate and culture, and that it is a long hard struggle to establish a truly facilitative environment.

The manager carries particular responsibility for promoting this facilitative environment. Two significant means of fulfilling this responsibility are the supervision of individual staff combined with attention to the staff team as a group. Hawkins and Shohet (1989) point out some of the complexities of the supervisory task.

Many analytic and psycho-therapeutic writers have used maternal care as the paradigm for the therapeutic relationship. Bowlby (1988, p.140) writes of the therapist as providing the patient with a secure base:

> this is a role very similar to that described by Winnicott as 'holding' and by Bion as 'containing'...the therapist's role is analogous to that of a mother who provides her child with a secure base from which to explore the world.

So family centre staff hold individuals and families in mind just as the good-enough parent not only holds the child physically but also mentally. Supervision is an important aid for supporting that holding and should provide a space where, among other things, a member of staff can think about and make sense of their interactions with the service-users. Supervision provides the place where a member of staff can integrate thinking and feeling with doing. The most basic of factors should not be overlooked such as availability, reliability and lack of interruption. Managers harassed by numerous responsibilities or preoccupied by a particular crisis may forget these most fundamental principles of good practice.

In supervision, issues of transference and counter-transference can be examined. The nature of family centre work means that many of the parents engaging in the centre's therapeutic services are likely to have experienced abusive and neglectful childhoods. Often they may be facing severe difficulties in parenting their own children. Transference and counter-transference can be particularly complex.

Comments, by Preston-Shoot and Agass (1990, p.168), about social workers apply equally to much work within a family centre: 'regardless of whether or not social workers see themselves as "therapists" they cannot escape the profound emotional or psychological impact that their clients are bound to have on them.'

Centre workers need time to examine the content and process of coun selling or therapy sessions to increase their effectiveness. Failure to attend to underlying dynamics can lead to 'distorted perceptions and bias; acting out of unexpressed feelings; impaired communication; blurring of facts, feelings and opinions; ignoring information; inadequate analysis; untested assumptions; action based on personal agendas, and polarization of professional networks' (Morrison 1997, p.200).

A crucial source of effectiveness for a family centre pursuing therapeutic aims is the ability of the staff to function as an effective group. If the different elements of family centre life are to combine together synergistically then the staff team must work collaboratively. This latter function includes attending to the processes of the staff group, recognising the maintenance needs of the team as well as both aspects of the task and the individual needs of each team member. It is necessary to set aside sufficient time for the staff to focus together on their shared task and to building the team.

Different workers providing services for the same family requires close co-operation. Individuals or families struggling to undertake hard and often painful work may employ unconscious strategies such as avoidance, projection or splitting. Communication between staff undertaking different pieces of work with the family is essential. Frequently, meetings to plan the work and review progress will involve the family as well, but sometimes staff will need to meet separately to clarify or reflect on issues particularly those arising from their co-working relationship. In addition to differences of race, gender, age and experience, a team will contain workers holding varied models and perspectives and demonstrating divergent styles of working. Such diversity offers richness to a centre's operation but also carries the potential for fragmentation and conflict.

At New Fulford we have found it particularly valuable to hold 'closed days' when in-depth planning and reviewing can take place and also important issues of team-functioning can be explored. The effective working of any group requires processes such as the development of trust and the handling of conflict. Roles within the group and attitudes to others' roles may both need exploring. Wider influences, such as society's estimation of different roles, can subtly influence individual esteem and a team's functioning.

The staff team did some team-building exercises with an external consultant. This included self-positioning on a line representing status. Staff whose responsibilities focused on the children's needs or community development work viewed colleagues primarily engaged in adult therapeutic work as possessing higher status. This exercise enabled the team to identify the factors contributing to these views and explore the effects both on the individual staff and on team-functioning.

A variety of models and exercises are available to assist in team-building and development. Sometimes work within the team is aided by an external trainer or consultant; this frees the manager to participate more fully and can help highlight issues within the team which the manager and other staff are either avoiding or failing to recognise.

The families using the centre and relationships within the centre

Many writers have commented on the fact that users of family centres are predominantly white women. Most centres need to give thought to how both men and black users are enabled to take up centre services. Both groups are likely to be particularly under-represented as users of therapeutic provision. In seeking to offer services to black users, managers and staff need to examine whether their approaches are Eurocentric. A study of the use of family centres by black families found that counselling and group-based parent programmes were among the services least attended by black users (Butt and Box 1998).

> A support group for black and multi-racial families at New Fulford Family Centre was well attended. However, staff became very aware that black users rarely accessed other groups or individual or family counselling. A black student undertook a survey with black and multi-racial families to obtain their views on how the centre's services could be more accessible to them.

The combination of families using a centre is obviously a significant influence on the culture created within a centre. A neighbourhood centre may have a large number of users accessing the centre for varied services. A centre mainly focusing on treatment may have a smaller total community of users. The degree to which a centre works with its users in groups will influence the opportunity for users to interact with each other. Where users are seen primarily within the context of individual or family work, other users may still have influence but this may often be more through fantasy and projection rather than direct interaction.

The image of the centre may be an over-emphasis of one feature or a distortion of certain aspects. Staff need to stay aware of how a neighbourhood centre is viewed as its image can be a powerful factor influencing both referral agencies and the engagement of families newly referred for services.

A health visitor expressed hesitancy in referring a parent to a group as a previous user of the centre had told her that the centre users encouraged people to go shoplifting. This reputation had developed from two unfortunate incidents involving a small minority of centre users.

The characteristics of a centre may alter over a period as the overall group composition changes. A few dominant users can have a crucial impact on the culture of the centre at any one time. The degree to which the overall environment of the centre is therapeutic will be affected by the culture and the staff team needs to work with users on values and other issues. Some form of user committee, which is made up of representatives of the centre, can be a central vehicle for this work. New Fulford Family Centre has a parents' council that is composed of representatives of each centre group. The council meets regularly and once a month a joint meeting is held with the staff group. These meetings cover a wide range of issues and provide a vital forum for addressing the culture of the centre and inter-group dynamics.

Staff had been made aware of two separate incidents where users had been distressed by personal information about them being shared by other parents more widely than they had wanted. In one instance this appeared to have been 'gossiping' and in other a group member sharing concern about another centre user's serious illness. These events highlighted for staff how a context where users belong to different centre groups and have varied local networks creates a complex milieu for pursuing confidentiality. A joint meeting was used to look at some of the intricacies involved. This was achieved by producing a series of scenarios focusing on issues of confidentiality. The meeting was divided into small groups to look at each scenario and suggest appropriate action. It was then suggested that similar discussions should be held in each centre group.

As indicated earlier, one of the advantages of undertaking therapeutic work within a neighbourhood centre is the potential for families to have a range of different strengths and vulnerabilities. Families under less stress can provide support for those who are particularly vulnerable.

Physical resources

The building and equipment are obvious factors in creating an environment conducive to therapeutic work. At a most basic level, the style and state of a building and the care taken of it are perceived by users as communicating something about the agency's views of the users. Fulford Family Centre was initially housed in three hard-to-let flats. Although the flats were transformed internally and the outside redecorated it was difficult to make the overall building appear attractive. On moving to a splendid purpose-built centre (and adding 'New' to our title), a number of families started using the centre for the first time. One of the parents said, 'I didn't come to your old centre. I thought it was just for problem families.' Another family centre user, commenting on the local housing and social services office, a building surrounded by barbed wire and appearing like a fortress, said, 'It's not very respectful to local people.'

It is well recognised that colours affect moods; in choosing decor, thought can be given to the appropriate hues for different activities.

Centres running very varied activities may find a number of challenges in managing the use of their building. Problems can arise both in terms of pressure on accommodation and conflict between differing uses. Shortage of space is stressful for both staff and users and needs addressing by a manager. The manager may sometimes be the only member of staff to have their own space and so may not personally experience the pressure and tensions of competing for limited rooms and working in cramped conditions. Staff commitment to users and services may result in them experiencing stressful working conditions for some time before making their complaints known vociferously.

> Fulford Family Centre was housed for 12 years in hard-to-let flats owned by the local authority. During the first six years the centre expanded in numbers of users, activities and staff. Various imaginative efforts were made to use every inch of available space. The pressure on staff was not fully recognised by immediate and senior managers until the team, highly committed to social work training, refused to take students any more.

Simple tools like room booking sheets are vital in a busy centre to ensure space is used effectively and activities are accommodated appropriately. Clear room signs indicating that a room is engaged are essential in protecting therapeutic space and creating a sense of safety. Using rooms for dual purposes can make appropriate protection much harder and where lack of space makes this unavoidable, thought needs to be given and time taken to create an appropriate environment before sessions start.

> Pressure on the play therapy room at certain times of day resulted in a member of staff needing to use a small play room for therapeutic work with one child. The room was usually used for crèches and contact visits. This meant a number of different workers and families had access to the room and consistency in its appearance was not a priority for most users. Before the play therapy session, the worker needed to spend additional time preparing the room to ensure that its layout and contents were reasonably constant from week to week.

Locating very different activities in close proximity can lead to problems. Thus providing counselling for a very distressed parent in the room next to an informal group meeting from which loud laughter emanates can be very distracting and intrusive. External noise may also result in the therapeutic space feeling unsafe. Such factors are not always apparent when designing a building or allocating activities.

> Fulford's Play Therapy room is located next to a tea station used by staff and volunteers. Staff can often forget that a session may be taking place next door and their lively conversation can intrude. The tea station sink outlet combines with the play therapy sink drain and staff washing up in the kitchen can cause a disconcerting gurgling in the play therapy sink. This extraneous noise can be particularly distracting to children feeling anxious or unsafe in their play therapy session.

The programme of services and activities

It is useful to consider the type of services needed for a family centre to be effective, while also exploring the possibilities for creating a combination of services for individual families. Experience at Fulford leads us to advocate a range of services. It is difficult to find a simple categorisation of services as they vary in terms of their focus, their context and their content. Thus a group context can have very different objectives; a group may aim to change intrapersonal, interpersonal or environmental factors. At the same time some similar aims may be pursued within the context of individual counselling or family play sessions. Fulford's programme includes:

- Services where the context for work is the individual or family – play therapy, individual counselling, couple counselling, family play sessions, risk assessments, welfare rights advice.
- Services where the context for the work is a group – parent support groups, carer and toddler groups, parenting group, educational or skills groups, community development groups.

This range both allows for individual difference in terms of type of family needs and difference in terms of scale of need. Some brief vignettes of families, below, will illustrate this point.

Anthea

Anthea was sexually abused as a child by her step-father and various other men. She spent a significant amount of her adolescence in the care of the local authority. She was parenting her young son fairly well, but was increasingly distressed by the memories of her abuse and anxious that her care of her son would deteriorate. She sought individual counselling and gradually over many months her distress abated and her confidence in her parenting increased. She only received a counselling service.

Valerie

Valerie's children had been removed following sexual abuse. Valerie had participated to a limited extent in this abuse. She had left her husband and was referred to Fulford following her arrival in the area with a child from a new partnership. The child was on the child protection register and work was requested in assessing the risks to the little girl. Work was undertaken with both Valerie and her partner, Zak. A detailed assessment looked at factors in each parent and the relationship between them. Their attitudes to the past abuse and their understanding and ability to protect their present and any future children were examined. The couple were new to the area and had no friends and limited social skills. They were encouraged to attend parent/child groups and parent support groups at the centre.

Holly

Holly was a lone parent with two children, the elder of whom suffered from a life-threatening illness. Holly was isolated and her own childhood had been full of separation and loss. William, the younger child, had an insecure attachment to his mother. Observation revealed that Holly found her son's sobbing very difficult. But she also welcomed the evidence that her absence was distressing and therefore her presence was important. This boosted her fragile self-esteem. Her behaviour maintained the insecure attachment. Counselling enabled some links to be made between Holly's childhood and her parenting behaviour. The transference demonstrated Holly's experiences of mismanaged separations and unresolved losses. The worker's consistency and dependability were vital and frequently challenged. William was given individual sessions parallel to his mother's counselling and the worker held William physically and by words and behaviour demonstrated her understanding of his anxiety and his anger. Family play sessions were also provided where Holly and William's interactions could be observed and Holly could be helped to change some of her behaviour. Holly's material circumstances were difficult and housing and financial problems were tackled through welfare rights advice. Holly was encouraged to attend a parent support group to lessen her isolation. This only became possible once counselling had addressed some of Holly's profound fears of abandonment and rejection.

The above case studies illustrate how a range of activities can provide the opportunity to work concurrently on different systems affecting a family's functioning and thus increase the factors targeting change.

The manager and staff team need to regularly review the family centre programme to ensure that it is balanced, coherent and offering the activities needed to achieve the centre's aims for users. It could be easy for regular activities to be maintained without exploring their effectiveness or for new services to be instigated without examining their impact on other parts of the overall programme. It is also important to consider the effect on individual users of different combinations of programme elements. The contribution of the 'spaces' between the formal programme elements cannot be ignored. The nature of a family centre is such that there are numerous interactions between users and between staff and users which are not 'timetabled' but either contribute to or detract from the therapeutic effects of a programme.

Competing needs

A varied programme, differing needs within and between families and finite resources provide the opportunities for competition and conflict.

There can be tensions between the needs of different family members, which have implications for the therapeutic work. Working with children and parents separately can raise issues of where to carry out that work. The child's needs and the parent's needs may be in conflict. Thus a child with an insecure attachment may find it very distressing to be separated from their parent for more than a very short space of time while therapeutic work with the parent may require uninterrupted sessions. Therapeutic work with a parent may recognise their need to regress but family centre staff will also be aware of the children's needs for a functioning adult to provide care for them. Staff undertaking therapeutic work with parents in a family centre setting are often faced with the arduous question of whether work with a particular parent can facilitate change within a timescale that meets their children's needs for 'good-enough' parenting.

A range of activities can also increases the potential for tension and conflict between services and sometimes between staff or between different groups of users.

High levels of need can easily result in competition for finite and sometimes scarce resources. In a centre undertaking both community development and therapeutic work this can sometimes lead to tension between approaches and staff representing those approaches. Recognising the source of the tension is important and accepting as appropriate individual staff or groups of users championing their services can be helpful. Obviously what is needed is an atmosphere where staff and users can advocate for their activity but also listen to the competing needs of other groups. This can be particularly difficult for users whose daily lives are often circumscribed by insufficient resources. Fantasies about and resentment towards other groups can easily be aroused. Some examples from New Fulford of inter-group rivalries and tensions have been given elsewhere (Stones 1989, 1994).

Some of the pressures on managers of social welfare services, in common with other services, are those of value for money and effectiveness. These are important principles, which would be hard to refute. However, they can lead to a simplistic notion that throughput is a priority and thus short-term approaches must be pursued. This is sometimes appropriate and efficacious, but sometimes the therapeutic task requires a long time and seeking to speed it up is counter-productive. Klein (1987, p.397) puts this powerfully:

> It is important not to be in too much of a hurry when faced with error or delusion or distress or disintegration. People come to therapy unready for a direct encounter with their deeper anxieties. If they had been ready, they would have faced them and contained them. When, encouraged by an unwise therapist or friend, they are made to drop the defences they need before they are strong enough to integrate new insights, they will awake the terror which has always surrounded this split-off part, a terror which includes the terror of disintegrating altogether. They will then tighten up more than ever, yet feel obscurely shamed and weakened by a sense of having failed to perform as expected.

The wider organization

Menzies (1970) drew attention to the role of socially structured defence mechanisms in the culture, structures and procedures of organisations. This occurs both within the micro-organization of the family centre and the wider establishment in which it is located. De Board (1978, p.143) points out that:

> Social defence systems evolve to meet a real need, the need to reduce anxiety. However, because these systems rapidly become institutionalised, it means that newcomers must adapt to them and have little chance to modify or contribute to them. For them, they are inappropriate and so they not only fail to temporarily reduce anxiety, but also can even cause it.

Large organizations' detailed policies and some managers' over-concern with attention to the finer points of policies and procedures can be understood in terms of such defences. Two areas of family centre work and working context, which clearly raise anxiety for both workers and managers, are child protection and health and safety. Both are issues for which most childcare organizations will have meticulous policies and procedures. Morrison (1997, p.210) applying Menzies' research and other insights to the management of child-protection work points out:

> Plainly there are no quick fixes or standardized remedies for the complex emotional turbulence of child protection work. What is clear, however, is that such processes are best understood as a triangular interaction involving agency, clients and workers. As such, the question is not whether organizations should be concerned for their emotional health but how to grow healthy organizational environments.

Parton (1998, p.23) reflecting on the emergence in child welfare policy and practice of an over-emphasis on assessment and management of risk argues for recognition of 'the central and pervasive concerns related to uncertainty and ambiguity'. He asserts, 'a commitment to uncertainty opens up creativity and novel ways of thinking which are in danger of being lost in a climate obsessed with concerns about risk, its assessment, monitoring and management.' Such a commitment values the professional judgement of workers as well as the careful adherence to organisational procedures.

The external environment

Systems theory reminds us that an organization is a living system in interaction with its wider environment. This requires essential work to be undertaken at the boundaries of the organization in order to maintain it in a state of dynamic equilibrium with its environment. This can be seen to be the responsibility primarily of the manager. A number of different forces are at work at the boundary and lead to several demands on the manager. They include factors essential to the very survival of a family centre. Among other external relationships, most centres must pay particular attention to:

- funding and funders
- referring agencies
- a complex network of other professionals and agencies.

There can be tensions between funding issues and the nature and content of therapeutic work. The tension may vary according to the type of funding. Thus public authorities may, as indicated earlier, want increased effectiveness in terms of more centre users and thus shorter interventions. There may be pressure only to engage in short-term work and solely to utilise models that support time-limited work.

Funding from voluntary organizations or raised from the private sector may carry requests for case studies of families or opportunities to observe the centre at work. A family centre manager may need to spend time explaining to funding partners the nature of the work and the inappropriateness of many forms of publicity. At the same time, in order to ensure good relationships with funders they may need to identify ways of both meeting their needs and protecting family centre users. If publicity requests are presented to users it is vital to help them think through the potential implications of participating in media or other interviews and to assist them in developing strategies for coping with questions.

> Amy volunteered to respond to a request from the local radio station to be interviewed about how the family centre had assisted her and her family. When she heard the recorded interview on the radio she realised that the interviewer's sympathetic questioning had resulted in her forgetting that the interview would be broadcast and probably heard by neighbours and friends. Subsequently she regretted her openness about her depression and family difficulties.

Centre managers will usually carry responsibility for regular liaison with referring agencies. This requires clarity about criteria for referrals including basic details such as catchment area, age of children and focus and methods of work. Referring agencies need to be informed of any significant changes in a centre's programme or in work allocation. It is also important in some areas of work to negotiate an agreement or contract with the referrer as well as the family. This particularly applies to situations such as a centre carrying out assessments for a referrer. In such a context clarity about what and how information concerning the work is shared is vital.

A family centre is part of a complex network of other professionals and agencies. Multi-agency work is not easy and joint work with colleagues from other agencies can be challenging. Families under stress may uses unconscious strategies such as splitting in their relationships with professional workers. Non-statutory workers in a voluntary agency family centre may find themselves viewed as the 'good parents' while the local authority social workers are the target for anger and criticism. This can be a seductive process and can be compounded by differences between agency perspectives. Misunderstandings and disagreements between workers from different agencies can easily arise and require a commitment from staff in different settings to respect each other's practice while also being willing to explore conflicting views.

Key features of the manager's role

In conclusion and summary, a few aspects of the manager's role can be highlighted as particularly significant in a centre undertaking therapeutic work:

1. Supporting and challenging individual staff in their varied roles

2. Facilitating staff in their work as a team

3. Holding together the various strands of work.

1. Supporting and challenging individual staff in their varied roles

This requires recognition of the contribution which each member of staff makes as important to the quality of the therapeutic services. The welcome which users receive from the receptionist, the care and attention given to cleaning and cooking, and the maintenance of the building and equipment, each influence the facilitative environment. A manager has responsibility for ensuring that appropriate standards are maintained in all aspects of centre services.

As the previous sections have indicated, in a neighbourhood family centre many staff will be involved in varied and demanding roles. The manager carries responsibility for supporting staff in fulfilling appropriate roles and moving between different roles. This movement between disparate roles can be difficult for both staff and users and the manager needs to support staff in identifying the difficulties and wherever possible overcoming them. Careful timing of activities and acknowledgement of the stresses for both users and staff in managing different roles and relationships are fundamental tasks.

A manager also carries responsibility for protecting staff from unreasonable demands and expectations. Some of these, of course, arise from the workers themselves as well as from other people. Centres are usually situated in areas of high need and cannot meet all the demands. Clarity is required about priorities and a centre needs transparent processes for setting these and wherever possible the processes should involve the key stakeholders of users and funders.

2. Facilitating staff in their work as a team

As indicated earlier the role of the team in creating a therapeutic environment cannot be over-emphasised. Facilitating creative teamwork requires time spent working together on, among other things: planning and reviewing the centre's work, exploring attitudes and values and resolving conflicts. The manager needs to identify any difficulties arising in team functioning as quickly as possible. Clues may be picked up in individual supervision, team meetings or observation of both formal and informal interactions. Effective teamwork needs the allocation of sufficient time and the manager may need to work hard to protect this time.

3. Holding together the various strands of work

In a busy neighbourhood family centre few, if any, individual project staff are likely to be engaged in all parts of the centre programme. As a result the manager carries particular responsibility for ensuring that the various strands of work are held together so that an integrated programme is available for users. This is a demanding activity. Smith (1996, p.187) in her study of six family centres, commenting on the success of family projects in combining work with 'referred clients' with work on an 'open access basis', states: 'links between the different types of work were often hard to make and opportunities were sometimes missed'. Ensuring links are made requires the manager to record and hold in mind complex networks of users, staff and services. While this responsibility may primarily rest with the centre manager it is also vital that the manager enables the team to accept shared responsibility for a coherent programme and integrated services.

Finally it should be said that creating a therapeutic environment in a neighbourhood family centre carries many challenges but it also provides immense opportunities and rewards for children, parents and staff.

Chapter 12

Managing the Impact of Anxiety on the Primary Task of a Family Centre

Rosemary Lilley

Introduction

> It is...our experience that even in the best run institution, not only within the human services but also in other sectors, there are pockets of irrationality and behaviour which undermines the work. (Obholzer and Roberts 1994, p.xvii)

If irrationality and undermining behaviour are prevalent in most workplaces these factors can be assumed to be prominent in settings where the recipients of the services are themselves struggling to conduct and maintain a semblance of individual and family life. This chapter, written from the perspective of my position as manager of a family centre, explores how those issues which impede the successful functioning of a family centre can be managed. I explore the nature of anxiety and consider the main issues and anxieties with which this family centre has to contend, identifying the recognised and less recognisable anxieties that affect staff individually and collectively. I give thought to the idea of the primary task and how it is affected by both conscious and unconscious anxieties. Finally I look at how the inherent anxieties in family centre work can be managed and contained. In particular I make use of the idea that workers 'need themselves to be contained in a system of meaningful attachments if they are to contain the children [and parents] effectively' (Menzies Lyth 1988, p.253).

The family centre and its primary task

The family centre in question is a project of a large national voluntary child care agency. Its remit has always been to provide for families with pre-school children who are regarded as 'in need', reflecting the central philosophy of the Children Act that 'the child in need can be helped most effectively if the local authority, working in partnership with the parents, provides a range and level of services appropriate to the child's needs' (DOH 1991 1.2). Our family centre is situated in an expanding former market town in southern England. The first written aims and objectives for the project are perhaps indicative of a euphoric phase in the centre's life, the aims being 'to create a therapeutic environment – offering an accepting, safe and secure milieu – in which children and parents are enabled to recognise and work on past and present experiences, so that each individual may mature and develop...'.

However, when the primary task is vaguely defined this can become anti-task. As Roberts (1994, p.32) observed in another example:

> the team behaved as if their task were to provide as much help as was needed to everyone who needed it. As the demands on the unit increased in both scope and numbers, this became impossible.

While the family centre increased in reputation for its ability to manage effectively highly disturbed parents this resulted in increased stress on staff – both the conscious stress of demands for more places and the corresponding unconscious stress of failing to provide for the many families requiring places. Consideration needed to be given to the primary task.

The task needs to be differentiated, recognised and defined or otherwise service development will be constrained (Balbernie 1966). However, defining task is far from simple, particularly in relation to outcomes. The open systems model is helpful in defining task in a group-care setting. It provides a base from which it is possible 'to enable the team to make firm connections between the intended outcome of the client's stay and the stated functions and actual roles of individual workers and of the team as a whole' (Ward 1993, p.134). Yet when addressing the primary task in a family centre there will be no one input or output. That the centre works for the benefit of both children and parents has to be accommodated. Grappling with this complexity led to our devising the following aims which set out a primary task which provides realistic boundaries for parents, children, staff and agency partner:

> The Family Centre aims to provide a day care service for families with pre-school children, who are in considerable distress or difficulties, to enable parents to positively manage their parenting role and children to develop and mature.

Anxiety and defences against anxiety

A dictionary definition of anxiety is 'a state of chronic apprehension'. Management literature tends to refer less to anxiety than to stress, which is seen to arise from concrete factors such as noise, fatigue, temperature, amount of work, unfamiliar situations or domestic troubles. Resolution of stress is said to lie in equally concrete practical techniques, such as the advice 'set your own objectives and life goals, decide what you want and go for it' (Stewart 1987).

Yet management texts based on an understanding of social systems give considerable credence to the impact of anxiety. Social-systems thinking is an extension of psychoanalytic knowledge from individuals to groups, institutions and workplaces. It recognises that anxiety and the defence mechanisms that arise to combat or avoid it have a harmful effect on the primary task unless they are understood and addressed. Menzies Lyth (1989) contends that the viability of a social system is determined by the containment of anxiety. She draws on Klein's (1975) view of anxiety as arising from a fear of annihilation, with each individual building their own defence mechanisms to reduce immediate distress.

Anxieties arising from external or conscious sources

One aspect of anxiety is a response to factors arising in the environment. Family centre work is made complex by its clients being both children and parents. This complexity is compounded by the impact of such factors as partnership arrangements, organisational policies, staff's vision of family life versus parents' vision. Mediating variable primary tasks calls for changes in what is the primary task at any given moment, so reducing levels of effectiveness in relation to the rightful demands of each task (Menzies 1979).

Family centre work is a constant balancing of children's and parents' needs. Ultimately the needs of children are paramount (DOH 1999b 1.1) but the provision of a service to address inadequate and failing parenting necessarily has to confront the needs of both children and parents. It is interesting to note that the Children Act Guidelines stress that therapeutic family centres are a place for parents to be helped to discuss their difficulties, while the agency's family centre policy emphasizes the child. Staff are daily facing this dilemma and permanently juggling.

The daily power of families' distress

The centre prepares for each day with a staff meeting. The meeting addresses practical business matters but also facilitates the expression of feeling. At one level the meeting is about the mechanics of the day – how many people to collect in the mini-bus; staff rota for setting up play equipment; and reminder (if domestic staff are absent) that care staff will have to clean the group rooms and cloakrooms at the end of the day; etc. At another level it is a process for getting in touch with the issues that families are likely to bring with them, and thereby an opportunity for staff pro-actively to defuse potential difficulties for families and for themselves. There are reminders: of users' birthdays and past (often painful) anniversaries; of the impact on a child, parent, family if the keyworker is absent; of the last time we had fish for lunch and the irrational response from a mother and how are we going to forewarn her it is fish today? It is a time for discussion: about how best to help a traumatised little girl, who is panicked by any move from one environment to another, make the transition from home to mini-bus to centre without her screaming and transferring her distress to everyone else in the mini-bus. It is a time when staff can voice their concerns and for other team members to be alerted to support: 'I'm worried about how some of the mums will react when I tell them about Sue going to a refuge – you remember how last time they all began talking about their own experiences of violence in front of the children?' or 'What shall I do if Charlie pushes Annie, like he did last week, and his mum threatened to smack him when they got home.'

The morning arrival of the families is a crucial time. There is an influx of families all carrying the events of, at minimum, the hours since last being at the centre the previous day, while some families may not have attended for three or four days. However much the staff team tries to prepare for and recognise potential issues or difficulties for individuals and the group, the power of families' distress never ceases to amaze and surprise. It is not uncommon for a staff group of three to be faced within half an hour with six or so families all struggling with personal crises. For example on one day there was a mother the worse for drug mis-use, a family where the baby had been admitted to hospital, a mother alleging that the lodger was 'touching' her child, a mother refusing to speak, a child with a prominent bruise. On a practical level workers were faced with seven adults and eleven children. Children and parents were all distressed by the immediate impact of their experiences. Whose needs do workers even begin to address?

Part of the problem here lies with inadequate resources. Family centres are a pro-active means of addressing complex family situations where children are concerned, but they are also a means whereby society can dump its problems. For workers under-resourcing provokes a conflict. On the one hand there is overwork, disappointment in poor outcomes, and high stress, and on the other hand there is the pain arising from not helping as many families as require help.

Responding to children where parents are present

Another constant source of anxiety for staff working with both parents and children is about how to respond to children when parents are present. Workers often feel inhibited, particularly if they and parents disagree about how to respond. For example, staff were confronted with a child asking the whereabouts of his father and his mother saying he had gone on holiday. In fact the father was in prison, but the mother was unable to tell the child. Staff were aware of the dilemma and the keyworker was working towards enabling the mother to tell or to give permission for the child to be told. However, before this could be negotiated, the child directly asked the worker, in front of his mother, where his father was. Previously she had prevaricated but this time she took courage and stated the facts. It was an anxious moment. The worker recognised that the mother could well feel undermined and also had the right to complain that staff had acted against her wishes. Such work is about an intricate pattern of powerful relationships.

Child protection

Child protection procedures are always a priority, but this can be at the expense of the emotional well-being of the children and parents concerned and of others in the group. Workers are mobilised by what could potentially affect them most. Child protection issues are controlled by strict procedures which concern the collation of facts. Workers' anxieties are immediately heightened. They are anxious to conduct themselves correctly; fear for themselves and their job, often openly acknowledged, overrides other considerations. Thus staff are preoccupied and so not emotionally available to children or parents. With parents themselves being so vulnerable they perceive the staff's preoccupation as not caring about them. The children respond similarly. Winnicott (1965, p.75) notes that when an infant suddenly finds the mother preoccupied this is very disturbing and 'an infant in this position can feel infinitely dropped'. For children caught up in such a situation there is the potential for them to be suffering the loss of two significant adults – the mother and the keyworker.

Child protection issues also create other anxieties. Where children are often left in the care of mothers who frequently change partners or male lodgers, the need to be vigilant to possible abuse is heightened. At the same time, workers have to struggle with the possibility of labelling or stigmatising men and not misreading the child's behaviour. A case in mind was a two-year-old child who was often looked after by her mother's male friends while her mother went out to work. Small children often openly masturbate, and workers are conversant with this situation, often needing to allay parents' confrontational responses.

They are also aware that masturbation could be a communication from a child of abuse. However, when the child in question masturbated once, staff became exceedingly anxious even though there was nothing to suggest that the child was behaving in any way out of the ordinary. They struggled with maintaining a balance and holding to their knowledge base. There were demands that I as project manager interview the child to ascertain if abuse had occurred and there was a notable questioning of the mother as to what was happening at home. Such situations threaten to overwhelm staff and become anti-task.

Conflicting views of family life

A final example of anxiety arising from conscious sources is the issue of vision. Family centres necessarily work with a client group who are experiencing considerable difficulties. The outcome of work is some level of impact on the parenting of the children concerned. As we all come from families, as workers we bring with us to the job our own vision of how families should function. The centre itself is a forum for acting out a form of family life (Burton 1993). Much of the work is about modelling to parents positive ways of managing and considering their own and children's needs. Difficulties arise when the family and staff visions conflict. The issue of smacking and its connotations of abuse and power are always around.

Less obvious but equally confrontational are other issues. For example, in supervision a worker discussed concerns that a mother had no ambition for her children whereas the worker recognised the children's intellectual potential and could see them doing well in school. Additionally, with both parents coming from delinquent families, the mother often saying proudly that the boys were 'just like their dad', the perceived expectation was for the children similarly to follow this route. Nothing the mother said suggested that she wanted her children to lead what staff considered to be successful lives. While we advocate self-determination it is not part of the family centre task to collude with parents' negative visions for their children. Yet to express the moral judgment is potentially to destroy the professional relationship (Winnicott 1965).

Anxiety arising from internal or unconscious sources

Family centre work raises a complex mixture of anxieties that are recognisable and acknowledged but for which there are often no straightforward resolutions. Anxiety can be a response to unrecognised factors in the self which can be stirred by unconscious repressed factors (Rycroft 1968). Any social work setting imports the distress, fragmentation and conflicts which clients carry, some of which staff absorb (Hawkins 1989). The impact of distress, conflicts and negative experiences has a powerful effect on how staff respond to families. In our family centre all parents, without exception, have suffered multiple abuse or trauma in their own childhoods. The projection of negative feelings from these experiences into individual workers, the staff group, and into the whole centre can be forceful. Likewise the primitive functioning of young children together with workers' own unresolved issues can arouse unrecognised anxiety that has a detrimental effect on the service provided.

The impact of projective identification is a constant issue for the staff group to address not least because they are constantly assaulted by clients' projections. If the process is not recognised workers may surrender to despair, illness or withdrawal. They are liable to become entangled in the process and therefore less likely to recognise the forces at play. As Moylan (1994, p.56) notes, 'The more distressed the client group, the more these unconscious communications are likely to predominate. When there is a lot of pain involved the natural reaction is to attempt to avoid it.' There is also the danger of workers responding similarly to the client's primitive feeling (Menzies 1979).

Two case studies

Family centre workers have striven for two years with a depressed mother, diagnosed as having an avoidant personality disorder. Much of the time she sits uncommunicatively in the family room or else totally withdraws, sitting for long periods on the stairs, often crying. Either situation is painful to observe. Her life history is horrendous, with not a month going by that is not the anniversary of some traumatic experience. Initially workers responded with pity, repeatedly re-enacting the avoidant problem by allowing her to miss groups. Then frustration set in. Time spent with her, listening to the depth of her distress but still not getting any spontaneous response was reacted to with growing condemnation and comments that she was deliberately playing games. Finally staff began to act out avoidance by not acknowledging her when she refused to speak or was sitting on the stairs; they did to her what she did to them.

Another family had potentially devastating effects on the family centre. The hostile and destructive fears of the mother were initially projected through her three-year-old child who continually attacked other children for no apparent reason – attacks that were vicious and caused injuries. At the same time the mother was a dominant person, on the one hand saying what a wonderful place the centre was but on the other complaining vociferously when staff, other parents or other children failed to meet her high expectations. From the first week she used the agency's complaints procedure against staff. As workers became increasingly fearful for themselves so the child became increasingly aggressive. Equally other parents became frightened of the family and children were similarly fearful. However, only the children's fear was recognised. Workers' and other parents' fear was projected in counter complaints against the mother. Not recognising the mother's fears but only regarding her as a trouble-maker led staff to pull back from interacting with her. The situation came to a climax when the mother made a complaint against me. While I had managed previous complaints and been able to protect a little, this complaint brought in external managers and the agency's users' rights officer. The situation was no longer contained. The centre, while functioning at some level, was unable to provide any meaningful holding: everyone felt threatened. While we had tried to hold on to the knowledge that the mother's difficult behaviour had some meaning, it became virtually impossible to retain such reasoning. Interestingly, in the midst of the turmoil the child became a little less aggressive, which the mother used as evidence of the effectiveness of the centre and their need to continue attendance.

It was only after the complaints procedure had been completed that the centre was able to re-focus on the family. With the help of a consultant it was possible to recognise that the fear that the staff team experienced was what the mother also felt. What emerged was that she had been abused as a child in a group-care setting. Coming into the group environment had stirred the unconscious, reawakened memories and unleashed the associated fears. The mother was enabled to realise that in reality the centre was a disturbing place for her and she decided to leave. Importantly she allowed the child to attend a different group provision.

Seeking the origin of feelings

It is easy for a child to become caught up in their parents' illness, as the previous example demonstrates. Family centre workers are daily faced with trying to unravel what are truly the child's and what are the parent's emotions. Additionally the usual primitive feelings that young children evoke in adults have to be addressed. Parental ambivalence is usual but often parents are unable to acknowledge this; neither are parents able to be the ideal parents they wish to be. 'It is practically impossible to sustain positive attitudes…when our emotions stir us strongly because we lose patience with what our child is doing' (Bettelheim 1987, p.23). Blaug (1989) describes his own feelings of helplessness and guilt when he was unable to control a group of pre-school children, and his concern as to what other staff would think. Parents have similar feelings and experience; so also do workers. For workers the issue is how to acknowledge this for themselves. Unless they are able to do so, the internal rage in the self becomes projected on to parents, whose inability to control their children is deplored. This potential for splitting (Obholzer 1994) can result in the situation becoming 'stuck', when no one is helped. In the centre it is noticeable that in those cases where workers blame the parents for their children's so called 'bad' behaviour, little maturational development takes place for the child. Where workers are able to express their own frustration with a child, then they and mother are able to work together to the child's benefit.

Workers also need to acknowledge their own unresolved issues. The worker who was able to come and say how much she disliked a child was able to consider what aspects of the child provoked her negative feelings. As the discussion went on it became evident that there were repeated references to events around meal-times. Asked if she had herself perhaps had difficulties as a child over food she recounted a history of feeding issues. From this it was possible to determine if the worker could get her dislike of the child into perspective or whether she needed to seek independent support. It was interesting that some weeks later she was, of her own accord, able to reflect on why she had been unable to establish a working relationship with several mothers in the past; she had recognised that all the mothers she had not been able to work with positively had a similar history of eating problems to herself.

Managing the anxiety

How then is the anxiety – conscious and unconscious – which has been identified, to be managed? Groups require a bounded space in which it is possible for participants to be enabled to raise their feelings in a tolerant and self-examining environment (Mawson 1994). Various factors have emerged in the examples given that suggest routes to enabling the inherent anxiety to be faced. Issues of management and leadership need to be explored, as does the question of boundary control. Satisfactory support and supervision available to the staff team is essential. Running through the discussion is the concept of 'holding', with anxiety being the chief feeling needing to be contained or held.

The concept of holding is related to a mother's capacity to identify with her baby; inadequate holding arouses negative feelings such as 'going to pieces', 'falling for ever', 'feeling unsafe' (Winnicott 1965). Applied to organisations the concept suggests that, unless they are reliably contained, organisations show these negative feelings in various disorderly ways (Stokes 1994). In group care, management can be said to equate with parenting. Thus when the manager is not adequately parenting the group, unsafe feelings are aroused in workers and in turn in the client group (Burton 1993). The case of the family described earlier illustrates how once the manager – myself – felt fearful, projective identification pervaded the entire project. The effect on the staff group was considerable. Dominant in my own emotions was fear of what I may have done to the family concerned, and also to the family centre; I know I became emotionally unavailable to the staff group.

A factor contributing to the impact of this case once the mother had complained was the ensuing confusion over boundaries. The interface between my role and that of the external line manager and users' rights officer increased uncertainty and thus anxiety. In such circumstances a collusive anxiety cycle occurs in which workers are liable to retreat into frozen professional competence (Balbernie 1966). The role of the consultant was a crucial factor in the recovery of myself and thus the centre. Recognising when one is out of one's depth is crucial (Ward 1993). Restoration of the capacity to again face the future and make plans although this future remained uncertain (Cardona 1994) enabled me to hold to the belief that behind the attacks/complaints the mother was communicating her distress. Having recognised the issue it was then possible to find a constructive outcome for all concerned. On reflection an important aspect of the recovery for the staff team was the recognition of the pervading anxiety to which we had all been subject and the decision to have some space before a new family was admitted. Worden (1992) notes the importance of grieving after a loss. The staff team needed time to face the loss, especially as it was a wanted loss.

Working with loss

Coping with loss is an important aspect of supervision. The importance of supervision in the holding environment cannot be overestimated. It is an interactive process on the part of supervisor and supervisee, with the supervisee wanting to learn about themselves as a worker as well as the families or group for which they have responsibility (Ward 1993). Facing loss is a recurring issue in the family centre. Families leave but not always having achieved all that was hoped for. More difficult is when the centre is instrumental in recognising that certain parents cannot adequately care for their child and the child is taken into the care of the local authority.

Experience also suggests that family centre work entails facing the death of centre parents or former parents. Important in coping with such difficulties is for workers to be enabled to recognise their own losses. Helping others face their bereavement may confront the worker with the depth of their own losses, but in looking at their own grief, workers can be enabled to know the extent of their capabilities (Worden 1992). Through addressing early in the supervision relationship the issue of loss as a constructive aspect of the work with families it has been possible to identify workers who have suffered early or traumatic losses. This has helped supervisors to be alert to the issue when the worker concerned faces the ending of a family's time in the centre, and in turn supports the worker in helping the family face their loss of the centre.

Conclusion

In considering managing the impact of anxiety on a family centre I have sought to demonstrate the links between the need to define a workable primary task and acknowledgement of the anxiety involved in carrying it out. We need to recognise both the inherent discernible anxieties and those arising from unconscious sources. How anxiety is confronted depends upon the ability of the staff team to recognise it and allow it to be acknowledged. The staff team in turn require effective management and leadership. It is this role that is critical to determining the family centre's ability to achieve the primary task.

A particularly crucial leadership function is to manage the boundaries between inside and outside. As we have seen, this is about managing the boundaries between parent and partner agencies, between the centre and external line management, and between workers' and families' experiences. More critically it is about enabling the manager herself and the staff team to recognise the boundary between the internal world of parents or children and of themselves. If there is no clear understanding of these boundaries, anxiety will be kindled.

> To take action in the moment of the first onset of anxiety is relatively easy, because anxiety is a powerful motivating force to action. But if action is delayed, the longer anxiety lasts and the more energy is spent on binding it, that is, on not acting to relieve it, the more a person is drained of vital energy and the less he feels capable of acting on his own. (Bettelheim 1960, p.268)

Further reading

Breen, D. (1989) *Talking with Mothers*. London: Free Association.

Handy, C. (1994) *The Empty Raincoat*. London: Hutchinson.

Handy, C. (1995) *Beyond Certainty*. London: Hutchinson.

Chapter 13

Soft Structuring
The NEWPIN Way of Delivering Empowerment
Anne Jenkins Hansen

Introduction

NEWPIN was pioneered in 1982 in the former Guys Health District in Southwark as a direct result of the rise in child abuse and the low take-up of the services to pregnant and post-natal women in the area. The original intention was to provide a centre in which mothers and their children referred to NEWPIN as being in need of support (or their children in need of protection) could come on a daily basis. The central idea was to create an environment which would alleviate social isolation, leading to befriending and mutual support. By this means the positive power of peer influence – which is so often suppressed by physical and social isolation and by the conventions and structures of mainstream social work – could be developed as an engine of positive personal development as well as emotional and practical support. As the majority of NEWPIN members are mothers the term 'mother' or 'women' will be used throughout, except when directly referring to work with fathers.

Note: Some of the material in this chapter draws on the revised (2000) NEWPIN practice manual.

The needs of parents referred to NEWPIN centres

The experience of the pioneer centre(s) demonstrated that the distress experienced by the mothers in the form of depression, low self-esteem, inability to connect positively with others and feelings of being persecuted, was linked to their early life trauma. For many women this had included separation at infancy from their parents. For some this meant frequent disruptive separations. Many had experienced multiple carers and frequent changes of home establishments. Relationships with their children were difficult and they could not communicate emotionally with them. There was little understanding of the children's needs apart from the need to be clothed and led. Most of the mothers revealed that their childhood had been frightening and or abusive in some way. Consequently, as adults they felt that they could not invest trust in another. They had few people to turn to when in need of support. The mothers had little comprehension of what is meant by a secure base or secure attachment – although they craved these vital forms of psychological support.

The NEWPIN model helps users to overcome the crippling effects of past guilt and shaming experiences, and to deal with the often overwhelming fear that these experiences will continue to haunt them by reappearing again and again. An instinctive reaction to this fear is concealment at all costs. This in turn can lead to a denial of responsibility by the parent (especially in a damaging parent-to-child relationship), as the fear of reprisal of the parent from 'authority figures' is very real in the minds or the experiences of the parents.

The environment of sympathetic peers with similar feelings, and staff who are prepared to be open about the emotional damage which has occurred in their own lives, helps the women to understand that such concealment is both self-destructive and unnecessary. This non-hierarchical, non-judgmental approach introduces a different perspective about oneself. The developing realisation of this possibility provides profound relief and really does open the door to subsequent stages of positive change.

Parents have the very rational fear that candour in front of statutory social workers can lead to the removal of their children into care. By contrast, candour in a NEWPIN centre results in sympathy and understanding and the reversal of attitudes, from habitual secretiveness and fear to open-ness and matter-of-factness together with the opportunity to step back from repetitive and destructive patterning. Validating the parent by accepting that within every parent who hurts their actual child there resides a child who has themselves been hurt (Jenkins 1987) is part of NEWPIN's soft structured approach. This does not imply that such acceptance *condones* destructive behaviour towards children (rather the reverse) but it is a starting point for change.

Another example of NEWPIN's soft structuring is the central role played by its five core values: support, equality, empathy, respect and self-reliance, referred to as SEERS. SEERS is one of the programmes which will be discussed in more detail later. These values and their everyday practice are central to the work of NEWPIN's effectiveness.

Parents referred to NEWPIN frequently have low self-esteem: they do not feel valued as members of society, they have largely gone through life feeling unsupported and misunderstood, and invariably they have not had the experience of feeling equal to others. To experience for themselves the core values in action makes the words meaningful. Consequently the values are not (as is so often the case) mere lip-service but are embedded in the work of each centre. Their application and implications are the subject of a specific 'SEERS' component in each user member's programme and each of the values is constantly referred to throughout the process. Parents are helped to remember them and to remind each other of them when situations develop which are abusive – and they continue to do so in life situations long after they have left their centre.

These core values were adopted in response to the real needs of parents and children. NEWPIN takes the view that emotional harm is the precursor to physical and sexual abuse and intentionally focuses on it through the core values which specifically address the damage of systematic emotional abuse – which was and still is the experience of most of the referred families. Although the NEWPIN approach has been in the main taken up in areas where there is severe social deprivation, poverty and crime, the model has proved to be equally applicable to more affluent families. Difficulties in parent relationships are endemic in our society and learning to enjoy one's children and to communicate well with them are not confined to those who are more likely to become a focus of attention to statutory organisations.

Each centre needs to be accessible to the local community, which is taken to be within pram-pushing distance. Some centres – especially those where transport is difficult to access such as the Greenwich and Lewisham centre – or where a lone centre covers a wide section of a borough or straddles more than one borough – such as the Walworth centre – are supported by a mini-bus service, or user members are brought in by the centre staff. This is not ideal for NEWPIN practice; the potential for drop-out is increased which can destabilise the centre. There is a psychological importance in creating a sense of 'nearness'. The fragility of the user member's experience of securely belonging to someone is very real and any minor incident can inhibit attendance. External evaluation of NEWPIN (Cox *et al.* 1987; Pound 1990) indicates that the first few months of attachment to a centre are crucial as it can take some time before a genuine sense of belonging and connectedness has developed within the parent. The proximity of the centre is an identifiable and familiar thread, which assists in the positive attachment process.

Coming to NEWPIN

After a referral is made (including self-referral) the family will be seen at home and at their convenience by the centre co-ordinator. This is called the 'pre-NEWPIN chat' which is in fact a carefully structured first step in personal empowerment, personal control and personal decision making. The parent will have already been prepared for the visit to be long and knows that the time is exclusively for her and her family. It is crucial that, at this point and throughout the future association with NEWPIN, the co-ordinator conveys to the parent a sense of her value and uniqueness. This is very important as many referred women have little self-esteem to begin with, and the self-loathing they have learned from childhood is frequently handed on to their children. The co-ordinator will be aware that, when a parent is speaking of their past and present often overwhelming distress, the children's reactions can be overlooked. So from the time of this visit and throughout involvement in NEWPIN, children are afforded equal respect. They are made to feel secure and emotionally comfortable and form a part of the interview.

Meaningful natural and spontaneous engagement with the children is a very important part of the NEWPIN chat. This purposeful interaction with the children puts the mother at her ease and reinforces the message to her that her children are as significant as she is herself. This may come as a surprise to a troubled parent, especially if she is having difficulties coping with her children. But she soon understands that this is a part of the NEWPIN ethos and it inevitably starts the process of her bonding with her child. By taking a relaxed time to listen and interact with the family the co-ordinator can get as full a picture as possible as to how the parent views her past and present life and how she might fit in the jigsaw of a NEWPIN centre. This is to say that each adult and child is seen as unique and special. It is not the bricks and mortar which makes a NEWPIN centre but every individual and their inter-relationship with each other. In this first face-to-face contact with the referred mother the co-ordinator will not be concentrating on the problems giving rise to the referral but will be looking for the woman's positive aspects and what she herself can contribute to her own personal growth.

> Mary was seen at home for the pre-NEWPIN chat. She had been referred to NEWPIN by the social worker who was concerned about her relationship with her six-month-old baby. Mary, a lone parent who had been abandoned by her partner when she became pregnant, said that she was very depressed. She had attempted to take her own life on two occasions and was on anti-depressants. She admitted to feeling worthless. She confided that her early life had been traumatising, having been cared for by social services on numerous occasions, and that she had endured serious abuse. She sat with her hair covering her face and her head down throughout the pre-NEWPIN chat. She could only talk about herself negatively and said that she was useless and that everybody thought she was no good. The co-ordinator observed that she was rocking her fractious baby to sleep and pointed out to Mary how caring she was being to her baby. She

remarked on Mary's gentleness and that the baby was responding to her. Mary looked surprised but appeared to listen as the co-ordinator talked about how this appeared to her.

If the NEWPIN chat takes place with a father or male partner present, he is encouraged to remain to hear about NEWPIN and the work his partner will undertake. The personal changes, although significant, generally have a positive outcome for the family as a whole in the long term. An important aspect of this is a more positive communication between partners. Most women say that they respond differently to their domestic situations as a result of their own personal progress and through this change of perception they avoid falling into circular destructive conflicts with their partner. Sometimes, however, a man will feel very threatened by the growing confidence of his partner. This is most likely to occur when the relationship is based on domination and control, and the mother's empowerment can create problems. Such a situation can cause some women to drop out of NEWPIN and stay in the relationship whereas others may leave their partners as they increasingly find their own self-respect and strength.

Great care is taken to avoid too much exposure of feelings and this is particularly important if the partner is present. Many of the referred families do not have trusting and open relationships between partners and sensitivity is required to prevent spontaneous revelations of past and current unhappiness. These may be too difficult for the parents to handle after the co-ordinator has left with the result that the women can be made more vulnerable to hostility. The co-ordinator will ensure that she leaves behind a sense of emotional security after the visit.

An open-door policy is always maintained at the NEWPIN centres; families are always welcome to return and when they do a further NEWPIN chat is offered to review the situation. Sometimes women are simply unable to attach at one or more attempts. These can prove to be not failures but preparation for a later, successful engagement with the centre and its programmes. This is another example of the firm results obtained by NEWPIN's soft structuring. Rigid 'rules of admission' would deter parents who are most in need of NEWPIN support.

When the parent decides she will come to NEWPIN, arrangements will be made to support her by attaching her empathetically to an established user member. Establishing such an 'artificial' friendship begins a process of forming other natural attachments with others who attend the centre and beyond. Sometimes it might not be possible to empathetically attach – particularly if the woman is very mistrustful of others. In such cases the co-ordinator will bring her to the centre herself and stay with her until she has integrated. At these times the co-ordinator will request established user members who have learned to relate to others without difficulty to help to ease the family in.

As soon as a decision is reached to attend the centre the member will complete the first of the set of 'My Progress Through NEWPIN' forms at home. This personal chronicle and self-evaluation of the time spent in NEWPIN provides an encouraging sense of progress. In addition to noting achievements it also records any falling back on what the user member decided she wanted to change for herself and her child(ren) at the time of the pre-NEWPIN chat. The 'My Progress Through NEWPIN' forms play a vital role in the defining change of mindset from a passive and reactive approach to one's personal life to one which is proactive. It underpins the initial decision to attend a NEWPIN centre to which the member comes not to pass the time but systematically to change one's life: the role of NEWPIN centres is not a palliative one – it helps users to effect positive changes in their lives. Certainly the process is structured, but in a way in which the individual is put in charge of her own progress. NEWPIN does not do things to parents, but rather enables them to undertake the positive re-shaping of their lives.

NEWPIN centres: safe havens for parents and children

The NEWPIN centres are designed to be warm and homely. They include a living room designed to feel like one's own home, including a kitchen where meals can be prepared and eaten together. The purpose of this is to create a safe and facilitating environment, which supports parents, and enables their children to feel cared for, while coping with either spontaneous or chronic distress, or both. Centre design also fosters a positive sense of social interaction, friendship and deepening relationships. It is of critical importance that the play room for the children should be adjacent to the living-room space. This is a deliberate policy to avoid the damage of premature separation of the children from the mothers, which could compound anxiety in children especially when their relationship with their parent is insecure.

It is also imperative that a child's time-scale for safe separation – as perceived by the child – is recognised and respected. Parents, carers and staff often make an assumption of the readiness of a child to be left by the parent or a child to be removed from the parent. This is frequently too speedy or without proper preparation and is often at the convenience of the staff or the parent. It is not right in NEWPIN to say such things as 's/he will be all right when you have gone'. Or, 's/he didn't cry for long'. NEWPIN play staff are trained to understand that a child who reacts with distress when a parent is leaving must be comforted with the maternal presence. Parents are therefore encouraged to come regularly to the play room so that their child is familiar with the centre, the staff and other children and mothers before the start of parental programmes. The staff will help the mother to manage her own ambivalent feelings, which may be exacerbating her child's separation anxiety.

It is a familiar feature of NEWPIN centres that some parents are uncomfortable in the play room and prefer not to go in. The play facilitators are trained to understand that for some parents the experience of playing when children themselves may have been unfamiliar, joyless and possibly fear-bound. The facilitators will help and encourage the parent in playing and point out that a child will settle into the play room if the mother initially comes in with her child for some period of the day. There is a play room rota where parents help the staff. This is usually when a group or programmes are taking place and more hands are needed to care for the number of children. Parents are encouraged to join the rota as a step in their own personal development and to begin the process of understanding the needs of children.

When the newly referred children are insecurely attached they will stay close to their mothers for long periods. They often seek to play but can't bear to leave the side of the parent. They will peer into the play room but not enter it. The play facilitator will bring toys into the living room and encourage a child to come to find for itself what they would like to play with. Through gentle persistence children generally settle happily themselves and without enforced distress. There is a deliberate policy to assist children and their parents to develop a sense of security within the centre as soon as possible. We have found that the provision of an environment to which members want to come voluntarily and regularly facilitates the process of positive emotional change and growth.

Each NEWPIN play room must reflect the same degree of comfort as the living room. Parents and children work with the play room staff to decorate the space and to provide themes. The play facilitator encourages each mother to work alongside her child and to join with other parents in making such things as mobiles or pictures or to take part in activities. It is of equal importance to take time with the parents as well as it is with the children. The degree of insecurity and fear will vary from person to person and both the co-ordinator and the play facilitator are conscious of the differing personalities of each individual mother and child.

The relationship between the play facilitator, the children and their parents is a finely balanced one. The play facilitator respects the parent and will only act as a surrogate mother when the parent is too distressed to provide adequate care for her child's emotional needs. Just as the co-ordinator is a positive role model to the parents, so the play facilitator can be a positive role model to the parents as they observe the way the facilitator and other play staff relate to the children.

> Tina had a doll and Katie snatched it from her. Tina began to cry but Katie firmly held on to the doll. Sharon, the play facilitator, knelt down beside the two children. She comforted Tina but did not ask Katie to hand the doll back. Rather she talked to her about the doll and Tina. After an unhurried interval during which Sharon communicated with Katie about general matters but without altogether letting Katie forget the purpose of the interaction, Katie voluntarily handed the doll back. Sharon thanked her and gave her recognition for her kindness, then asked her if she would like Tina and herself to come with Katie to find another doll, which they did. Both girls played happily together. Throughout this time Katie was not shamed or made to feel guilty and Tina was comforted and respected.

This happened to be an interlude between two girls but a similar situation could occur between either a boy and a girl or between two boys. The manner in which the situations are handled would be the same – no violation of either of the children.

This incident became an ad hoc learning session, or an example of opportunity-led work with young children. The observing parents – who had themselves experienced belittling and shaming as children – viewed Sharon's approach as something of a revelation. A discussion ensued and they all admitted that their response would have been to shout and take the doll from Katie, removing it from both children since they could not manage to sort out the emotional dynamic between the two children. They also felt that they might have lashed out and most certainly would have been verbally abusive. The parents' honesty indicates their receptiveness to new ways of managing their children – far different from the way they were treated when children themselves. Such 'on the hoof' (Pound 1994) experiences at the centres are of comparable importance to the more structured courses which the parents undergo.

To support the family beyond the centre the new member will be invited to add her name to the 24-hour support network to which all centre members belong including the co-ordinator. This has proved vital in the prevention of crises. Not only does the telephone network act as an emotional buffer when the centre is closed, it also serves as a link between centre members and creates a community network. Through it members contact each other for practical purposes such as baby-sitting, shopping and arranging social events. The telephone connection to the co-ordinators is rarely abused. If it is, then the matter is discussed with the member concerned to unearth the underlying problems.

The characteristic approach of NEWPIN staff is to listen to and respond to the dilemmas which the members experience empathetically, but with constructive challenge about their own part in the dilemma they present. For parents who are listened to for what they are saying and are accepted for being themselves, and who feel heard without fear of condemnation, there nonetheless may be a need to test out the validity of such an experience. This can take the form of provoking a self-destructive situation in the centre living room, which leads to conflict, or reacting negatively to her child in front of others. Such behaviour is similar to the child who invokes disapproval from the adult world, which s/he doesn't understand and who needs to push the boundaries further to test out the reaction from that adult world. Initially the parent who is in conflict with their own emotional immaturity may also test out any apparently validating messages she receives from the staff by destructively acting out in the centres with other members, with the co-ordinator, or with other staff members. The co-ordinator will be expected to respond to this without judgemental behaviour but also to balance this with direct supportive challenge. It is the reinforcing of a message which says 'you matter' in such a softly structured way it brings reflective change within the parent.

The Personal Development Programme (PDP)

When a parent joins a NEWPIN centre she is committing herself to making major changes and participating in programmes which, because they uncover profound and often distressing feelings, are very taxing. A typical remark of a former user member is, 'I've never worked so hard in all my life.'

All the elements of the Personal Development Programme (PDP) are interlinked and follow each other sequentially. This mirrors the individual emotional maturation of the members. The programme runs for about a year with natural breaks occurring during the school holidays. The participants – the optimal number being 10 to 12 – are encouraged to view the theoretical parts of the programme as 'academic'. This helps to boost self-esteem, especially for those women for whom schooling was a bad experience.

The therapeutic support group

This is the first of the formal activities which a parent will engage in. She will be able to join in the group when she has been coming to NEWPIN consistently, is comfortable in the living room and when her child is able to settle in the play room for a period of two hours without distress. Her readiness and emotional robustness to embark on this difficult personal work is crucial. Until this time – and if the co-ordinator thinks it is necessary – she will offer the mother one-to-one counselling.

The group is run on slow open lines. When a new member is ready to join, both she and the group members will have been prepared for some weeks before. Although relationships in the living room will have been made and friendships developed, relationships take on a different colouration in the groupwork as much more of personal life histories are slowly revealed. Initially there is limited trust because of the degree of loss and separation that many members have experienced: hard experiences have created hard defences against further disappointment. This is constantly tested out. Because of the degree of mistrust and the intermingling nature of the NEWPIN process, confidentiality is paramount.

The group rules will have been drawn up with the members. These always consist of no smoking, eating or drinking while the group is in progress; regularity and punctuality of attendance and the agreement that confidential revelations in the group room are confined to the group room. Although members generally treat the groupwork with respect there will be some 'acting out' – particularly when a member is going through a difficult time in self-revelation. It is at these times that lateness or being absent will occur. Other manifestations will be silence, passive or verbal aggression or non-communication. All of these will be gently but firmly explored and challenged.

The aim of the group is to help members to get rid of the guilt and shame of past lives. They become aware that the painful things, which have happened to them in childhood, are not their fault and learn to turn past negative experiences to positive use. They are encouraged to communicate and challenge each other's behaviour constructively and to give support and encouragement to work through emotionally painful experiences. They learn to recognise that attacking each other is a distorted projection. This groupwork is very effective in showing members how the perceptions of self can begin to be changed. Children are symbolically a part of the group. Mothers are challenged or praised for their behaviour towards their children and links are made between aspects of their own upbringing and how this may reflect on the way they bring up their children.

If a group member is absent the other members will be encouraged to make contact by phone and home visiting to support her back into the group. The co-ordinator herself will also actively encourage her to return and help her to bring the troubling issue to the group.

Personal development

This section is a term of 12 weeks and is participatory. It starts the process of looking at oneself as a person and as a parent. It is a structured course, which has a 'homework' component during the course of which each member completes a journal, which is a living testament to her progress. The journal is made up of both pictorial and written sections. Members who have few literary skills are helped by other members to complete them and individual design is encouraged. Everyone is urged to keep adding to the journals throughout their time in NEWPIN. The co-ordinator will help the members to focus on the journal as a living testament of her own changes and the value of the journal to her children in later life. Those journals which are badly kept or left lying around often reflect the state of low self-worth and the co-ordinator will be able to use this observation constructively. She will ask what this means and will explore with the member whether it reflects the way she feels about herself. This exploration often opens the door for the member to voice deep and painful feelings.

Family play

This important element of the programme was developed on the basis of the observation of parent–child dynamics within the centre. Centre staff are aware of the impact of how the validation of the parent reverberates on to the children as a sort of emotional chain responsiveness. Small details such as a parent actually stopping shouting at her child, or observing her child playing and remarking about the child in a caring and non-abusive way are noticed by the staff and other mothers and used to encourage and support parents. Through the centre network other parents care for each other's children. When a mother through depression or despair can't manage her child herself, the mother will be supported both in the centre and at home. For instance mothers will look after each other's children over night to give each other a break. The children appear to flourish with this multi-parenting and also through the care which they receive in the play room and through the stable peer relationships they form with each other. The value of multiparenting is significant. The pressures of parenting are shared and mental space to reflect and relax from the tensions of parenting are the outcome. This sharing and caring of each other can be seen as marking changes in both the parental attitudes and child behaaviour. It will indicate whether some respite from the total grind of day to day care of their children assists toward the emotional growth of the parents and can be used to record success and monitor the child/parent relationship. Nevertheless it is tacitly acknowledged that some parents take longer to begin to value their children to the point where they can reduce their destructive behaviour towards them. Nevertheless the staff feel that the children actually do benefit from the esteem-building and validation they receive from other mothers and the staff, even when their mothers are unable to respond positively and consistently to them. However, for some years there was no formal programme for this work.

When NEWPIN was evaluated (Cox *et al.* 1987 – 'Evaluation of a Home Visiting and Befriending Scheme') it was not possible to demonstrate change in the parent–child interaction within the six-month period of the evaluation. Cox in his summary of the evaluation states that the time given for the study was probably insufficient to demonstrate change, and NEWPIN would concur with this. (As a consequence of this and their knowledge of NEWPIN two of the research team, Mills and Puckering (1995), went on to devise the Mellow Parenting Programme.)

So the Family Play Programme (FPP) was devised partly as a result of the findings from the research but also because NEWPIN itself was observing changes in the children irrespective of there being no real improvement in the way some mothers related to their children. The FPP has now been incorporated as a more structured part of the PDP. It spans ten weeks and is a two-hour session. The parents are divided into pairs. They work in the play room with the play facilitator and the play room is closed at this time to other members. The essence of this work is to support the parent to discover how to play intimately, creatively and have fun with their child. Many members whose experiences of 'play' in childhood were frightening or abusive have difficulty with this programme. But completing this work is viewed by the parents as very rewarding. This is conveyed by the parent's personal evaluation of their progress. One mother wrote 'Until I did the family play I saw my child as if he was an animal – I have now learned to see him as a little person in his own right.' Parents say that they carry the experience home and use their new-found knowledge to help them through the day. The programme is used not only for the children who are attending the NEWPIN centre with the parent but also if a parent is having difficulties with a school-age child. The child will come to the NEWPIN centre after school and also during the school holidays. The programme is then adapted to suit the age of the child.

However, powerful if anecdotal evidence of the lasting nature of the changes which NEWPIN effects was given at its national conference (1998). At the conference former user members and former NEWPIN children of 12 years ago spoke eloquently of the permanent nature of the positive changes they had made for themselves. The children all spoke of the strong and healthy relationship they had with their mothers. These were members who were involved *prior* to the introduction of the formalised play component of the PDP.

NEWPIN's long experience strongly indicates that adverse psychological problems – which usually are deeply entrenched in a family or societal culture – can only be resolved through deliberate commitment to a structured programme over at least a year, one which incorporates the development of meaningful relationships starting with those in the centre.

The effect of permanent positive change through the combination of key elements described here which work together are necessary if the emotional maturing of parenting is to be permanent. The carefully structured development programmes, the design of the centres, the training and quality control of staff, and the length of the programmes all contribute to ensuring that the total effect is lasting and life long. Short-term programmes can be useful but at a different level. Monetary constraints on social welfare budgets may favour these but in NEWPIN's experience short courses do not have the power to influence the randomness of life adversity. The key lies in the emotional maturation of the adult and this takes time.

SEERS module

This part of the programme emphasises the importance of NEWPIN's core values. These are strong strands in the psychological cord of attachment to meaningful others beginning in childhood with significant carers. Such a connection may be damaged or even lost through the passage from childhood to adulthood. The core values speak of respect for oneself. Through their constant application each individual is eventually enabled to grow sufficiently within the self to look outward to the needs of others. Through this section of the PDP parents learn to recognise the value of others in relation to their own personal emotional growth through the development of communication skills. This recognition begins from the interactions with each other within the living room, experience of the 24-hour mutual support network and through the intimate and trusting relationships which the NEWPIN centre as a secure base encourages. Understanding the importance of meaningful and honest discourse with each other enhances positive emotional connection with the children, from which the children will ultimately benefit. There is anecdotal evidence from nursery school teachers that a NEWPIN child can be recognised for being able to articulate difficulties for themselves and on behalf of others in distress, and for their capacity to reason.

Another advantage of the SEERS programme is the preparation of members who are ready to consider moving on and out of the supportive and accepting

NEWPIN centre into the world, a process that was bleak and mistrustful prior to engagement within NEWPIN. Members who want to continue to develop themselves within NEWPIN start by contributing to the running of the centre – a sort of giving back by supporting the co-ordinator to support others. There is a regular workshop for members befriending new members where relationships are explored and where ways to encourage attendance at the centre are discussed. Role playing of situations which occur in centres between members and ways of handling conflict are part of this workshop. Training is given to some members who are keen to open their horizons further. This is the Foundation Course described on page 236.

Supporting the co-ordinators and the play facilitators

The attitude of society in general is that those mothers who as main carers 'fail', regardless of their circumstances, should be punished rather than understood. NEWPIN's notion of parenting validates the mothers for what they have achieved in their parenting, irrespective of the need to improve upon it. This is a tricky balance. This means that NEWPIN centre work can be emotionally demanding with intense involvement with the user members. Unlike other family work, which, although intensive, may not be as continuous – NEWPIN co-ordinators are on call 24-hours a day and therefore require a high level of support.

NEWPIN operates away from the mainstream of family care, and to that it owes and owns its success. The supervision of co-ordinators is therefore crucial and attendance at supervision sessions is mandatory. For NEWPIN to work effectively for families in distress it is essential that centre staff are prepared to understand their own psychological and emotional processes and to be capable of insight. Because of the open and non-hierarchical nature of the work, co-ordinators and play facilitators working with conviction about the NEWPIN approach can be in opposition to what constitutes accepted forms of parenting by legally regulated statutory services.

Cluster supervision takes place with three members in weekly two-hour sessions. These are facilitated by a member of NEWPIN's Quality Assurance Team (QA) – most of whom have been former user members and who are specially trained into the work. Each member of the QA team has responsibility for a group of centres and the setting up of twice-yearly centre evaluation days to ensure good practice. In supervision, co-ordinators are encouraged and expected to bring issues that are concerning them within their centre management. These may be relationship issues between mothers or mother and child or problems occurring between staff members and mothers. Or in fact any issue which is affecting their centre management. The emphasis is on honesty in an atmosphere that is supportive and understanding. But it is also challenging – not condoning or turning a blind eye to bad practice, but responding constructively, in a way which supports the centre and does not negate the individual approach of the co-ordinator. If personal issues seem to be negatively influencing practice (and expressing these is also encouraged), the facilitator would suggest that time be sought with an experienced counsellor or therapist. The facilitator would help the individual co-ordinator to access appropriate support outside NEWPIN if this proved necessary.

It is of crucial importance that play facilitators and other play staff should fully support the NEWPIN ethos. We have found that some people who express an interest in working exclusively with children are ambivalent with their relationships with the children's parents. They can covertly give off (and sometimes overtly) a superior knowledge above the parent concerning the child's needs. This can negate the parent and leave an anxiety within the parent that the play worker appears to know more about one's child than the parent themselves. This in NEWPIN terms is not only useless but can contribute to the notion of 'failed' parenting. The continuing importance of recognising a mother's positive changing relationship with her child, however small each step may be, cannot be undermined by the attitudes of play staff or other judgemental mothers.

Some of this practice has to some extent grown out of the statutory expectations of what good child-care standards should be and therefore recruitment of play staff must be sympathetic to this. NEWPIN aims to secure play workers who have sufficient emotional awareness themselves so that they can explore their own feelings as to the child–parent relationship without over reaction, in a process which involves both the parents and their children in an equal interaction. Play facilitators and play workers are supervised by their centre co-ordinator along similar lines. As part of their induction they will spend time in other centres both as user members and observing practice. Additionally there are four training days a year each – for co-ordinators and play facilitators.

Like the centre members all staff have an informal network of support to discuss concerns with each other as well as having access to their Quality Assurance supervisors. The NEWPIN culture is in an important sense non-hierarchical, enabling staff to move between posts, without feeling they are moving 'up' or 'down'. User members to become co-ordinators and central office managers.

Outcomes of NEWPIN's approach

A remarkable feature of NEWPIN users is that they have a lively idea of what they are doing and where they are going; and an impressive fluency of expression. Six months after the NEWPIN centre was started in Bidwill, a depressed suburb of Sydney, several user members appeared on national television speaking calmly but forcefully about the terrible personal problems they had experienced and about how they were overcoming these with the help of the centre. To appear in such a public way – talking about matters of great sensitivity – was beyond their imagination when they entered the NEWPIN process. Such remarkable personal development is characteristic of NEWPIN users everywhere.

Looking back to the positive message that the co-ordinator gave to Mary in the pre-NEWPIN chat described on pages 223–224 – this began Mary's process of increasing self-validation. Mary has now been involved with the NEWPIN centre for one and a half years and has completed the programmes. Although she does not find it easy to befriend others into the centre she is an active supporter in the NEWPIN living room and can care for new members well until they are successfully attached themselves. Her relationship with her toddler is warm and interactive and the toddler is no longer on the child protection register. Mary is confident enough to be considering further opportunities provided through the NEWPIN training department and will say frankly that she dreads to think what would have happened to her and her child if she hadn't come to NEWPIN. When asked about this she said that she would be dead and possibly her daughter as well as she could see no future for either of them.

Mary is fairly typical of some of the NEWPIN members insofar as she was initially hard to engage, ambivalently attached to the centre and needed constant affirmative messages about herself and her mothering of Clodagh – her baby. She would often fall back and feel defeated. Although not aggressive in herself she initially attached herself to outwardly stronger women who could behave aggressively. When she began to make sense for herself of why she needed to identify with other members in this way she was able to challenge their behaviour in a constructive manner without losing their friendship and could support their own capacity for self-reflection. Giving positive affirming messages is at the heart of NEWPIN's work. Eventually these messages become absorbed and members gain a new perception of themselves.

The Foundation Course

This 14-month course has been designed for members who are ready to move on from their centre to a position in NEWPIN and acts as a bridge between being a user member and being a paid member of staff. Members participating in this course also act as a visible role model to other members. They will have completed all the modules, supported other mothers and will be on the point of leaving the Therapeutic Support Group. This course enables them to consider a future – but not at cost to the parent–child relationship which is the fulcrum of NEWPIN's work. Course members leave their centre and begin working for three days a week at another centre, where they will develop further through shadowing the centre's co-ordinator, learning how to conduct pre-NEWPIN chats, running supporters' groups and participating in the SEERS programme. The theoretical component consists of levels 2 and 3 of the National Vocational Qualifications in Child Care and Counselling Skills. They will be helped to put together a CV and to develop their writing skills.

All the Foundation Course students will be members of a facilitated experiential group. This gives them personal support as they come to terms with their changing role. To this group they bring personal and work issues, which may affect their performance at work. Through the group they help each other in handling sensitive issues surrounding membership in the centre. They are encouraged to express themselves directly toward staff and other user members and to learn to openly challenge adverse behaviour in the centre. The experiential group enables them to form strong and supportive bonds with each other.

The Foundation Course is a prerequisite for members hoping to go on to train as NEWPIN co-ordinators. Currently 70 per cent of NEWPIN co-ordinators are former user members. That women who originally appeared with sometimes severe degrees of dysfunction can hold down such demanding jobs is a measure of the efficacy of the NEWPIN model.

Recent developments

Work with Fathers

Since 1982 the work of NEWPIN has developed significantly. There are now fathers' personal development programmes, which are separate from the mothers' activities. These take place in the evenings and at weekends using the same centre that the mothers attend. The same consideration and recognition of human vulnerability applies for the fathers as to the mothers and children who attend the centre in the daytime. Fathers also have a deep craving for a warm caring environment in which to work through past and present emotional damage.

Along with the Personal Development Programmes and the Therapeutic Support Groups the programmes are specifically tailored to the needs of men with particular emphasis as to what are known as male problems such as male violence. A different approach is needed for men whose childhood culture suppressed the expression of emotion. Fathers who were taught as children that it is weak to cry – 'stop behaving like a baby' – have developed a strong defensive front when faced with painful life situations. Our experience has shown us that they need much more time to get to know each other before they can open up and express freely and deeply how they feel. All this is taken into consideration when devising programmes. Men in the fathers' groups are particularly grateful for the opportunity to share and to deal with some of their innermost feelings which have no place among their peers, a problem which is much more severe for men than it is for women.

When NEWPIN began, the brief was to support main carers of children and these were preponderantly women. Fathers were initially accepted, but unlike the mothers they had the benefit of statutory child-care facilities so they did not bring their children when they accessed the programmes. However, the integration of fathers was found to be disruptive: invariably, isolated and lonely women sought to create a relationship with the usually sole male member. This set up an adverse dynamic, as patterns of past destructive relationships were re-worked. NEWPIN's measured response was to restrict the centres to mothers and children only. However, NEWPIN is now seeking to incorporate fathers who have participated in their own Personal Development Programme into the established centres as they will have developed a clear perception of the personal dynamics of the integrated centre and will be able to deal with adverse situations which inhibit the development work.

Very young parents

NEWPIN has established its first young mothers' centre in Peckham in south London and this project will link into the local schools to enable the young mothers to learn about themselves and the needs of their children. It has also started an antenatal project working with vulnerable pregnant women from Guys and St Thomas' Hospital Trusts. This work will be extended to other areas – especially to those proximal to NEWPIN centres. All of these programmes focus primarily on positive re-building of the self and forging healthy emotional relationships with their children and important relationships in their lives and that of their children.

Conclusion

NEWPIN is as much prey to the many imponderables as is any family centre work. But through the 'soft' nature of its centres its organisational structure appears to work well with a wide range of family distress. It underlies a vigorous programme deriving from some hard analyses of the realities of life in distressed families. The success of any enterprise which is dedicated to supporting troubled families needs a flexible but containing model and must be prepared to accept that each individual parent will react differently when facing life adversity.

NEWPIN's soft structured approach for distressed families relies on reciprocal support and equality regardless of rank or pay. It recognises human needs and strengths irrespective of supposed 'failed or faulty parenting'. Parents become aware of the value of respecting their children's need for autonomy even in their dependency as they parent them to a mature safe adulthood.

The success of NEWPIN's approach is borne out by the fact that of the children on the child protection register, and of others who would have been placed on the register had they come to the attention of the authorities, or who have been removed from the register but require parenting supervision, not one has experienced serious abuse at home when their parent is well-attached to a NEWPIN centre. Application of the core value of 'equality' invests in each user member a positive role in the running of her centre and its programmes. This is an essential part of the shift to a proactive mindset in an environment where people feel valued. This is the basis of positive personal change.

Further reading

Bowlby, J. (1969) *Attachment and Loss.* London: Tavistock.

Bowlby, J. (1988) *A Secure Base: Clinical Applications of Attachment Theory.* London: Routledge.

Cox, A. *et al.* (1987) *The Evaluation of a Home Visiting and Befriending Scheme.* NEWPIN.

Jenkins, A. (1987) 'Recognising and treating the hurt child within the parent.' In R. Whitfield and D. Baldwin (eds) *Families Matter.* Collins Fount.

Marrone, M. (1998) *Attachment and Interaction.* London: Jessica Kingsley Publishers.

Mills, M. and Puckering, C. (1995) 'Bringing About Change in Parent–Child Relationships', Chapter 12 in J. Trowell and M. Bower *The Emotional Needs of Young Children and Their Families.* London: Routledge.

Pines, M. (1998) *Circular Reflections.* London: Jessica Kingsley Publishers.

Pound, A. (1994) *NEWPIN: A Befriending and Therapeutic Network for Carers of Young Children.* London: HMSO/NEWPIN.

PART 4

Conclusion

Chapter 14

Transfer of Learning

Reflections on a Student Placement in a Family Centre

Laraine Beavis

Looking back at my social work training, some years after qualifying, one of the most significant experiences in shaping my practice was a six-month placement at a therapeutic family centre in the third year of my social work degree course. Social work placements always caused great difficulties as there were barely enough opportunities to accommodate all students. I was told that I was to work at a therapeutic family centre; not my first choice! Fellow students' attitudes were varied but on the whole were not very positive. I recall such comments as 'You'll be bored' and 'It will be like childminding' and 'There'll be very few qualified workers'. A couple of lone voices told me that I would learn a lot and enjoy the placement. I therefore began the placement with some wariness and uncertainty as to what to expect. However, my experiences over that time have consistently influenced and informed my post-qualifying work, initially as a paediatric social worker and currently as a family placement practitioner.

My aim in this chapter is to reflect on my placement at the family centre, focusing particularly on what I consider to be special about such a setting that facilitated such valuable and influential learning experience. However, since the list could be long I will concentrate on two specific areas: first, family dynamics and second, poverty and discrimination.

Family dynamics

For six months I worked for three days a week at a therapeutic family centre, managed by NCH. The centre operated on a referral basis for families with children under five years of age and they (almost exclusively mothers and children) attended from 10 a.m. to 3 p.m. two, three or even four times a week. A cooked lunch was provided and staff and families ate together. Being in the company of the same families three or four times a week for often as long as five-hour periods and being keyworker to one particular family gave me an insight into some of the struggles that are not always apparent in the brief contact of much social work interaction. Family members can be observed interacting with their peers, with staff and with each other. They can be observed at informal breaks, over a meal-time, in activity groups and during both individual and group counselling. With such an intensive opportunity to interact, observe and assess families, the worker is generally more able to gain an impression of the dynamics within that family and may then begin to have some understanding as to what changes are needed to protect and preserve the family and keep the children safe. It is difficult over long periods for family members to maintain a facade.

Throughout the placement I was keyworker for a young woman who was referred to the centre with her son aged four and her daughter aged ten months. There were concerns about her relationship with her son. He was felt at risk of physical abuse and was small in stature and underweight. The mother herself was asking for help and had been referred by her health visitor. An example of the interactions that can be observed and assessed in such a setting is shown in the following scenario.

The mother was observed over a meal-time without interference until it became necessary to protect her son. As lunch-time approached, the mother began to watch the clock very closely and her conversation turned to food. She was eager to be sitting at the table as soon as the food was being served but was rather slow in helping the other mothers and staff to set the table and organise the room. It was clear that her priority was to feed herself not her children. She did not prepare the baby's food beforehand so that when the baby began crying with hunger at the same time as her own food appeared, she became visibly irritated at having to make up the baby's food and feed her. Instead of concentrating on the baby's needs, she 'shovelled' the food into her daughter as quickly as possible while watching her own food being served. She then greedily ate her own food, wanting to finish before the other mothers and staff so that she could claim any 'seconds'. The baby ate well and the mother appeared to hold her frustration in check about the 'interference' with her own meal. However, her control slipped very easily when her son became far from co-operative.

Initially she ignored his needs and clearly expected him to be quite independent. Although he had earlier demonstrated the ability to feed himself, he generally chose not to do so. He vied for his mother's attention and only seemed to be able to gain it by misbehaving. He kept getting off his chair and moving around, and used his fingers to eat with rather than utensils. He played with his food, pushing it around his plate, and hardly ate a thing. He would then 'accidentally' knock his drink over. His mother grew visibly more angry with him until she lost her temper completely and appeared oblivious to the other families and staff around her. She shouted loudly at her son, handled him roughly and threatened him. Without staff intervention there was every indication that she would have hit him. The boy's reaction was to shout back at her and try to get out of reach. He did not cry. The baby showed no reaction to the outbursts and continued finger-feeding and watching the scenario.

Observing this drama unfold was quite painful to watch without interfering and helping in the first instance. It revealed the mother's intense desire to satisfy her own need of nourishment above all else, a need arising not from under-nourishment or hunger from lack of food. Her anger was clearly visible and physical violence an observable risk. The vehemence with which this was directed against her son was disturbing. The boy could be seen to be deliberately increasing his disruptive behaviour until he obtained his mother's full attention, which was when she lost her temper. Although he then tried to avoid his mother to shield himself from her verbal and threatened physical assault, his verbal and non-verbal communication was also predominantly expressing anger rather than fear or upset. The baby's indifference to the uproar gave an indication that such interactions were not uncommon in that household. Subsequent days showed that this pattern of behaviour was not an isolated incident and gave a basis to explore with the mother on a behavioural basis how to manage meal-times better but also to explore her own emotional needs and the intensity and origins of her negative feelings towards her son.

This 30-minute meal-time, where several families and workers were together, enabled an observation to take place without the mother being too aware of any focus of attention on herself. The behaviour unfolded to reveal the problems but in a way that intervention could take place at an appropriate time to protect the child. Once things had calmed down an individual session with the mother could look at what had happened, acknowledge her difficulties and start to plan how meal-times could be better managed. As a team, with several members who were present at the meal-time, we discussed what had taken place and shared ideas on how to handle the situation, identifying strategies to try to bring about change. This required skilled negotiation with other mothers and staff as much of the work was undertaken in the group setting. For example a decision was made that the boy would not be allowed to get down from the table or we risked all the children copying this, but that providing he began to eat we would not worry too much if he did not use the utensils or just wanted to use a spoon, bearing in mind there were concerns about his weight. Peer advice, although sometimes unhelpful, was generally a positive influence; sometimes mothers who had been part of the family centre for longer would encourage a mother to co-operate and try to work things out. At one stage the mother with whom I was working began to ask for her son to attend the centre on his own and made excuses as to why she could not attend herself on that particular day and this had to be addressed. While working with these families it was inevitably a fine line between enabling and de-skilling or creating over-dependence.

Applying the learning in family placement work

In my current post of family placement worker I assess both prospective foster carers and adoptive parents and have been able to build on the valuable skills of observation that was an integral part of family centre work. Prospective carers have a vested interest in trying to portray themselves as what they perceive the 'ideal' family that social services are looking for; none more so than couples who are desperate to adopt. Any facade has to be seen through and as accurate assessment as possible be made of their skills and weaknesses, together with their interpersonal relationships, attitudes, values and either parenting or potential parenting skills in order not just to be approved as carers but particularly with adoption, to assist in the matching process which is so critical to the success of a placement.

In supporting foster placements, the experiences of striving to work with children and families in a constructive partnership rather than a dependent or de-skilling relationship is revisited. Not only are these aims important in guiding and supporting the foster carers in my role as link worker to care for and manage the often difficult behaviour of distressed children placed in care but also, since the majority of fostered children return home, in supporting the carers to work alongside the birth parents in a way that does not undermine their confidence but is a constructive partnership. A significant number of children are accommodated during periods where their parent is suffering from mental health problems and to see their child more relaxed and happy and more controllable in a placement can further dent the parent's confidence and self-esteem.

I am able to draw on my experiences of facing similar dilemmas when working with the children and mothers at the family centre. I learnt always to remember who was the parent and to ask their permission, for example if they were happy for me to take their child to the toilet or to check with them about what they wanted their child to drink. In similar ways foster carers can work so as not to undermine the parents by discussion and inclusion, for example by saying 'perhaps you could try x or y' rather than 'don't do that, do this'. It is perhaps one of the most difficult balances to achieve and the family centre placement gave me an excellent overview of the problems of the dynamics involved. I learnt some of the strategies used by the experienced workers which gave me a good foundation on which to build.

Poverty and discrimination

Both formal and informal group sessions with mothers in the family centre gave a clear insight into the difficulties faced by many families because of poverty, class and discrimination. The depth of their feelings and unhappiness at the way they perceived the system to be treating them helped me to understand the barriers that can exist to change and to effective working. The women expressed views, for example, regarding the way in which they had to queue at the Benefits office. They commented on the fact that there were no facilities for children, which frequently caused problems when the wait was a long one, and that they sometimes felt intimidated by the men in the queues. They added that they felt as if they were not entitled to the money and disliked the grilles on the counters.

Another discussion centred around one woman's experience of only being given a week's notice to move accommodation. She was living in a crowded flat and had been waiting a long time to be re-housed. She did not want to lose the house offered and therefore did not complain to the housing authority about the short notice, but her distress and anxiety around the logistics of getting everything organised so quickly was clearly expressed with her peers. The feeling in the group was one of anger at her not being given enough time to sort schools out for children and to get packed and physically move, together with anger at her powerlessness to express any unhappiness for fear of losing the new home. In another discussion a mother described how it had taken a substantial length of time to summon police help following an incident of domestic violence. Mothers believed that they were discriminated against because they lived on a deprived estate in a particular area of town in which domestic violence was not uncommon and the police did not protect as quickly as the women felt that they should.

The conversations between these mothers helped me to gain a sense of perspective of issues and to begin to understand how their feelings of low self-esteem, powerlessness, vulnerability and anger at the system were fuelled. Over the six-month placement many similar incidents were discussed and the discrimination experienced because of poverty and class was evident. All these incidents helped me to be aware of how often families who are already struggling to cope are so often expected to fall in with the way social services systems work or be penalised when the expectations are unrealistic. Many of the mothers struggled to have themselves and their children ready in the morning to be picked up by the centre mini-bus between 9.30 and 10.00 a.m., yet they were often given other appointments at inconvenient times without any help with transport, and with no follow-up if an appointment was missed.

Applying learning in another social work setting

These experiences helped me to continually assess what I was expecting a family to do and to try to ensure that I was not setting them up to fail or arranging to see them at a time when it was going to cause them a lot of problems. It also helped me to consider when working with families the impact of other agencies' expectations and to consider at times whether liaison or advocacy might be required. In subsequent work as a social worker for a maternity and special care baby unit, this experience enabled me to empathise with many families who had problems with housing. In one particular case I was able to support and advocate for a young single pregnant girl whose parents refused to allow her to continue living at home. I accompanied and supported her in an interview with the Homeless Officer and helped her to obtain accommodation. I believe that I was more sensitive to the impact on this young person, and I hope a better advocate, because of my experiences at the family centre.

I was also more aware of the discrimination encountered from many quarters by young single mothers who found it difficult to access ante- and post-natal services because of the culture of these services, which were geared to older women in a stable relationship with a planned pregnancy. Further problems were often witnessed when mothers had themselves or their babies transferred to another hospital, sometimes up to 30 miles away, when the special care baby unit was at capacity. Not all the mothers had support, transport or money to use public transport. Financial help could be given but again a bureaucratic process was in place and various forms had to be filled in and documents produced, and offices to be visited at a time of immense emotional stress. It is one thing to know the theory of this but working in the close environment of the family centre I was able to experience directly the powerful feelings associated with this uphill struggle and be more empathetic to subsequent families facing similar problems.

The family centre staff, both qualified and not, were skilled and experienced workers. They worked very much as a team. The value of reflective practice within the team group was an integral way of working and became an important part of the way I have subsequently worked.

It is now several years since I was a student at the therapeutic family centre but I continue to draw on the lessons learnt about systems theory, psychodynamic principles, team work, groupwork, observation and assessment, family dynamics and discrimination...the list is almost endless. I consider myself fortunate to have experienced such a formative placement. I was not bored! It was nothing like childminding! I learned a tremendous amount and thoroughly enjoyed the placement.

Endpiece

Linnet McMahon and Adrian Ward

We hope that this book has shown that therapeutic work in family centres is not the preserve of a small band of experts who work behind closed doors. On the contrary it is a way of working that is open to all workers who wish to be helpful to young children and their families. In fact it is most successful when all workers share an understanding of the therapeutic task and work openly and as a team in carrying it out. We hope that this book has provided a theoretical framework that links directly to practice, which can support the team of family centre workers in making sense of what they are trying to do, and gives them tools to do the work.

Working therapeutically is not incompatible with empowerment and 'rights' work. On the contrary, working in partnership with parents, with respect for open and two-way communication, and with continuing regard for the way in which people, families and cultures differ, and with awareness of the effect of (and our own part in) racism and other forms of oppression, is an essential part of helping create change.

We hope too that this book will contribute to the beginning of a 'climate' change in child care in the UK towards re-valuing therapeutic approaches to work with young children and their families. In some areas family centres' very existence is still under threat and many more are under pressure to abandon long-term work with families in favour of brief interventions. Workers feel de-valued. Some excellent work teams have been disbanded, and such skilled team work cannot easily be replaced even when the policy pendulum swings back in their favour.

We have seen that early intervention is important and can make a difference to the lives of children and their families. However, it is clear that short-term interventions are not enough to help the most needy families and that for them work over the longer term is essential if real change is to be achieved. These families, with their capacity to engender stress and the inability to think, make enormous demands on those setting out to help them, Kindness and goodwill, although crucial, are not enough. Thorough and appropriate training and ongoing support are needed for this complex work. Society cannot afford simply to paper over the cracks. Public concern about and for children who are troubled and may become troublesome must be backed by the kinds of help which can make a difference and by the training and support which makes this possible.

Narrative Stems for Pre-schoolers

Using miniature toy animals and bendy dolls, start the story, enacting it at the same time, and then ask the child to 'show me what happens next'. At the end of each story ask 'how does the animal/child feel?'

Note: Acknowledgement to Jill Hodges 1997 and McArthur Battery of Tests.

The Lost Little Pig
Set out where the big and little pigs live together, describing it as you do. Say 'The little pig goes for a walk' (and enact this), 'and gets lost, and doesn't know how to get back. Show me what happens.'

Going Home
'A child is taking a nice picture home from school, and knocks at the door. Show me what happens.'

Hot Gravy
'The child is in a hurry for supper, grabs the pan off the stove, and gets burned... Show me what happens.'

Lost Keys
'Mum and Dad come home and are standing outside the front door arguing over who lost the keys... Show me what happens.'

Crying Outside
'The child goes out the back of the house and cries... Show me what happens.'

Stamping Elephant
'The elephant is in a bad mood and stamping around, so the other animals are scared... Show me what happens.'

Provide a doll's house and miniature toys for the child to use:

- 'Tell me a story about bed time.'
- 'Tell me a story about a time that was really happy.'
- 'Tell me a story about a time that was really sad.'

Narrative Stems for School Years Children

These stories (from Farnfield 1994, based on Bretherton, Ridgeway and Cassidy 1990) are particularly useful for work with children in care or children who have had changes in carer. They require a selection of doll people, two doll's houses, furniture and a car.

1. Ask The Child To Choose A Family

'Will you choose a family from the figures here in this box…'

(*Prompt*: 'As many or as few as you like.')

It is a family (not their family).

'Would you like to put the family in one of the houses?'

'And put some furniture in the house; use as much or as little as you like.'

(*Taking each room in turn*) 'Tell me what is going on there.'

'Now I am going to tell you the beginning of a story. What I would like you to do is tell me or show me how the story ends.'

2. The Spilt Drink Story (Mother)

'One of the children in the family wants a drink. Would you choose one of the children. Do you want to give her/him a name?'

'His/her mother gives X a drink and says don't take it up to your room because you might spill it on the new carpet. X says s/he won't but then takes it up to his/her room and spills the drink on the new carpet. Will you tell me or show me what happens next.'

(*Prompt, if the mother doesn't find out*: 'Supposing X's Mum did find out, what happens then?')

'How does X feel?'

3. The Spilt Drink Story (Father)

'X wants a drink and this time asks his/her father. He gives him/her a drink and says don't take it up to your room because you might spill it on the new carpet. X says s/he won't but then takes it up to his/her room and spills the drink on the new carpet. Will you tell me or show me what happens next'

'How does X feel?'

4. The Noise In The Night

'X is in bed one night. Everyone else is in bed and X hears a loud noise downstairs. Tell me or show me what happens next?'

'How does X feel?'

5. The Protection Story

'X comes home from school. S/he has been bullied. Both his/her parents are at home. Tell me or show me what happens next.'

(*Prompts*: 'Does s/he tell Mum or Dad?'

'Then what happens?' (e.g. *child says parents see the head*)
'Does the bully stop?'
'Tell me how.'
'What should s/he do about the bully then?'
'How does s/he feel?')

6. The Separation Story

'Now X goes to stay with another family. Will you choose this other family from the dolls in the box. And would you like to put them into their house?' (i.e. *the second house*).

(*Note composition of the new family.*)

'Why do you think X has gone to stay with this family?'

(*Prompt*: 'Can you think of any reason why s/he might?')

'Do any of the other children in X's family go too?'

'Can you say why?'

'How does s/he feel?'

7. The Hurt Knee Story

'Outside this (*second*) house X falls off his/her bike and cuts his/her knee. There is a lot of blood and it hurts. Tell me or show me what happens next.'

'How does s/he feel?'

8. The Re-Union Story

'One day X's Mum and Dad come to the door and say they want her to come home with them again. Tell me or show me what happens next.'

(*Prompts*: 'Why...doesn't s/he like them?'
'What does X want?'
'Does X know?'
'Can you tell me what X wants?'
'What do her Mum and Dad do now?'
'How does s/he feel?')

9. The Child Is In Trouble Story

'Think of a situation where X is in a lot of difficulty or danger. Something pretty serious has happened and s/he needs the help of a grown up. What sort of thing might happen?'

(*Finally*: 'Let's put all the children and families back in the box.'

'Do you think those stories were too young for you, or too old for you or just about right?')

Questions Excerpted from the Adult Attachment Interview (George, Kaplan and Main 1985)

Note: Additional questions by Crittenden (1997) are marked with an asterisk. See also Hesse 1999, p.397.

What is the earliest memory that you have as a child?* (This taps *imaged memory*)

Can you give me five adjectives or phrases to describe your relationship with your mother/father when you were young? (*semantic or script memory*)

Can you tell me about a particular occasion when your relationship was x? (*episodic memory*)

Which parent did you feel closest to? Why? (*integrative memory*)

When you were upset as a child what did you do? For example, what happened when you were ill? When you were hurt? Can you remember a particular time? (*semantic* then *episodic memory*)

Could you tell me about the first time you remember being separated from your parents? (*episodic*)

When you were young did you ever feel rejected by your parents – even though they might not have meant it or been aware of it? (*semantic*)

Can you remember a time when this happened? (*episodic*)

Why do you think your parents did this? (*integrative*)

Can you think of a time when your parents were angry with you, or you were angry with them?* (*episodic*)

Questions about potentially dangerous experiences

Did your parents ever threaten you, for example, for discipline or even jokingly?

Did you ever feel very frightened or unsafe?*

Do you worry about something like this happening again?*

(*semantic/episodic: probing unresolved trauma*)

Questions about loss

When you were young did you experience the loss of someone close to you?

How did you respond at the time?

Have your feelings regarding this death changed much over time?

Integrative questions

Looking back on it now do you think your parents loved you?*

Why do you think your parents behaved as they did, during your childhood?

Taken as a whole how do you think your childhood experiences have affected your adult personality?

References

Ahmed, S., Cheetham, J. and Small, J. (eds) (1986) *Social Work with Black Children and their Families.* London: Batsford.

Ainsworth, M., Blehar, M., Waters, E. and Wall, S. (1978) *Patterns Of Attachment: A Psychological Study Of The Strange Situation.* Hillsdale, N.J.: Erlbaum.

Anderson, H. and Goolishian, H. A. (1988) 'Human systems as linguistic systems: evolving ideas about the implications for therapy practice'. *Family Process 27,* 371–393.

Anthony, E. and Bene, E. (1957) 'A technique for the objective assessment of the child's family relationships.' *Journal of Mental Science 103,* 541–555.

Audit Commission (1994) 'Seen but not heard: Coordinating community child health and social services for children in need – Detailed evidence and guidelines for managers and practitioners.' London: HMSO.

Axline, V. (1947 and 1989) *Dibs, in Search of Self.* Boston: Houghton Miflin; Edinburgh: Churchill Livingstone.

Axline, V. (1969) *Play Therapy.* New York: Ballantine Books.

Axline, V. (1982) 'Entering the child's world via the play experience.' In G. L. Landreth (ed) *Play Therapy: Dynamics of the Process of Counselling Children.* Illinois: Charles C. Thomas.

Bain, A. and Barnett, L. (1980) *The Design of a Day Care System in a Nursery Setting for Children Under Five.* London: Tavistock Institute of Human Relations, Document No. 2T347.

Bain, A. and Barnett, L. (1986) *The Design of a Day Care System in a Nursery Setting for Children under Five,* Part 1 Abridged version of Bain & Barnett 1980; Part 2 Application of Principles in Devon: *TIHR Occasional Paper 8.*

Balbernie, R. (1966) *Residential Work with Children.* London: Human Context Books.

Batchelor, J. and Kerslake, A. (1990) *Failure to Find Failure to Thrive.* London: Whiting and Birch.

Bates, J. (1997) 'Men, masculinity and child care', (Cited in Pringle, K. (1992) *Danger! Men at (Social) Work,* p.2) In J. Bates, R. Pugh and N. Thompson (eds) *Protecting Children: Challenges and Change.* Aldershot: Arena.

Berrueta-Clement, J., Schweinhart, L., Barnett, W. and Weikart, D. (1984) *Changed Lives: The Effects of the Perry Pre-school Program on Youth Through Age 19.* Monographs of the High Scope Educational Research Foundation No 8, Michigan: High Scope. (See also Lazar and Darlington (1982) on Home Start.)

Bettelheim, B. (1960) *The Informed Heart.* Glencoe, USA: Free Press.

Bettelheim, B. (1987) *A Good Enough Parent.* London: Thames and Hudson.

Bion, W. (1962) *Learning from Experience.* London: Heinemann/Karnac.

Binney, V., McKnight, I. and Broughton, S. (1994) 'Relationship Play Therapy for Attachment Disturbances in Four to Seven Year Old Children.' In J. Richer (ed) 'The Clinical Applications of Ethology and Attachment Theory.' *Association for Child Psychology and Psychiatry Occasional Papers 9*.

Blaug, R. (1989) 'Staff Anxiety and its Management in a Day Nursery.' *Journal of Social Work Practice*, May 1–10.

Boston, M. and Szur, R. (eds) (1990) *Psychotherapy with Severely Deprived Children*. London: Karnac.

Bower, M. (1995) 'Psychodynamic family therapy with parents and under-fives.' In J. Trowell and M. Bower (eds) (1995) *The Emotional Needs of Children and Families*. London: Routledge.

Bowlby, J. (1969 and 1982) *Attachment and Loss* – vol 1 (second edition, 1984); *Attachment* – vol 2 (1973 & 1985); *Separation: Anxiety and Anger*, – vol 3 (1980) *Loss, Sadness and Depression*, London: Hogarth Press and Penguin.

Bowlby, J. (1988) *A Secure Base: Clinical Applications of Attachment Theory*. London: Routledge.

Boyd-Franklin, N. (1989) *Black Families in Therapy*. New York and London: The Guilford Press.

Brazelton, T. and Barnard, K. (eds) (1986) *Touch*. New York: International Universities Press.

Brazelton, T. and Cramer, B. G. (1991) *The Earliest Relationship: Parents, Infants and the Drama of Early Attachment*. London: Karnac.

Bretherton, I., Ridgeway, D. and Cassidy, J. (1990) 'Assessing internal working models of the attachment relationship.' In M. Greenberg, D. Cicchetti and E. Cummings (eds) *Attachment in the Preschool Years*. University of Chicago Press.

Bretherton, I. and Waters, E. (eds) (1985) *Growing Points of Attachment Theory and Research*. Chicago: University of Chicago Press.

Briggs, S. (1995) 'From subjectivity towards realism: Child observation and social work.' In M. Yelloly and M. Henkel *Learning and Teaching in Social Work*. London: Jessica Kingsley Publishers.

Briggs, S. (1997) *Growth and Risk in Infancy*. London: Jessica Kingsley Publishers.

Britton, R. (1983) 'Breakdown and reconstitution of the family circle.' In M. Boston and R. Szur (eds) (1990) *Psychotherapy with Severely Deprived Children*. London: Karnac.

Broughton, S., McKnight, I. and Binney, V. (1992) *Manual for Relationship Play Therapy*. Family Psychiatry Department, Doncaster Royal Infirmary, Armthorpe Road, Doncaster.

Brown, A. and Clough, R. (ed) (1989) *Groups and Groupings: Life and Work in Day and Residential Centres*. London and New York: Tavistock/Routledge.

Bruggen, P. and O'Brian, C. (1987) *Helping Families: Systems, Residential and Agency Responsibility*. London: Faber.

Brummer, N. (1988) 'White social workers, Black children: Issues of identity.' In J. Aldgate and J. Simmonds (eds) *Direct Work with Children*. London: Batsford/ BAAF.

Buchsbaum, H., Toth, S., Clyman, R., Cicchetti, D. and Emde, R. (1992) 'The use of a narrative story stem technique with maltreated children: Implications for theory and practice.' *Development and Psychopathology 4*, 603–625.

Burnham, J. (1986) *Family Therapy*. London: Tavistock Publications.

Burr, V. (1995) *An Introduction to Social Constructionism*. London: Routledge.

Burton, J. (1993) *The Handbook of Residential Care*. London: Routledge.

Butt, J. and Box, L. (1998) *Family Centred: A Study of the Use of Family Centres by Black Families*. London: REU.

Byng-Hall, J. (1995) *Rewriting Family Scripts: Improvisation and Systems Change*. London: Guilford Press.

Byng-Hall, J. (1997) 'The Secure Family Base: Some Implications for Family Therapy.' In G. Forrest (ed) *Bonding and Attachment: Current Issues in Research & Practice*. London: Association for Child Psychology and Psychiatry.

Cannan, C. (1992) *Changing Families, Changing Welfare: Family Centres and the Welfare State*. Hemel Hampsted: Harvester Weatsheaf.

Cardona, F. (1994) 'Facing an uncertain future.' In A. Obholzer and V. Z. Roberts (eds) *The Unconscious at Work*. London: Routledge.

Carroll, J. (1998) *Introduction to Therapeutic Play*. Oxford: Blackwell Scientific.

Chrystal, J. (1998) 'Child Protection versus Therapy: the impact of this dilemma on parents attending Greenham House Family Centre.' (Dissertation for MA in Advanced Social Work Studies) University of Reading.

Chrystal, J. and Ward, A. (1999) 'The therapeutic family centre: do child protection concerns inhibit the therapy?' *Issues in Social Work Education 18*, 2, 70–74.

Cigno, K. (1988) 'Consumers' views of a family centre drop-in.' *British Journal of Social Work 18*, 361–375.

Cole, T. (1998) *Thrive Line Acetates and Cole Calculator*. Child Growth Foundation, 2 Mayfield Avenue, London W4 1PW.

Copley, B. and Forryan, B. (1987/1997) *Therapeutic Work with Children and Young People*. London: Robert Royce/Cassell.

Coulter, H. and Loughlin, E. (1999) 'Synergy of verbal and non-verbal therapies in the treatment of mother–infant relationships.' *British Journal of Psychotherapy 16*, 1.

Cox, A., Puckering, C., Pound, A., Mills, M. and Owen, A. (1990) *The Evaluation of a Home Visiting and Befriending Scheme*: NEWPIN. Final Report to the DOH Research Group.

Crittenden, P. (1992) 'Treatment of anxious attachment in infancy and early childhood.' *Development and Psychopathology 4*, 575–602.

Crittenden, P. (1995) 'Attachment and Psychopathology.' In S. Goldberg, R. Muir and J. Kerr (eds) *Attachment Theory: Social, Developmental, and Clinical Perspectives*. London and New York: The Analytic Press.

Crittenden, P. (1997) *Modified Adult Attachment Interview*, Unpublished. Miami: Family Relations Institute.

Crittenden, P. (1999) *Patterns of Attachment in Adulthood: A Dynamic-Maturation Approach to Analyzing the Adult Attachment Interview*. Unpublished. Miami. Family Relations Institute.

Crittenden, P. and Ainsworth, M. (1989) 'Child Maltreatment and Attachment Theory.' In D. Cicchetti and V. Carlson (eds) *Child Maltreatment: Theory and Research on the Causes and Consequences of Child Abuse and Neglect*, pp.432–463. New York: Cambridge University Press.

Dacre, V. (1996) 'A study of practice within family centres by means of a literature search.' (Dissertation for MA in Therapeutic Child Care) University of Reading.

Dale, P., Davies, M., Morrison, T. and Waters, J. (1986) *Dangerous Families: Assessment and Treatment of Child Abuse*. London: Tavistock.

Dasgupta, C. (1999) 'Listening to children through play.' In P. Milner and B. Carolin (eds) (1999) *Time to Listen to Children*. London: Routledge.

Davis, M. and Wallbridge, D. (1981) *Boundary and Space*. New York and London: Karnac Books.

De'Ath, E. (1985) *Self Help and Family Centres*. London: National Children's Bureau.

De Board, R. (1978) *The Psychoanalysis of Organizations*. London: Tavistock.

Deco, S. (1990) 'A family centre: a structural family therapy approach.' In C. Case and T. Dalley (eds) (1990) *Working with Children in Art Therapy*. London: Routledge.

Department of Health (1991) *1989 Children Act Guidance and Regulations: volume 2 – Family Support, Day Care and Educational Provision for Young Children*. London: HMSO.

Department of Health (1995) *Child Protection – Messages from Research*. London: HMSO.

Department of Health (1998) *Families in Focus: Evaluation of the Department of Health's Refocusing Children's Services Initiative*. London: HMSO.

Department of Health (1999) *Getting Family Support Right: Inspection of the Delivery of Family Support Services*. London: HMSO.

Department of Health (1999b) *Working Together to Safeguard Children: Government Guidance in Inter-Agency Cooperation*. London: HMSO.

Department of Health (2000) *Framework For The Assessment Of Children In Need And Their Families*. London: HMSO.

DiPhillips, N. and Elliott, V. (1987) 'The Amersham Family Centre.' *Child Abuse Review* 1, 5, 13–16.

Dockar-Drysdale, B. (1968) *Therapy in Child Care*. London: Longman.

Dockar-Drysdale, B. (1990) *The Provision of Primary Experience, Winnicottian Work with Children and Adolescents*. London: Free Association Books.

Downie, A. and Forshaw, P. (1987) 'Family Centres.' *Practice 2*, 140–147.

Eichenbaum, L. and Orbach, S. (1983) *Understanding Women.* New York: Basic Books.

Erickson, Beth (1993) *Helping Men Change: The Role of the Female Therapist.* Newbury Park: Sage.

Farnfield, S. (1994) *Narrative Stems Schedule· Children in Care.* Unpublished.

Farnfield, S. (1996) *Can You Tell Me? Some Useful Approaches To Eliciting Children's Views.* The University of Reading.

Farnfield, S. (1997) *Guide To Using Can You Tell Me. Version 1* (updated June 1997). The University of Reading.

Farrington, D. P. (1995) 'The development of offending and antisocial behaviour from childhood: key findings from the Cambridge Study in Delinquent Development.' *Journal of Child Psychology and Psychiatry 36,* 6, 929–964.

Ferenczi, S. (1933, 1999) 'Confusion of tongues between adults and the child: The language of tenderness and of passion.' In J. Borossa (ed) *Sandor Ferenczi: Selected Writings.* London: Penguin.

Fonagy, P. (1996) 'Attachment and theory of mind: Overlapping constructs?' Address to Association for Child Psychology and Psychiatry, London, 26 June 1996.

Fonagy, P., Steele, H., Steele, M., Higgitt, A. and Target, M. (1994) 'The Theory and Practice of Resilience.' *Journal of Child Psychology and Psychiatry 35,* 2, 231–257.

Forehand, R. and McMahon, R. (1981) *Helping the Non-Compliant Child: A Clinician's Guide to Parent Training.* New York: Guilford.

Fraiberg, S. (1968) *The Magic Years.* London: Methuen.

Fraiberg, S. (1980) *Clinical Studies in Infant Mental Health: The First Year of Life.* London: Tavistock.

Gaber, I. and Aldridge, J. (eds) (1994) *Culture and Identity and Transracial Adoption: In the Best Interests of the Child.* London: Free Association.

Gambe, D., Gomez, J., Kapur, V. Rangel. M. and Stubbs, P. (1992) *Improving Practice with Children and Families: A Training Manual.* Anti-racist Social Work Education 2. Leeds: CCETSW.

George, C., Kaplan, N. and Main, M. (1985) *Adult Attachment Interview.* (Unpublished) Department of Psychology, University of California, Berkley.

Ghate, D., Shaw, C. and Neal, H. (2000) *Fathers in Family Centres: Engaging Fathers in Preventive Services.* York: Joseph Rowntree Foundation/YPS.

Gill, O. (1988) 'Integrated work in a neighbourhood family centre.' *Practice 2,* 3, 243–255.

Green, A. (1998) 'Four years in a family centre.' *Outlook,* Quarterly Journal of the NCVCCO, Winter 1998.

Green, J., Stanley, C., Smith, V. and Goldwyn, R. (2000) 'A new method of evaluating attachment representations in young school-age children: The Manchester child attachment story task.' *Attachment And Human Development,* 2, 1, 48–70.

Green, V. (2000) 'Therapeutic space for re-creating the child in the mind of the parents.' In Tsiantis *et al*, (eds) *Work with Parents: Psychotherapy with Children and Adolescents*. London: Karnac.

Greenberg, M., Cichetti, D. and Cummings, E. (eds) (1990) *Attachment in the Pre-school Years*. Chicago University of Chicago Press.

Greenberg, M., De Klyen, M., Speltz, M. and Endgriga, M. (1997) 'The role of attachment processes in externalizing psychopathology in young children.' In L. Atkinson and K. Zucker (eds) *Attachment and Psychopathology*. New York: The Guilford Press.

Greenhalgh, P. (1994) *Emotional Growth and Learning*. London: Routledge.

Grice. H. (1975) 'Logic and conversation.' In P. Cole and J. Morgan (eds) *Syntax And Semantics: Volume 3, Speech Acts*. London: Academic Press.

Gutridge, P. (1995) 'Gender issues in social work. Skewed view denies men a service.' *Professional Social Work*, February, p.6.

Hampton, D. (1995) *Failure to Thrive: Recognising and Resolving Non-Physical Feeding Disorders*. London: The Children's Society.

Hampton, D. (1996) 'Resolving the feeding difficulties associated with non- organic failure to thrive.' *Child Care, Health and Development 22*, 4, 261–271.

Hanlon, D. (1995) '"Him outdoors": A study of men's experiences of a family centre.' (MA dissertation) University of East London.

Hannah, C. (1992) 'The context of culture in systemic therapy: An application of CMM.' Cited in *Human Systems 5*, 1–3, 70.

Hansburg, H. (1986) *Researches In Separation Anxiety*, Vol. 3. Robert E. Krieger Publishing Co. Inc.

Hardiker, P. (1996) 'Typology of family centres.' Presented to NCCVO Conference, Leicester, December 1996.

Hardwick, A. and Woodhead, J. (1999) *Loving, Hating and Survival*. Aldershot: Arena.

Hardy, K. (1997) 'Steps Towards Becoming Culturally Competent.' *Family Therapy News 28*, 2, 13–19.

Harris, G. and Booth, I. (1992) 'The nature and management of eating problems in pre-school children.' In P. Cooper and A. Skein (eds) *Feeding Problems and Eating Disorders in Children and Adolescents*. Monograph of Clinical Paediatrics. Harwood Academic Publishers.

Harris, G. and Johnson, R. (1997) 'Summary of the proceedings of three one day conferences presented by Cow & Gate.' Unpublished.

Harwood, R. and Miller, J. (1997) *Culture and Attachment*. NY: Guilford Press.

Hawkins, P. (1989) 'The social learning approach to residential and day care.' In A. Brown and R. Clough *Groups and Groupings*. London: Tavistock/Routledge.

Hawkins, P. and Shohet, R. (1989) *Supervision in the Helping Professions*. Milton Keynes: Open University Press.

Hay, J., Leheup, R. and Almudevar, M. (1995) 'Family therapy with "invisible families".' *British Journal of Social Work 68*, 125–133.

Hesse, E. (1999) 'The Adult Attachment Interview.' In J. Cassidy and P. Shaver (eds) *Handbook of Attachment: Theory, Research, and Clinical Applications*. New York: The Guilford Press.

Hinshelwood, R. (1987) *What Happens in Groups. Psychoanalysis, the Individual and the Community*. London: Free Association Books.

HMSO (1989) Children Act 1989 *Working Together*. London: HMSO.

Hodges, J. (1997) 'The inner world of maltreated children: Research on assessment through narrative stems.' Paper presented at United Bristol Healthcare Trust, 8th Annual Infancy Conference: 'New Developments in Attachment Theory – Implications for Adoption and Fostering.'

Holman, R. (1988) *Putting Families First: Prevention and Child Care*. London: Macmillan.

Holmes, J. (1993) *John Bowlby and Attachment Theory*. London: Routledge.

Holmes, J. (1996) *Attachment, Intimacy, Autonomy: Using Attachment Theory in Adult Psychotherapy*. London: Jason Aronson.

Home Office (1993) 'Convictions for offending.' Cited in T. Newburn and G. Mair (1996) *Working with Men*. London: Russell House.

Hopkins, J. (1987) 'Failure of the holding relationship: Some effects of physical rejection on the child's attachment and on his inner experience.' *Journal of Child Psychotherapy 13*, 1, 5–17.

Hopkins, J. (1992) 'Infant–Parent Psychotherapy.' *Journal of Child Psychotherapy 18*, 1, 5–17.

Hopkins, J. (1999) 'Some contributions on attachment theory.' In M. Lanyado and A. Horne *The Handbook of Child and Adolescent Psychotherapy*. London: Routledge.

Horne, A. (2000) 'Keeping the Child in Mind.' In Tsiantis *et al.* (eds) *Work with Parents: Psychoanalytic Psychotherapy with Children and Adolescents*. London: Karnac.

Howe, D. (1995) *Attachment Theory for Social Work Practice*. London: Macmillan.

Howe, D. (1996) *Attachment and Loss in Child and Family Social Work*. Guildford: Avebury.

Hoxter, S. (1983) 'Some feelings aroused in working with severely deprived children.' In M. Boston and R. Szur (eds) (1990) *Psychotherapy with Severely Deprived Children*. London: Karnac.

Iwaniec, D. (1983) 'Social and Aetiological Factors in the Management of Children Who Fail to Thrive.' (PhD thesis) Department of Psychology, University of Leicester.

Iwaniec, D. (1995) *The Emotionally Abused and Neglected Child*. Chichester: Wiley.

Iwaniec, D., Herbert, M. and McNeish, A. (1985) 'Social Work with Failure to Thrive Children and their Families.' *Psychological Factors 15*, 1, 247.

Jacobs, M. (1988) *Psychodynamic Counselling in Action*. London: Sage Publications.

Jenkins. A. E. (1987) 'Recognising and treating the hurt child within the parent.' In R. Whitfield and D. Baldwin (eds) *Families Matter*. London: Collins/Marshall Pickering.

Jenner, S. (1992) 'The assessment and treatment of parenting skills and deficits: Within the framework of child protection.' Association for Child Psychology and Psychiatry *Newsletter 14,* 228–233.

Jenner, S. and McCarthy, G. (1995) 'Quantitative measures of parenting. A clinical-developmental perspective.' In P. Reder and C. Lucey (eds) *Assessment Of Parenting: Psychiatric And Psychological Contributions,* 136–150. London: Routledge.

Joseph Rowntree Foundation Findings (1996) 'A survey of group-based parenting programmes', *Social Policy Research 91;* and 1998 Evaluating Parenting Programmes.

Joseph Rowntree Foundation Findings (2000) *How Family Centres are Working with Fathers.* York: YPS, and www.jrf.org.uk.

Kennard, D. and Lees, K. (2000) 'Audit checklist' Unpublished. Website: http://www.pettarchiv.org.uk/atc-klac.htm

Kennedy, R. (1987) 'The work of the day.' In R. Kennedy, A. Heymans and L. Tischler (ed) *The Family as In-patient: Families and Adolescents at the Cassell Hospital.* London: Free Association Books.

Klein, Josephine (1987) *Our Need for Others and Its Roots in Infancy.* London: Tavistock.

Klein, M. (1940) 'Mourning and its relation to manic depressive states.' In *Love, Guilt and Reparation: The Writings of Melanie Klein* (1955), Volume 1. London: Hogarth.

Klein, M. (1975) *Envy and Gratitude.* London: Hogarth Press.

Lanyado, M. (1991) 'On creating a psychotherapeutic space.' In *Journal of Social Work Practice 5,* 1, 31–40.

Lazar, I. and Darlington, R.B. (1982) 'Lasting Effects of Early Education.' *Monographs of the Society for Research in Child Development 47,* 195, 2–5.

Ledger, D. (2000) 'A family centre approach to early therapeutic intervention for young children and their families.' (Dissertation for MA in Therapeutic Child Care) University of Reading.

Macdonald, D. and Roberts, H. (1995) *What Works in the Early Years – Effective Interventions for Children and Their Families in Health, Social Welfare, Education and Child Protection.* Ilford: Barnado's.

McGuire, J. and Earls, F. (1991) 'Prevention of Psychiatric Disorders in Early Childhood.' *Journal of Child Psychology and Psychiatry 32,* 1, 129–154.

McMahon L. (1992) *The Handbook of Play Therapy.* London: Routledge.

McMahon, L. (1992b) 'Play in under-fives and family work.' In *The Handbook of Play Therapy.* London: Routledge.

McMahon, L. (1994) 'Responding to defences against anxiety in day care for young children.' *Early Child Development and Care 97,* 175–84.

McMahon, L. (1999) 'Healing Play.' In A. Hardwick and J. Woodhead *Loving, Hating and Survival.* Aldershot: Arena.

McMahon, L., Dacre, V. and Vale, J. (1997) 'Reflection and Emotional Containment: Therapeutic Work in Family Centres.' *Early Child Development and Care 132*, 21–31.

Main M. (1986) 'Parental aversion to physical contact with the infant: Stability, consequences and reasons.' In T. Brazelton and K. Barnard (eds) (1986) *Touch*. New York: International Universities Press.

Main, M. (1991) 'Metacognitive knowledge, metacognitive monitoring, and singular (coherent) vs. multiple (incoherent) model of attachment: findings and directions for future research.' In C. Parkes, J. Stevenson-Hinde and P. Marris, (eds) *Attachment Across the Life Cycle*. London: Routledge.

Main, M. and Goldwyn, R. (1994) *Adult Attachment Scoring and Classification Systems*, Version 6.0. (Unpublished) University College London.

Main, M., Kaplan, N. and Cassidy, J. (1985) 'Security in infancy, childhood, and adulthood: A move to the level of representation.' In I. Bretherton and E. Waters (eds) *Growing Points Of Attachment Theory And Research*. Monograph of the Society for Research in Child Development 50, Nos 1–2.

Main, M. and Solomon, J. (1990) 'Procedures for identifying infants as disorganized/disoriented during the ainsworth strange situation.' In M. Greenberg, D. Cicchetti and E. Cummings (eds) *Attachment in the Preschool Years*. Chicago: University of Chicago Press.

Main, T. F. (1946) 'The hospital as a therapeutic institution.' Bull Menninger Clinic 10, 66–70. Reprinted (1989) in T. F. Main *The Ailment and Other Psychoanalytic Essays*. London: Free Association, 7–11.

Mair, G. (1996) *Working with Men*. London: Russell House.

Manolson, A. (1992) *It Takes Two to Talk: A Parent's Guide to Helping Children Communicate*. Toronto: Hanen.

Manolson, A., Ward, B. and Dodington, N. (1995) *You Make The Difference*. Toronto: Hanen.

Mattinson, J. (1975) *The Reflection Process in Casework Supervision*. London: Tavistock/IMS.

Mawson, C. (1994) 'Containing anxiety in work with damaged children.' In A. Obholzer and V. Z. Roberts (eds) *The Unconscious at Work*. London: Routledge.

Menzies, I. (1970) *The Functioning of Social Systems as a Defence against Anxiety*. Centre for Applied Social Research. London: Tavistock Institute of Human Relations.

Menzies, I. (1979) 'Staff support systems: task and anti-task in adolescent institutions.' In R. D. Hinshelwood and N. Manning (eds) *Therapeutic Communities: Reflections and Progress*. London: Routledge and Kegan Paul.

Menzies Lyth, I. (1988) *Containing Anxiety in Institutions: Selected Essays* Vol. 1. London: Free Association.

Menzies Lyth, I. (1989) *The Dynamics of the Social: Selected Essays* Vol 2. London: Free Association.

Miller, E. J. (1993) *From Dependency to Autonomy: Studies in Organisation and Change.* London: Free Association Press.

Miller, E. J. (1993b) *Creating a Holding Environment. Conditions for Psychological Security.* London: Tavistock Institute.

Miller, E. J. and Gwynne, G. V. (1972) *A Life Apart: A Pilot Study of Residential Institutions for the Physically Handicapped and the Young Chronic Sick.* London: Tavistock.

Mills, M. and Puckering, C. (1995) 'Bringing About Change in Parent–Child Relationships.' Chapter 12 in J. Trowell and M. Bower *The Emotional Needs of Young Children and Their Families.* London: Routledge.

Modell, A. H. (1975) 'A narcissistic defence against affects and the illusion of self sufficiency.' *International Journal of Psychology 56*, 275–282.

Modell, A. H. (1978) 'The conceptualization of the therapeutic action of psychoanalysis – the action of the holding environment.' Cited in I. Stamm (1985) 'The hospital as a holding environment', *International Journal of Therapeutic Communities 6*, 4, 219–229.

Monson, S. and Baylis, M. (1997) 'Working together with parents and young children.' In *AIMH (UK) Newsletter 1*, 1 June.

Moores, J. (1997) 'Summary of the proceedings of three one day conferences presented by Cow & Gate.' Unpublished.

Morrison, T. (1997) 'Emotionally competent child protection organizations: Fallacy, fiction or necessity?' In J. Bates, R. Pugh and N. Thompson (eds) *Protecting Children: Challenges and Change.* Aldershot: Arena.

Moylan, D. (1994) 'The dangers of contagion: Projective identification processes in institutions.' In A. Obholzer and V.Z. Roberts (eds) *The Unconscious at Work.* London: Routledge.

Murray, L. and Cooper, P. J. (1994) 'Clinical applications of attachment theory and research: Change in infant attachment with brief psychotherapy.' In J. Richer (ed) 'The clinical applications of attachment theory', *ACPP Occasional Paper 9.* London: ACPP.

Murray, L. and Dymond, M. (2000) 'Attachment, maternal depression and early interventions.' Talk at Oxford ACPP Study Day on the Clinical Implications of Attachment Theory, 22nd September 2000.

NCH Action for Children (1995) *Family Centre Policy.* London: NCH.

NCVCCO (2000) 'Fathers at the family centre: Family centres, fathers and working with men' Conference Report. London: NCVCCO and Family Centre Network and Policy Research Bureau.

Nelson, K. (1996) *Language In Cognitive Development: The Emergence Of The Mediated Mind.* Cambridge University Press.

Neville, D., King, L. and Beak, D. (1996) *Promoting Positive Parenting.* Aldershot: Ashgate.

NEWPIN conference report (1998) 'NEWPIN 16 years on – Family mending that works.' London: NEWPIN publication.

NEWPIN (2000) Revised practice manual.

Oaklander, V. (1978) *Windows to our Children.* Utah: Real People Press.

Oates, R. K. and Bross, D. C. (1995) 'What have we learned about treating child abuse – a literature review of the last decade.' *Child Abuse and Neglect 19*, 463–473.

Obholzer, A. (1994) 'Fragmentation and integration in a school for physically handicapped children.' In A. Obholzer and V.Z. Roberts (eds) *The Unconscious at Work.* London: Routledge.

Obholzer, A. and Roberts, V. Z. (eds) (1994) *The Unconscious at Work.* London: Routledge.

Offord, D. (1987) 'Prevention of behavioural and emotional disorders in children.' *Journal of Child Psychology and Psychiatry 28,* 1, 9–19.

O'Hagan, K. (1997) 'The problem of engaging men in child protection.' *British Journal of Social Work 27*, 1, 25–42.

Oppenheim, D. (1997) 'The attachment doll – play interview for preschoolers.' *International Journal of Behavioural Development 20*, 681–697.

Parton, N. (1998) 'Risk, advanced liberalism and child welfare: The need to rediscover uncertainty and ambiguity.' *British Journal of Social Work 28*, 5–27.

Pearce, W. B. (1989) *Communication and The Human Condition.* Southern Illinois University Press.

Pearce, W. B. (1994) *Interpersonal Communication: Making Social Worlds.* New York: HarperCollins.

Peterson, L. (1995) 'Stop think do: Improving social and learning skills for children in clinics and schools.' In H. Bilsen, P. Kendall and J. Slavenburg (eds) *Behavioural Approaches for Children and Adolescents: Challenges for the Next Century.* New York: Plenum Press.

Phelan, J. (1983) *Family Centres: A Study.* London: Children's Society.

Phillips, A. (1988) *D W Winnicott.* London: Fontana Press.

Pithouse, A. and Lindsell, S. (1995) 'Specialist referred family centre and field social work: a comparative study of user views on service impact and outcome.' *Research Policy and Planning 13*, 1–2, 13–18.

Pithouse, A., Lindsell, S. and Cheung, M. (1996) *Family Centres: Their Impact and Effectiveness.* Aldershot: Avebury.

Platt, T. (1999) 'Durley Family Support Centre', Family Centre Network 45, in *NCVCCO Quarterly Journal 6,* Winter 1999.

Pound, A. (1990) 'The development of attachment in adult life – the NEWPIN experiment.' *British Journal of Psychotherapy 7*, 1, 77–85.

Pound, A. (1994) *NEWPIN A Befriending and Therapeutic Network for Carers of Young Children.* London: HMSO/NEWPIN.

Pound A., Puckering C., Cox T. and Mills, M. (1989) 'The impact of maternal depression on young children.' *British Journal of Psychotherapy 5*, 241–252.

Puckering, C., Evans, J., Maddox, H., Mills, M. and Cox, A. D. (1996) 'Taking control: A single case study of Mellow Parenting.' *Clinical Child Psychology and Psychiatry 1*, 4, 539–550.

Preston-Shoot, M. and Agass, D. (1990) *Making Sense of Social Work. Psychodynamics, Systems and Practice.* London: Macmillan.

Pritchard P. (1999) 'Helping parents with severe parenting difficulties.' *Community Practitioner 72*, 248–251.

Provence, S., Naylor, A. and Patterson, J. (1977) *The Challenge of Day Care.* London: Yale University Press.

Rack, P. (1982) *Race, Culture and Mental Disorder.* London and New York: Tavistock Publications.

Rashid, S. P. (1996) 'Attachment viewed through a cultural lens.' In D. Howe *Attachment and Loss in Child and Family Social Work.* Aldershot: Avebury.

Reder, P. and Duncan, S. (1995) 'The meaning of the child.' In P. Reder and C. Lucey (eds) *Assessment of Parenting: Psychiatric and Psychological Contributions.* London: Routledge.

Reder, P. and Lucey, C. (eds) (1995) *Assessment of Parenting: Psychiatric and Psychological Contributions.* London: Routledge.

Redl, F. (1966) *When we Deal with Children.* New York: Free Press.

Rice, A. K. (1958) *The Enterprise and its Environment.* London: Tavistock.

Richman, N. and McGuire, J. (1988) 'Institutional Characteristics and Staff Behaviour in Day Nurseries.' *Children and Society 2*, 138–151.

Richman, N., Stevenson, J. and Graham, P. J. (1982) *Pre-school to School: A Behavioural Study.* London: Academic Press.

Roberts, V. Z. (1994) 'The organisation of work: Contribution from open systems theory.' In A. Obholzer and V.Z. Roberts (eds) *The Unconscious at Work.* London: Routledge.

Robertson, J. and Robertson, J. (1989) *Separation and the Very Young.* London: Free Association.

Rogers, C. (1958) 'The character of the helping relationship.' *Personnel and Guidance Journal 37*, 6–16.

Russell, G., Treasure, J. and Eisher, I. (1998) *Mothers with Anorexia Nervosa Who Underfeed Their Children: Their Recognition and Management.* Psychological Medicine: Cambridge University Press.

Rutter, M. (1981) *Maternal Deprivation Reassessed.* Harmondsworth: Penguin.

Rutter, M. (1989) 'Pathways from childhood to adult life.' *Journal of Child Psychology and Psychiatry 30*, 1, 25–31.

Ruxton, S. (1992) *'What's He Doing at the Family Centre?' The Dilemmas of Men Who Care for Children.* London: NCH.

Rycroft, C. (1968) *A Critical Dictionary of Psychoanalysis.* London: Nelson.

Sauter, J. and Franklin, C. (1998) 'Assessing post-traumatic stress disorder in children: Diagnostic and measurement strategies.' *Research in Social Work Practice* 8, 3, 251–270.

Saywitz, K. and Snyder, L. (1996) 'Narrative elaboration: Test of a new procedure for interviewing children.' *Journal of Counsulting and Clinical Psychology 64*, 6, 1347–1357.

Schneider-Rosen, K. (1990) 'The developmental reorganization of attachment relationships: Guidelines for classification beyond Infancy.' In M. Greenberg, D. Cicchetti and E. Cummings (eds) *Attachment in the Preschool Years.* Chicago IL: University of Chicago Press.

Shapiro, E. and Carr, A. (1991) *Lost in Familiar Places.* New Haven and London: Yale University Press.

Shotter, J. (1994) *Cultural Politics of Everyday Life: Social Constructionists Rhetoric and Knowing of the Third Kind.* Milton Keynes: Open University Press.

Shuttleworth, J. (1989) 'Psychoanalytic Theory and Infant Development.' In L. Miller, M. Rustin, M. Rustin and J. Shuttleworth (eds) *Closely Observed Infants.* London: Duckworth.

Sinclair, R., Hearn, B. and Pugh, G. (1997) *Preventive Work with Families.* London: National Children's Bureau.

Smith, E. M. J. (1985a) 'Ethnic minorities: Life stress, social support and mental health issues.' *The Counselling Psychologist 13*, 4, 537–79.

Smith, T. (1996) *Family Centres and Bringing Up Young Children.* London: HMSO.

Solomon, J. and George, C. (1999) 'The Measurement of Attachment Security in Infancy and Childhood.' In J. Cassidy and P. Shaver *Handbook of Attachment: Theory, Research, and Clinical Applications.* New York: The Guilford Press.

Solomon, J., George, C. and De Jong, A. (1995) 'Children classified as controlling at age six: Evidence of disorganized representational strategies and aggression at home and at school.' *Development And Psychopathology 7,* 447–463.

Speller, B. (1994) 'Managing therapeutic work in a family centre.' In G. Pugh and A. Hollows *Child Protection in Early Years.* London: National Children's Bureau.

Stamm, I. (1985) 'The Hospital as a Holding Environment.' *International Journal of Therapeutic Communities 6*, 4, 219–229.

Stern, D. (1985) *The Interpersonal World of the Infant.* New York: Basic Books.

Stern, D. (1997) *The Maternal Constellation.* New York: Basic Books.

Stevenson, J. (1999) 'The Treatment of the Long-term Sequelae of Child Abuse.' *Journal of Child Psychology and Psychiatry 40*, 1, 89–111.

Stewart, A. M. (1987) 'Stress at Work.' In D. Stewart (ed) *Handbook of Management Skills.* London: Gower.

Stokes, J. (1994) 'Institutional chaos and personal stress.' In A. Obholzer and V. Z. Roberts (eds) *The Unconscious at Work.* London: Routledge.

Stones, C. (1989) 'Groups and groupings in a family centre.' In A. Brown and R. Clough (eds) *Groups and Groupings.* London: Tavistock/Routledge.

Stones, C. (1994) *Focus on Families: Family Centres in Action.* London: Macmillan.

Thoreau, Henry David (1854) *Walden.*

Trowell, J. (1995) 'The Monroe young family centre.' In J. Trowell and M. Bower *The Emotional Needs of Children and Families.* London: Routledge.

Trowell, J. and Bower, M. (eds) (1995) *The Emotional Needs of Children and Families.* London: Routledge.

Trowell, J., Hodges, S. and Leighton-Laing, J. (1997) 'Emotional abuse: the work of a family centre.' *Child Abuse Review 6,* 357–369.

Truax, C. and Carkhuff, R. (1967) *Towards Effective Counselling and Psychotherapy.* Chicago: Aldine.

Tsiantis, J., Boethious, S., Hallerfors, B., Horne, A. and Tischler, L. (eds) (2000) *Work with Parents: Psychotherapy with Children and Adolescents.* London: Karnac.

Tulving, E. (1972) 'Episodic and semantic memory.' In E. Tulving and W. Donaldson (eds) *Organization Of Memory.* New York: Academic Press.

Van IJzendoorn, M., Juffer, F. and Duyvesteyn, M. (1995) 'Breaking the intergenerational cycle of insecure attachment: A review of attachment-based interventions on maternal sensitivity and infant security.' *Journal of Child Psychology and Psychiatry 36,* 2, 225–248.

Van der Vlugt, H., Pijnenburg, H., Wels, P. and Koning, A. (1995) 'Cognitive behaviour modification of ADHD: A family system approach.' In H. Bilsen, P. Kendall and J. Slavenburg (eds) *Behavioural Approaches for Children and Adolescents: Challenges for the Next Century.* New York: Plenum Press.

Vygotsky, L. (1962) *Thought and Language.* Cambridge, MA: MIT Press.

Vygotsky, L. (1978) *Mind in Society: The Development of Higher Psychological Processes.* Cambridge MS: Harvard University Press.

Ward, A. (1990) 'The role of physical contact in childcare.' *Children and Society 4,* 4, 337–351.

Ward, A. (1993) *Working in Group Care: Social Work in Residential and Day Care Settings.* Birmingham: Venture Press.

Ward, A. (1995) 'The "matching principle": Exploring connections between practice and training in therapeutic child care: Part 1 – Therapeutic child care and the holding environment.' *Journal of Social Work Practice 9,* 2, 177–187.

Ward, A. (1995b) 'Opportunity led work: 1. Introducing the Concept.' *Social Work Education 14,* 4, 89–105.

Ward, A. (1996) 'Opportunity led work: 2. The Framework.' *Social Work Education 8,* 1, 67–78.

Ward, A. (1998) 'The inner world and its implications.' In A. Ward and L. McMahon (eds) *Intuition is Not Enough: Matching Learning With Practice in Therapeutic Child Care.* London: Routledge.

Ward, A. and McMahon, L. (eds) (1998) *Intuition is Not Enough: Matching Learning with Practice in Therapeutic Child Care.* London: Routledge.

Warren, C. (1991) *The Potential for Families at the Centre: A Study of Seven Action Projects.* London: Bedford Square Press.

Waters, E. (ed) (1995) *Caregiving, Cultural and Cognitive Perspectives on secure Base Behaviour and Working Models: new growing points of attachment theory and research.* Chicago: Society for Research In Child Development.

Waters, E., Weinfield, N. and Hamilton, C. (2000) 'The stability of attachment security from infancy to adolescence and early adulthood: General discussion.' *Child Development 71,* 3, 703–706.

West, J. (1992) *Child Centred Play Therapy.* London: Edward Arnold.

Widerstrom A., Mowder, B. and Sandall, S. (1997) *Infant Development and Risk.* Baltimore: Paul H. Brookes Pub. Co.

Willmott, P. and Mayne, S. (1983) *Families at the Centre.* London: Bedford Square Press/NCVCCO.

Wilson K., Kendrick, P. and Ryan, V. (1992) *Play Therapy: A Non-directive Approach for Children and Adolescents.* London: Bailliere Tindall.

Winnicott, C. (1968) 'Communicating with children.' In R. Tod (ed) *Disturbed Children.* London: Longman.

Winnicott, D. W. (1960) 'The theory of the parent–infant relationship.' In D.W. Winnicott (1965) *The Maturational Processes and the Facilitating Environment.* London: Hogarth Press and the Institute of Psycho-Analysis.

Winnicott, D. W. (1964) *The Child, The Family and The Outside World.* London: Penguin.

Winnicott, D. W. (1965) *The Maturational Processes and the Facilitating Environment.* London: Hogarth Press and the Institute of Psycho-Analysis.

Winnicott, D. W. (1965b) *The Family and Individual Development.* London: Tavistock.

Winnicott, D. W. (1971) *Playing and Reality.* London: Tavistock.

Winnicott, D. W. (1988) *Babies and Their Mothers.* London: Free Association.

Worden, J. W. (1992) *Grief Counselling and Grief Therapy.* London: Routledge.

Wright, C. (1996) *Amplified Growth Percentile Charts.* Harlow Printing Ltd, Maxwell St, South Shields, Tyne and Wear, NE33 4PY.

Wright, C, and Talbot, E. (1996) 'Screening for failure to thrive, what are we looking for?' *Child Care Health and Development 22,* 223–234.

Wright, J., Binney, V. and Smith, P. (1995) 'Security of attachment in 8–12 year-olds: A revised version of the separation anxiety test, its psychometric properties and clinical interpretation.' *Journal of Child Psychology and Psychiatry 36,* 5, 757–774.

The Contributors

Laraine Beavis is a paediatric social worker for Wokingham Family Placement Team.

Yvonne Bailey-Smith is a social worker, psychotherapist and groupwork consultant, Queen's Park Family Service Unit.

Paul Collett is a social worker and Guardian ad Litem for Hampshire, Portsmouth and Southampton.

Viv Dacre is a social worker and lecturer in child care at Deeside College and was manager of Castlefield Family Centre, High Wycombe.

Steve Farnfield is Lecturer in social work, Department of Health and Social Care, University of Reading, and was until recently a social worker at Hester Road Family Centre, Portsmouth.

Anton Green is Manager of Penn Crescent Family Centre, Haywards Heath, W. Sussex, and Co-ordinator of the Mid-Sussex Feeding to Thrive Service.

Anne Jenkins Hansen is the founder of NEWPIN. She has written extensively about NEWPIN.

Denise Ledger is a teacher and social worker and is Family Services Manager for Exeter and Mid-Devon based at Buddle Lane Family Centre.

Rosemary Lilley is Project Manager, Greenham House Family Centre, a project of NCH.

Linnet McMahon (editor) is Lecturer in social work and course leader of the MA in Therapeutic Child Care, University of Reading. She has written *The Handbook of Play Therapy*, and co-edited *Intuition Is Not Enough: Matching Learning with Practice in Theraputic Child Care*.

Sarah Musgrave is a social worker at Gladstone Street Children's Resource Centre in Swindon. She is completing training in psychotherapy.

Christine Stones is Project Leader of New Fulford Family Centre, a Barnardo's project in Bristol. She is a qualified social worker and psychotherapist. She has written with other Centre staff *Focus on Families: Family Centres in Action*, Macmillan/BASW 1994.

Adrian Ward (editor) is Senior Lecturer in the School of Social Work and Psychosocial Studies, University of East Anglia. He was formerly at the University of Reading, where he founded and for many years was course leader of the MA in Therapeutic Child Care. He is author of *Working in Group Care* and co-edited *Intuition Is Not Enough: Matching Learning with Practice in Therapeutic Child Care*.

Subject Index

Author Index